LIBERATING THE ENCLAVE

D. C. Zook

SHANTIWALA
BOOKS

Berkeley, CA

Aside from brief quotations for media coverage and reviews, no part of this book may be reproduced or distributed in any form without the author's permission.

Text copyright © 2018 by D. C. Zook
All rights reserved.
Published by Shantiwala Books (Berkeley, CA)
Cover design by James, GoOnWrite.com
ISBN: 1947609092
ISBN-13 (print): 9781947609099
ISBN-13 (E-book): 9781947609013

Ourselves Among Others:
The Extravagant Failure of Diversity in America
and An Epic Plan to Make It Work

Understanding the Misunderstanding (vol. 1)

Liberating the Enclave (Vol. 2)

Writing the Past Imperfect (vol. 3)

Unpoisoning the Well (vol. 4)

To the one and only Wole Soyinka, whose plays showed me how words could be fiercely eloquent and eloquently fierce

TABLE OF CONTENTS

Preface to Part 2	Liberating the Enclave	ix
Chapter 1	Happy Slaves and Other Oddities	1
Chapter 2	Heritage and the Strange Notion of Pride	33
Chapter 3	Heroine Addiction	54
Chapter 4	LGBTQI+ and Its Discontents	91
Chapter 5	Coming in First: Indigenous Identities and Diversity	172
Chapter 6	Fear, Ignorance, Stupidity, Diversity	213
Index		247
About the Author		251

PREFACE TO PART 2
LIBERATING THE ENCLAVE

For reasons I discussed in Part 1 of this series, diversity has turned America into what is in essence a country of enclaves. Each of these enclaves is like a gated identity community, where only those with the right credentials are allowed to enter. And yes, there may be many different gated communities, many different enclaves, so to speak, but the biggest mistake we make—and the fatal flaw in the architecture of diversity—is to mistake the diversity of enclaves for diversity itself.

But wait, the critical voice might say, what's wrong with just having a diversity of enclaves? What's wrong with a bunch of different groups coexisting side by side? Isn't that diversity? Isn't that close enough? The answer is, well, no, that's not diversity, and no, that's not close enough. A bunch of different and separate homogeneous communities is not an approximation of diversity. It's a bunch of different and separate islands of homogeneity, and islands of homogeneity are the opposite of what a diverse society should be. Think, for instance, of how we even filter our sense of social justice by separate identities— Ferguson becomes a "black" issue, immigration reform becomes a "Latino" issue, and so on. By this logic, if I'm not black, then Ferguson isn't my concern. And if

I am black, then immigration reform is someone else's problem. The enclaves of America preclude inter-cultural social empathy. We seek a separate justice for each different community, rather than, as we should be doing, one justice for one society.

What we need now, and what this whole series offers, is an alternative vision of diversity that takes us out of our enclaves, rather than seeking shelter and comfort within them. So long as we retain our enclaves as a safe space in which to retreat in order to escape the tensions and challenges of interacting with others, what we end up doing is ignoring those tensions and challenges rather than confronting them and resolving them. The more we ignore them, the worse they get. And the worse they get, the more we desire to find security among those just like ourselves. The failure of diversity becomes a self-fulfilling prophecy.

Why aren't enclaves good enough? Why won't they work to give us diversity? First of all, if we take the Supreme Court case *Grutter v. Bollinger* (2003), discussed in detail in Part 1, as our standard, the whole point of diversity—and this was a case about the use of affirmative action to create diversity on college campuses—is to create a more inclusive and *integrated* society in America. Enclaves both exclude and separate, so enclaves therefore move in the opposite direction of diversity.

Second, enclave societies lack any substantive sense of diversity. Within each of these identity enclaves we find people who are just like one another, and we find activists and community leaders who work hard to ensure that the community, the enclave, speaks with "one voice," ironically suppressing diversity in the name of empowerment. Creating a larger society out of a number of communities that lack diversity within does not and cannot give us diversity at large—not now, not ever.

Lastly, if we all exist in our separate communities among our own kind, tolerating but not understanding all the other communities that exist around us, what this actually amounts to is a reassertion of the idea of "separate but equal"—separate communities with equal rights to exist. But the idea of separate but equal was struck down long ago, and for good reason. For diversity to work, we've got to have the equal, it is true, but we can't have the separate. Separation is the death knell of diversity.

Part 2 is an in-depth look at several different enclaves—how and why they are formed, the problems that are created through self-segregation, and the obstacles that self-segregation creates for meaningful dialog and understanding. Chapter 1 gets things rolling by discussing how the narcissism created by our current version of diversity stifles opportunities for meaningful dialogue. The narcissism of diversity has over time created a brittleness that makes each identity-based community unable to accept or consider any critical perspective from outside the enclave. The result is a strange and unsustainable library of narratives from each separate enclave, each of which tells the story of endlessly beautiful and unblemished selves. Only people in other enclaves have flaws and make mistakes, these stories say, never ourselves.

Chapter 2 confronts the very foundation of this narcissism by questioning the pride we often associate with our heritage. We are always told to be proud of our heritage, but what role if any does heritage play in making us who we are (or think we are)? Even if heritage does play a role, even a profound one, to what extent should this generate a sense of pride? Many things go into making us what and who we are, yet diversity encourages us to cling to the one thing that draws us further and further into our enclaves. Cultivating pride within the enclave is only one step short of identity-based chauvinism, and chauvinism rarely produces anything other than hatred, resentment, and anger. Perhaps it's time to rethink the importance of heritage and the pride we attach to it.

Chapter 3 examines gender-based enclaves, focusing specifically on the place of women within the larger framework of diversity and identity. Drawing on ideas about unblemished narratives of separate identities developed in Chapter 1, this chapter shows how narratives and perspectives that endlessly extol the positive virtues of women end up replicating rather than resisting the narratives they claim to question and oppose. By introducing the idea of negative equality—an equal capacity in all persons for both good and bad things—we end up with a balanced narrative that mitigates narcissism and encourages interactive dialog.

Chapter 4 wades into the many complicated layers that compose the LGBTQI+ community, layers that in many ways cannot bear the weight of one another in building what claims to be a unified community. This chapter also goes into detail about how the desire to build a unified LGBTQI+ narrative shuts down dialog with others, thus rendering an incomplete conversation that leaves many feeling frustrated. As with the perspective of so many other enclaves in the world of diversity, the "I don't have to explain, but you have to accept" approach shuts down the central thing that diversity is supposed to provide—the robust exchange of ideas (in the words of the Supreme Court). Just because things are difficult to talk about doesn't mean we shouldn't talk about them.

Chapter 5 discusses the idea of indigenousness and shows how ideas we have about indigenousness actually complicate and even undermine the work of diversity. Indigenous identities are separate identities, so they are a part of the enclave problem, but their separateness is also different from all other forms of separateness and therefore represents a special type of enclave. That raises the question of how we are to situate the idea of indigenousness within the larger project of diversity—whether we will need an entirely separate toolkit or whether we should instead stop viewing indigenousness as something that is entirely separate from other narratives of diversity.

The last and final chapter, Chapter 6, returns to the general idea of how the language we use to talk about diversity actually works against the goals of diversity. The word "homophobic," for instance, refers to an irrational fear of homosexuality, but over time it has come to refer to anything that questions homosexuality or any aspect thereof. If we can't ask questions of one another, or if anything or anyone that challenges even one aspect of our identity can be dismissed as "phobic" (much like some people dismiss as "fake news" anything they don't want to hear), then we render any type of mutual understanding impossible. In other words, the language of diversity causes diversity to fail. We therefore need to learn to speak differently when we speak of diversity.

CHAPTER 1

HAPPY SLAVES AND OTHER ODDITIES

Underneath all the relentless examples of how diversity continues to fail and how the current practices and policies associated with diversity continue to produce results that undermine the very aspirations of diversity, there remains the fundamental question of how all this came to pass. It would be easy to ascribe the whole disaster of diversity to the intrinsic stupidity of government and the myopic disconnect that policy-makers often have with their constituencies and with reality in general, but that would be too facile an explanation to explain the current quagmire of identity politics in America. Even if policy-makers in government consistently got things wrong and issued an endless stream of poorly-designed policies that asked us to adopt identities that we never had in the first place, it would still raise the question of why anyone would follow those policies rather than, as intelligence and ethics would both require, reject them out of hand. Indeed, this is a central question in identity-based politics around the world. Looking at the identity-based conflicts that emerged in the disintegration of Yugoslavia in the 1990s, for instance, there is always the difficult question of trying to discern why anyone would have ever have fallen for the idea that one's ethnic group was the epitome and essence of one's existence, and then to think it was not just acceptable but also necessary to kill anyone who even questioned that idea. Fortunately the state of identity politics in the United States is nowhere near to the situation that brought Yugoslavia to its knees, but the experiences of Yugoslavia (and so many other countries around the world) remain a sobering reminder of just how quickly misguided notions of identity can spiral out of control and devolve into murderous hate and bilious rage.

But if we cannot blame the government for the failures of diversity, then whom can we blame? Although it would be possible to draw up a list of persons who have been instrumental in stirring up anything from identity-based narcissism to outright race-hatred, I think that would be the wrong approach. It too easily transforms into the idea that specific individuals are responsible for ruining diversity in America and the rest of us are the innocent victims of those misguided individuals. Instead, I think it is far more effective to show just how pervasive these misguided notions of identity and diversity have become in American society using everyday examples of willful compliance and connivance with those misguided notions. The current miasma of diversity in America is widespread and systemic, and the most important medium through which identity is distorted and manipulated is the medium of education. Yes, education. This is all the more alarming since education is supposed to teach critical thinking, and any sort of critical thinking should be able to take one whiff of current diversity practices and tell that something is rancid. I am sure there are many skeptics who would argue that education is nothing to worry about since students retain the knowledge imparted to them about as well as meth addicts retain teeth, but the reality is that by the time most American students enter society, the damage is already done. Whether through formal channels of education in the classroom, or through more informal peer-to-peer learning networks, we are taught and in turn teach each other an unfortunate string of lies about who we are and why we are who we are, with little concern for the short-term or long-term consequences of those lies. Yet another facet of the difficult work of fixing diversity reveals itself in the unlikely project of re-crafting the entire educational apparatus—from formal to informal, from top to bottom, from side to side, from inside to out—to help us *unlearn* everything we thought about who we thought we were. Only through the dissolution of the ties that bind can we learn that we were never bound in the first place, and only then can we rebind ourselves anew with bonds of our own choosing. Only then can we discover a diversity that works equally as well for ourselves as it does for others.

Happy Slaves?
Shortly after I joined the faculty at UC Berkeley, I had an experience that in many ways was a crash-course in just how misconstrued and perverted the politics of identity had become, even in, or perhaps especially in, the hallowed halls of institutions of so-called "higher" education. One of my teaching assistants had come to me with a paper she had graded—graduate students learn the craft of teaching and evaluating exams and papers through their roles as teaching assistants—and asked me to give the paper a second read since her first impulse was to give the student a very poor grade (either a D or an F). My teaching assistant said she really had no idea of what to do with the paper, since the topic was "just so strange." I took the paper from my teaching assistant and gave the paper a second read. In fact I gave it a third read and a fourth read and multiple other reads because I wanted to make sure that the paper was actually saying what it appeared to be saying. In a nutshell, the paper argued that slaves in Asia were happy slaves, unlike African slaves in America, because they were enslaved by people from their own ethnic group. Slavery in Asia was therefore a positive experience that helped to strengthen and build ethnic communities throughout Asia. Therefore, while slavery in America

was racist, exploitative, and bad, slavery in Asia was ethnic, beneficial, and good.

To understand where such a bizarre and horribly contorted argument might have come from, I need to provide a bit of background to the situation. The course for which the student wrote this paper was an introductory survey course on "modern" Asia, which means pretty much anything from around the sixteenth century to the present. The course attracts a large number of students of Asian heritage, especially since it satisfies the breadth requirement of the university curriculum. I suppose I should pause briefly and point out the irony that the breadth requirement is designed for students to explore something different by broadening their horizons, and yet a large number of Asian students flock to the course because the topic is already familiar to them and hence allows them to minimize how much breadth they actually experience (and the same is true of introductory courses on Latin America, Africa, etc.). In one of the readings I had assigned, there was a long discussion about systems of slavery in Asia, focusing mostly on the region of Southeast Asia. Throughout the semester, students were required to write short papers based on the topics covered in the course, and so it was in response to the discussion of slavery in Southeast Asia that this student, who was of Southeast Asian heritage, wrote her paper.

The general intent of the paper was to argue that systems of slavery in Southeast Asia were positive forms of ethnic camaraderie: being enslaved by someone from your own identity-group—ethnic, racial, or religious—was a positive experience, a way of cultivating a strong culture within and a way of preserving traditional practices, especially since slavery was "traditional" in Southeast Asia. Slavery in Southeast Asia, in other words, was "good" slavery. By contrast, the enslavement of Africans by white Europeans and Americans was "bad" slavery because white people had taken Africans away from their communities and transported them elsewhere, to other parts of the world, where they had to live among racial and ethnic groups other than their own. Slaves in Southeast Asia were therefore happy slaves, unlike those in other slavery systems who did not have the pleasure of being enslaved by their own kind.

The argument had multiple flaws—more on which in a moment—but the central reason for the poor grade was that the paper had not used any sources from the class itself and did not back up any of the broad assertions made in the paper, both of which were required for the paper. It was in essence a five-page rationalization of why being among your own kind, even as a slave, was the happiest way to be. The absence of diversity was apparently so intoxicating and comforting that even slaves did not mind their status in life as long as they could exist in their own little homogeneous world. The pedagogical awkwardness came from the fact that even though the grade was based on structural flaws in the paper that had little to do with the argument itself—a lack of sources from the course and a lack of any historical support for the assertions made in the paper—my teaching assistant was concerned that the student would not see it that way. As a result, the teaching assistant wanted me to sign off on the poor grade (which I did) to show my concurrence with my assistant's evaluation for the paper.

Not surprisingly, after the papers were returned to the students, the student who wrote the paper on happy slaves showed up in my office hours to contest the grade. In the course of the conversation, I learned that the student had been upset by the readings for the course, and was angry to learn that there were other kinds of slavery besides the African slave trade that she had learned about earlier in school. She wrote her paper the way she did to prove that slavery in Asia was nothing like and was not "as bad as" the African slave trade. She felt that the grade was not fair and also hinted that it might be based on a racial bias. When I asked why she felt that the grade was based on racism rather than on the lack of academic merit, she replied that if the course had been taught by an

Asian faculty member the grade would have been much higher, apparently because an Asian faculty member would have been more sympathetic to the claims of the paper. Sadly, on the last point there is a pervasive sentiment among students that faculty from similar ethnic groups can or should be supportive of their work as an expression of ethnic or racial solidarity. I once had a graduate student of Indian heritage student walk out of a class I taught on the political economy in India—on the first day of class—with the statement: "I can't believe they let a non-Indian teach this class."

But back to the paper on happy slaves. I tried to offer an alternative perspective to the student as we talked over her paper in my office hours. I did point out that the lack of sources and the lack of any course materials in the assignment were the primary reasons for the grade, but she seemed insistent that her grade was based solely on the fact that both I and my teaching assistant (who was also not Asian) had graded her harshly because of her "pro-ethnic" point of view. And so I tried a different tactic, mostly in the form of common sense and logic, to see what that would do. First, I pointed out the absurdity of comparing systems of slavery to determine which forms of slavery were "good" or "bad." Comparing systems of slavery is a bit like comparing genocides: if more than six million people were killed in the Holocaust during World War II, but only two million were killed in the Cambodian genocide that occurred between 1975-1979, is there really someone so vapid and so callous who would claim that the Cambodian genocide was not "as bad" as the Holocaust? Pushing this further, along the lines of reasoning offered by the student in her paper, I asked her if she thought the Cambodian genocide was a "good" genocide because most of the killing was done by Cambodians against other Cambodians. Surely there was a sense of comfort in knowing that you were being slaughtered and tortured by someone from your own ethnic group, right? Then I switched to the more contemporary practice of child sex trafficking, which is endemic in parts of Southeast

Asia, including Thailand. Was the student really suggesting that an eight-year-old Thai girl, sold to a brothel as a child sex slave and repeatedly raped and treated in unimaginably twisted and vile ways by her captors until her young spirit and body were broken beyond repair—was that young girl somehow a "happy sex slave" as long as her captors and customers were also Thai?

Unfortunately this conversation ended with one of the more common phrases that emerges in discussions of diversity, which is the dismissive and defeatist phrase that a person—in this case me—just "doesn't get it." The idea that all identities have outsiders and insiders, and that outsiders can never understand or "get" insiders, and that insiders automatically and intrinsically "get" it, leads in education to the idea that only insiders can and should teach anything about their own group identity. This of course is completely anathema to the idea of education and to the idea of diversity, but it is paradoxically a persistent idea in diversity education. If you devote even a single brain cell to this idea, you can see clearly just how utterly nonsensical the suggestion is: if only insiders can teach about insider things, and if outsiders can never understand how insiders think, then cross-cultural understanding and multicultural learning of any sort are both impossible. The "robust exchange of ideas" promised by university administrators can never happen because no exchange is possible. In other words, meaningful diversity is actually impossible—*if* we accept this line of reasoning (and many do). If you take that line of thought to its illogical conclusion, you end up with something like the following. If a course on Chinese politics is offered at the university, then only Chinese students, as insiders, could "get" the material and thus receive an A. Perhaps Chinese-Americans, at least with those who maintain some element of Chinese-ness, could get a B, while everyone else, no matter how hard they try and no matter how much mastery they display over the material, could at best get a C or below. As outsiders, there is just no way they could "get it." I shudder to think that there are people who are stupid enough or racist enough to believe that makes even a modicum of sense.

And yet, there are variations of that line of thinking creeping into educational institutions every day. It might not be as extreme as the illogical "happy slave" mess I just described, but it is certainly the kind of reasoning that creates, cultivates, and entrenches the very sort of narcissism and myopia that lie at the bottom of identity-based involution.[1] To offer but one thematic example, I will discuss what is no doubt the most difficult and divisive identity-based issue in all of my courses: the discussion of Islam and all things related.

Life in the fast lane to denial
Given the nature of the courses I teach at the university—human rights, international law, war and terrorism, regional security, and a few others—I attract a very large and diverse array of students into my courses. I have always worked hard to attract a large variety of students and I have always been grateful for their continued interest in my courses. Among those students are of course a number of Muslim students, some from abroad and some who are American-born (or who have become American citizens). Nearly all of my courses offer at least one assignment in which students are allowed to choose their own topic, provided that it addresses the general theme of the course (thus, if it is a human rights course, it has to be on a human rights-related topic, etc.). If I had to make a list of the top three topics that most Muslim students choose for my courses, it would be an easy and predictable list: (1) the oppression of Palestinians by Israel, (2) the oppression or victimization of Muslim minorities in Europe or America, or pretty much any

---

[1] Involution was covered in detail in the first volume of this series, *Understanding the Misunderstanding*. It refers to the tendency of identity-based groups to turn inward and embrace sameness rather than face outward and embrace diversity.

country that has a Muslim minority, and (3) Islamophobia. Those three topics cover about 95% of the papers I receive from Muslim students, when the choice is theirs to make. I don't have a problem with the topics themselves, and would never think to disallow a student from pursuing them as a topic. It's their choice to make.

What I do have a problem with is *the lack of diversity* in the choice of topics and the extreme one-sidedness that emerges when Muslim students focus only on themselves. From time to time, for instance, I will suggest something in office hours that would require a Muslim student to adopt a different perspective, to see things from a different point of view—something that any constructive platform of diversity should be able to do. When I do this, the reactions are quite striking and illustrative of how diversity in education fails to challenge students to understand the experiences of others. If I suggest to a Muslim student that instead of writing about how Muslims are discriminated against in, say, the Netherlands, they write instead about how non-Muslim minorities such as Christians or Hindus or Copts are discriminated against in Muslim-majority countries—something that is pervasive and systematic—the suggestion will be rejected out of hand. If I suggest that instead of writing about hate crimes against Muslims in America they write instead about hate crimes against Jews, something that might potentially open up even the smallest amount of empathy for the Jewish community, again, the suggestion will be rejected out of hand. There is a strong filter on what is to be accepted or rejected as a possible topic of inquiry: either good things are done *by* Muslims, or bad things are done *to* Muslims. Anything that suggests that bad things are done by Muslims or good things are done to Muslims by non-Muslims is to be covered up and occluded from view.

To push this to the most absurd conclusion, I should note that there are many proponents of diversity who would claim that encouraging a Muslim student to take a critical perspective on their own culture and history is itself an act of Islamophobia. To battle Islamophobia, according to this line of reasoning, Muslim students should refuse to look critically at their own identity and culture and instead accept and assert only the parts that are good and perfect. Resistance to oppression takes the form of ignorance. And in case you haven't heard the news, ignorance is never a good foundation for anything.

Since we started this whole discussion with the happy slaves topic, highest on the list of topics that are simply not written about would be the Islamic slave trade of black Africans, something that predated the Atlantic slave trade by centuries and in fact still continues to this day.[2] On the rare occasion a Muslim student writes on this topic, it is either another "happy slaves" type of paper, in which it is argued that (1) the slave trade was somehow benevolent in helping blacks in Africa economically and spiritually, or (2) that the Islamic slave trade was not "as bad as" the slave trade perpetuated by whites, or even (3) that the phrase "slave trade" should not be used at all because slavery is forbidden in Islam and therefore the slave trade could not possibly have existed (not kidding on the last one). Part of the reason for this is just historical ignorance or willful blindness. As scholar Ronald Segal has pointed out in his study of the Islamic slave trade in Africa, the existence of the Islamic slave trade, with all of its concomitant exploitation and violence, is overlooked or unrecognized for the simple reason that it falls "outside the historical confines of the Atlantic Trade and the survival of racism in American society."[3] Like Al Gore's work on

---

[2] Consider most recently the slave markets that sprang up in Libya to exploit and sell refugees trying to get to Europe. See, for instance, Ali Younes, "African refugees bought, sold and murdered in Libya," *Al Jazeera* (November 29, 2017) at http://www.aljazeera.com/news/2017/11/african-refugees-bought-sold-murdered-libya-171129103602048.html

[3] Ronald Segal, *Islam's Black Slaves: The Other Black Diaspora* (2002), p. 241

climate change, the Islamic slave trade is an inconvenient truth. But that raises the more important question of motive: why do so many identity groups filter all of human history through the lens of narcissism? And more disturbingly, why is this considered acceptable only for minority or non-dominant groups? How is this a foundation for diversity? There seems to be a belief that minority groups are already oppressed or at least depicted unfavorably (only by the dominant group), and so we should not look at any parts of their current or past situations that might lend credence to any sort of negative viewpoint. Only positive things can be shown or discussed, and if something negative does emerge, such as slavery, it gets airbrushed or caked over with rhetorical makeup and then rewritten into something like a "happy slaves" type of narrative.

Seeking selves in the diversity of others
If narcissism is the acid that corrodes diversity, then it is not difficult to understand why diversity continues to fail in the classroom. Narcissism is amply rewarded while critical thinking is not, at least in relation to identity. Here for instance is another illustrative example from my professional experience in the classroom. In one of the first courses I taught at UC Berkeley, a course on contemporary South Asia, I had two African-American students in my class. I noticed the two African-American students right away because their appearance in a class on South Asia was something of an anomaly. The reality of most universities is that students usually self-select their courses by identity. If I teach a course on India, it will attract Indian students and students of Indian heritage. If I teach a course on China it will attract Chinese students and Chinese-American students, and so on. So when I ended up with two African-American students in a course that would focus on India, my first thought was that for once someone took the idea of diversity seriously and had decided to take a class that was outside of their own narcissistic comfort zone. But when I went around the room to ask students why they were in the course and what

had attracted them to the subject matter, I then learned that these two students were in the class only because the class they actually wanted to take—on African-American history—was already full, so they had to find something else instead. That at least answered the question of why they were in the class, but when I asked if they had any interest in India or South Asia in general, the response I got, in the form of a question, was as indicative as any as to why diversity keeps failing. The question was this: *Were there black people in India?*

Take a moment to appreciate the layers of non-diversity that exist in that question. If you are wondering, for instance, how anyone could ask such a question in the first place, the answer is found once again in the way diversity is practiced in the classroom. Students almost always seek out courses that focus on their own identity and heritage, and so they develop a strong sense of narcissism in their education, which means that the wide variety of course offerings that supposedly offer diversity to the student body end up having the opposite effect: diversity teaches anti-diversity. And note also that in this scenario, the only way India could have any interest for non-Indian students would be, as the question implies, if there was something in India that was sufficiently close to their own comfort zone of identity that you could avoid learning too much about a different culture. And so, for an African-American student, the first thing to do is to find a way to make India less Indian and also make it as African as possible. In spite of the riches that diversity is supposed to offer, most people immediately seek to impoverish the experience by grasping onto anything that looks like themselves in order to avoid the unease of trying to understand others. If it's somebody else's culture, then somebody else should learn about it. In other words, diversity ends up encouraging students to find classes that "look like me," which is actually the opposite of what diversity should do.

As it turns out, by the way, the question of whether there are black people in India has a positive answer: there is in fact a small community of black people in India. The *Siddi* community in India comprises descendants of Africans who were slaves, some brought through the Islamic slave trade and some bought from Portuguese slave traders by wealthy Indians (yes, you read that correctly, Indians bought African slaves), mostly of royal lineage, and still others who arrived in India through other means such as regional trade routes. There are about 40,000 *Siddis* currently in India. Some are Muslim, some are Hindu, and some are Christian—it's a diverse community. Some even formed separate communities in India after escaping their conditions of enslavement. So yes, there are black people in India and yes, their story is an interesting one, and one composed of many diverse pathways to the same point of arrival in India. But note the sad irony here: for these two students, India had now become interesting, not in and of itself, not because of its different culture or history and not because of its people or cuisine or politics, but only because it had black people. Only the peculiar type of narcissism produced by our current programs and practices on diversity could create such a distorted view of India whereby the existence of black people becomes the one thing that redeems India as an interesting place. The other 1.2 billion people who are not of African descent, who are just "Indians," are apparently just non-black distractions and ethnic ornaments.

Unfortunately, this narrative doesn't end there. If you really want to understand how diversity plays out in the classroom, what will happen is this. Muslim students, whether from India or Pakistan, will again disagree that there was an Islamic slave trade and will point out that the arrival and presence of Islam in South Asia was peaceful and benevolent. They will then point out that if any of the blacks from Africa were slaves, that must have been something done by the Hindus. The Hindu students, already uncomfortable with the idea that Indian royalty were complicit in the European slave trade, since most of them want to believe that India was perfect until the Europeans arrived to ruin their utopia, will then try to shift the blame to the European part of things or else create a new version of the "happy slave" narrative of history in which Indian slavery was somehow a good form of slavery. For the African-American students, India has no existence on its own but is now reinvented as a footnote to African history. India is now important because it has black people. The discussion therefore goes nowhere, as diversity creates a situation in which the ugliness which is deeply and equally embedded in pretty much every historical narrative from every culture and every civilization that has ever existed in history is passed around from one group to the next, hoping to offload the burden of historical guilt onto others so they can continue their own mythology of narcissism. What diversity teaches in the classroom is that if something bad turns up in your history, then it must be someone else's fault.

It would be hard to underestimate the long-term damage that these fissiparous viewpoints do to any viable or constructive program of diversity. They insert fissures into the social fabric where before there were none, they take the integrative project of diversity and invert it into one of separation, ignorance, and narcissism, and they ask us to substitute unsubstantiated falsehoods for tangible facts in the name of cultural tolerance. The reality of history is that everyone is complicit in the countless tragedies of human history; at one point or other, our histories create moments where we wish we would have been different and better people, rather than the ruthless bastards that we invariably and disappointingly were. History is as diverse as it is ugly.

If diversity is designed to cultivate equal respect, then we have to have equal honesty and openness in the way we each tell our historical tales. There are no happy slaves in human history, and the unsettling truth is that slavery and exploitation are inextricably linked and are shared diversely among many cultures and civilizations. All slave trades are based upon exploitation and discrimination, and if we could go back in time and ask each person who was ever enslaved if they would rather have a different life, one that involved their freedom, I can guarantee that each and every one would say yes. The Atlantic Slave trade was ugly and it was a disgrace to the entire premise of humanity, but we have to remember that it was one slave trade among many (and one of the few to be stopped by its own practitioners). Diversity, if it is to have any substance at all, requires us to tell every disgraceful story, no matter how painful, one after another after another. If on the other hand we want a diversity that tells only some stories but not others, one that gives us flawed and selective histories that allow us to believe in happy slaves and other fantasies, then we will have created a peculiar form of diversity that exists never as an edifice and only and always as a ruin.

The blurred vision of racism
If the road to hell is paved with good intentions, as is so often heard, then what can be said about the road to heaven? I don't know much about that road, and I am not even sure if it's paved. I can't imagine that it is, for everything I have heard about the possibility of getting to heaven tells me that it is a very difficult and arduous journey, and even if you can make it through that perilous journey and reach the much coveted point of arrival, you end up standing at the entrance of what must be the world's most exclusive gated community, wondering nervously if the management are going to let you in. Not everyone believes in heaven, of course, because there are other religions with other pathways to other destinations, and there are also those who do not practice any religion at all. But most people, with the exception of the inveterate cynics who just stay home and vent about all the celestial road work, have some idea of a better place in their mind: if it isn't heaven, then it is

some sort of utopia, or if nothing else, a world that will be slightly better tomorrow than the one we have today. But since the original proverb tells us of the road to hell, I'll stick with that metaphor to make some sort of assessment of the road to heaven, and here is what I conclude: *If the road to hell is paved with good intentions, then the road to heaven is paved by people who think everyone else is going to hell.*

On the road that leads to the heaven of diversity, that is, on the road where we find ourselves traveling among others, there is a lot of self-righteous shouting and sanctimonious posturing. If the road to diversity were smooth enough to drive on, it would likely be a festival of pious road rage. And what would be the cause for this hullabaloo of invective and acrimony? The most likely culprit, and the one that rears its head almost immediately when a discussion about diversity turns to the topic of why diversity is not working, is the specter that haunts every aspect of diversity: namely, *the specter of racism*. Racism is something like the evil twin of diversity, the bête noire of a diverse society, the villain who spoils the romantic ending. Like a mouse in a roomful of elephants, the smallest trace of racism can wreak havoc and mayhem in the house of diversity. In a world where diversity could be heaven, racism would certainly be hell. I have no quarrel with that argument and I believe it to be true. If the goal of diversity is to integrate a complex society, then this cannot possibly reconcile with racism, the intention of which is to divide and denigrate.

What I do have a quarrel with, however, is the incomplete and truncated concept of racism that is invoked to explain why a more constructive form of diversity has not yet been achieved. In part this is because racism is always seen as something someone else does or some other group cultivates: every person and every group that interacts in some way with diversity knows the acidic and acerbic nature of racism, but responsibility for the ubiquitous presence of racism is always foisted onto other groups and individuals. It is as if everyone says, "I know that racism exists and is a problem, but

I am not racist and my group is not racist and so the responsibility for causing the problem and also fixing the problem lies with someone else." The biggest obstacle to the attainment of diversity is not racism. It is rather the way in which racism is conceived by those who would consider themselves the heroic champions of diversity. Until the architects and practitioners of diversity acknowledge that racism exists equally among all identity-based groups, there will never be any sort of diversity that can make even the weakest claim to the idea of social justice.

A simple plan
One of the ways through which racism is masked or hidden or blame-foisted onto others is through the use of simplistic and convenient formulations to define what racism is in order to manipulate the pathways of responsibility so that they lead to others rather than to ourselves. Consider on this point one of the most common definitions of racism that shows up in lecture after lecture on university campuses and at meeting after meeting of self-appointed diversity activists: *Racism = Power + Prejudice*. This definition is as simplistic as it is dubious, and the idea behind it is that racism is the product of hierarchy and stratification (power) and discriminatory attitudes (prejudice) that flow from the top down to the bottom. This definition is also favored for what it says about the responsibility for racism: since power flows from the top downward, only the group on top—the dominant group—has enough power to be racist. All other groups, which are by definition non-dominant, are considered to lack power or to be expressly disempowered by the dominant group, and thus lack one or more of the essential ingredients to be considered racist. By their very nature, at least according to this definition, minority groups simply cannot be racist. In plain terms, since "whites" are considered the only dominant group in America, racism is defined as what whites do to others, to non-whites, to people of color. Since people

of color lack power, comparatively or absolutely, there can be no talk of their racism, and nor any discussion of "reverse racism" (racism from non-dominant groups toward the dominant group) or even of the possibility of "racism of color."

There are so many problems with this approach that it would almost take a separate book to explain how this simplistic caricature of what racism actually is undermines the very idea of diversity. But for now, a short discussion should suffice. The first problem we have here is that with all the obsession on who has power and who does not, the definition glosses over the pervasive existence of prejudice. The definition seems to have no problem with people being prejudiced against others, just as long as they come from groups that don't have power. But prejudice is in fact the central problem, and it is inconceivably bizarre that we should be willing to accept or overlook the pervasiveness of prejudice within the architecture of diversity. Racism is just one variant of prejudice, one variant among many, and we should be battling all forms of prejudice as much as we are battling all forms of racism.

The second problem I have with this definition is that it assumes that power flows unidirectionally and uniformly from the dominant group downward to all other non-dominant groups. In reality, even if we accept the premise that all communities of color are disempowered, they are certainly not *equally* disempowered. If power flows necessarily from top to bottom, then if some minority groups have more power than others (which is true), and if the relatively more powerful groups also harbor prejudice, then there must also be the possibility of minority-on-minority racism (which by the way is prevalent everywhere). But those other forms of racism, the ones that complicate and confuse our childishly simplistic beliefs about diversity, those other forms of racism are either shoved into happy slave narratives or else simply censored out of the picture. Those other forms of racism remain as one of the most forbidden and suppressed topics in all of the ongoing discussions of diversity in America.

The last problem we have comes in the form of one other peculiarity of this formulation of racism that points to its utter uselessness. If we were to ask leaders and activists in the various communities of color in America what their most ardent demand would be, a demand that is consistent and common across all communities of color, it would be without doubt the demand for empowerment. But with that, we end up with something odd: since the original formulation of *racism as power + prejudice* seems to have no problem with prejudice (as long as it exists in places without power), then fighting to get that power, to gain empowerment, would equate to little more than a fight for the right to be racist. Put differently, for any community of color that already has any element of prejudice in it—and that's pretty much every community of every color—the moment they achieve the power they seek through empowerment, they will also in that moment achieve racism. So perhaps the element of power is not the issue here, and quite frankly, it might be completely irrelevant. A more effective approach would be to focus on prejudice whenever and wherever it is found. But that would require a radical retooling of the way we conceive of both diversity and discrimination. And sadly, that retooling, which is absolutely essential for the type of social justice that diversity ought to provide, will be fought against tooth-and-nail by the many vested interests in identity-based communities whose self-proclaimed leaders purport to fight for absolute equality—as long as it is not equality of responsibility for racism. Racism, it seems, is always something that others do, never ourselves.

Who constructs racism?
Another argument that is often raised to show that only certain communities can be racist starts with the premise that race is a

social construct. The idea behind this argument is that while genetic differences may exist among all the different ancestral groups of humanity, these differences do not support any taxonomic hierarchy in the biological sciences but only explain at best physiognomic differences (such as skin color). The concept of race, the argument goes, developed out of an attempt and a desire to justify a qualitative hierarchy of identity-based groups based on innate (genetic) characteristics. The hierarchies that emerged around the evolving concept of race were constructed out of predominant social values of the group constructing the hierarchy itself, and thus ideas linking superiority of some groups over others with racial purity became the foundation for pejorative judgments about groups believed to be lower down on the race-based hierarchy, thus producing the modern phenomenon of racism.

The key part of the race-as-social-construct argument is that the ideologies and belief systems that generated the concept of race and along with it racial hierarchies—neither of which have any justification in medical or biological sciences—were distinctly European or "Western," and therefore racism is something that can only naturally occur in the West or can only be inflicted naturally by Westerners. Since no other culture or identity-based group invented the concept of race, non-Western cultures are either naturally or intrinsically non-racist. Or, if they are found to be engaging in racist acts or sentiments (which happens quite frequently), then they must have experienced some sort of distortion, manipulation, or oppression that forced them to adopt the "foreign" beliefs of racism. Combating racism among non-Western or non-white cultures is thus seen as a project of expunging the unfortunate stain or taint of Western culture on non-Western peoples and recovering the pure and authentic and inherently non-racist cultures of those different cultures and peoples.

There is some strangely circular logic embedded in this argument: non-Western people are inherently non-racist, but if they are seen engaging in racism, it is because they have been somehow rendered non-non-Western or culturally inauthentic. They are victims of racism, and if they are racist themselves, then their racism only shows that they are still victims of racism. Thus, the current proponents of racism-as-social-construct conveniently place themselves outside of the realm of responsibility, so that no matter what they do and no matter how racist they may be, they can never in fact actually be racist. And so paradoxically, many of those who claim to be opposing racism are in reality constructing it anew. The counterargument to racism is itself racist. It might be a different building with a new set of architects, but it's still ugly.

I accept much of the argument that racism, wherever it is found, is a social construct. I also accept the claim that the origins of racism as we know it lie in specific parts of European and Western cultural history. The concept of race emerged out of biological and medical research being conducted in the West in the eighteenth and nineteenth centuries that influenced and was then in turn influenced by the prevailing sociocultural attitudes of the time. So far, so fair. What I do not accept is the argument that only Europeans or Westerners or "whites" can be racist, since that was the part of the world and the cultural environment where the concept of race as we know it first emerged. Everywhere else in the world where we find racism, the argument goes, it must either have been imposed by Westerners or else mistakenly imbibed by non-Westerners to create a derivative and hence non-intrinsic ideology that remains always and everywhere "foreign" to authentic local values. This perspective is something of a paean to willfully convenient amnesia, a militant form of ignorance, a panegyric of the exorbitantly stupid. In simpler terms, it's rubbish. And here's why.

First of all, how easy is it really to make someone a racist, especially someone for whom racism is supposedly a "foreign" concept? Is it really so easy to get people to hate each other, especially people that have allegedly lived in harmony for centuries if not for millennia? My own guess, based on my years of experience in conducting social research around the world, is that this is not an easy thing to do at all. In fact, if we accept the original premise that all non-Western peoples had no racism and lived harmoniously with each other before the Europeans arrived, the whole concept of converting entire cultures to racism against their will becomes difficult to fathom. The usual answer that is given to explain how this conversion was possible and how it happened so quickly is "oppression." This answer does not satisfy and it is extraordinarily incomplete. Just as the argument that racism is a combination of prejudice and power masks the complexity of racism by asking us to focus on only one part of the problem (the power differential between one dominant group and all non-dominant others), the oppression argument similarly occludes the complexity of global racism by asking us to look at only one fragment of one moment in historical time: the arrival of Europeans into non-European cultures and societies. I agree that oppression is a part of the equation, but as with my views on racism, if you want to open up the question of who is or was oppressing whom, you need to open up the question in its entirety, no matter how much that unsettles the way we see the world around us, past or present.

When I read accounts that try to describe how racism was transferred from Western to non-Western peoples, my intuition and my experience tell me that there is more at work in this process than just oppression. *The reason that racism translated so readily into non-Western cultures was not because Western cultures used so much oppression to make it so, but because racism was so similar to any and all of the systems of prejudice, discrimination, and oppression that already existed in non-Western cultures long before any Europeans arrived.* Those systems might not have been based on race, but they were based on structures and beliefs that were similar in their manner of discrimination, exploitation, and oppression, all of which were, like racism in its original cultural context, socially-constructed. In other words, they might not have used the word race and therefore might not be called racist, but their systems worked in ways that would have sounded very familiar to Europeans who did think in terms of race and would have been analogous to the ways that racism emerged out of conveniently-constructed hierarchies and conveniently-justified forms of prejudice. Race as a concept simply replaced pre-existing structures of hierarchy and discrimination. So in a sense, it would be true to argue that the introduction of European values destroyed or dismantled pre-existing cultural belief systems, but it would be equally true to argue that many of those pre-existing cultural systems were just as much in need of dismantling and just as deserving of resistance against them as the ideology of racism that replaced them, both historically and presently. Oppression is a social construct, in the sense that one cannot engage in oppression without first inventing a reason for it, and race is just one version from among a sadly long list of candidates produced by a wide variety of cultural actors in human history. Racism transferred so readily to non-Western cultures because oppression, like racism, is as ubiquitous as it is iniquitous. Adding racism to the mix doesn't really require much effort at all.

So when I hear that racism has tragically spread around the globe, along the routes of European imperialism, and when I think of the oppression that made that possible, I think quite differently about it than the simplistic gibberish that many contemporary advocates of diversity profess. When I hear that racism has emerged in the past or the present in some other part of the non-Western world, and has somehow replaced whatever cultural system had been there before, what it tells me is that either the culture in question did not have very strong cultural values, considering how easily they fell to a new cultural influence; or that sufficient oppression was already present in the cultural system to allow racism an easy entrance. Or it tells me that the cultural system in question had produced enough disaffection and discontent that certain segments of the population seized upon the idea of racism as a fulcrum to destroy the system that kept them down and to create a different hierarchy that would put them up. Internal disaffection did as much to spread racism around the world as did external oppression. Once that happens, and once racism is adopted into a new cultural environment, whoever adopts that ideology becomes authentically racist.

It is a logical fallacy to argue that only Westerners, and specifically white Westerners, can be racists because race only makes sense in the cultural environment of Western civilization. That would be like arguing that Indonesians cannot be "true" Muslims because Islam originated in the different cultural context of the Arabian peninsula. If you profess the values of Islam, regardless of your culture, then you are a Muslim. And if you profess the twisted message of racism, regardless of your culture, then you are a racist.

How more racism is necessary to get less racism
The idea that members of dominant communities are *genuinely* racist while members of non-dominant communities are *mistakenly* racist, which in a country like the United States means that only whites can be racist, has created a considerable amount of complacency among communities who consider themselves non-dominant minorities. That complacency is as corrosive to the project of building diversity as is racism itself because it gives rise to the belief that racism is always someone else's responsibility to fix because it is always and invariably someone else's creation. To a certain extent, this complacency is just another variant of the happy slave narrative: just as slaves in non-Western cultures who were enslaved by their own group were not "really" slaves (or if they were they were at least happy about it) persons from non-Western cultures who express racist viewpoints are not "really" racists. But this line of argument confuses different projects: spending time on the historical

origins of racism, or quibbling over which cultures can be racist and which cannot, overlooks the very real fact that however we got here, there is a tremendous amount of racism in the world and in the current state of things only a surprisingly small portion of that racism is Western, or for lack of a better word, "white." Even if we restrict our viewpoint to the United States alone, and even if diversity as hitherto practiced succeeds in eliminating every form of white racism in America, we will still be left with a lot of racism, which means we would only be fixing a part of the problem. *We need to identify more racism if we want to have less of it.*

Where does all this other racism hide? Primarily it hides in two places: the first is in racism projected from non-dominant minorities (so-called communities of color) to the dominant majority (usually called "white"), and the second is in minority-on-minority racism. The first is often referred to as reverse racism, though this epithet is generated by the erroneous belief (discussed earlier) that racism exists only in the form of prejudice + power. Since racist sentiments projected from minority to majority do not fit this pattern, because the hateful sentiments flow in a backwards direction that the inventors of the formula did not envision, it is given a special qualifying adjective and referred to as *reverse* racism. While there are those who think that reverse racism cannot and does not exist, I think the real problem is in adding the qualifying adjective. As I explained earlier, I do not think the original formulation of racism as prejudice + power has any heuristic validity, primarily because power is not the issue. Prejudice is independent of power, and prejudice packs all the ugly and destructive power toward diversity that racism does. Think about it: is there such a thing as reverse prejudice? Personally I do not think differentiating racism from reverse racism helps anything, and I think it is just another variation on the theme of trying to claim that only certain communities can be racist. I think anyone and any community can be racist, and so rather than quibble over the direction of power, we ought to just call something racist if it is racist, from whatever community it is voiced and in whatever direction its venom is spewed. Reverse racism is just more racism.

The second place that racism hides is in minority-on-minority racism, which is pervasive and yet receives scant attention both in colloquial discussions and in formal scholarly literature. Every time I bring this issue up, there are many who rush in to shut down the conversation as quickly as possible. "Don't even go there," goes the standard protest. I don't think it would be too much of a stretch to say that this type of racism is diversity's dirty little secret. Most people deny it exists, either because it threatens the idea of solidarity and unity among people of color or because it lays bare the falsehood of the formula that racism consists only in the lethal cocktail of prejudice + power. Community-based scholars won't touch it, because if they go public with the evidence for racism *within* their communities they will be excommunicated *from* their communities. Or, if they do approach it with a scholarly lens, it is to show that minority-on-minority racism is not genuine but rather the disaffected residue of a white racism through which communities of color have been unwittingly coerced into emulating their oppressors.

I think these lines of argument infantilize communities of color, something that does far more harm than good in generating the type of equal respect that diversity is supposed to generate. While there are a plethora of narratives lionizing those who have resisted oppression against communities of color, the fact of the matter is this: if a community is capable of skillful resistance then it is also capable of willful adaptation. You cannot force racism on someone any more than you can force religion, so the focus of our efforts in identifying the forces that undermine the premise of racism should be on identifying the agents of racism whenever and wherever they occur. Sorting them out by color to determine which are genuine and which are not makes as little sense for racism as it does for slavery. The lack of white skin does not make a person "innocent." At best, it simply makes them guilty of a different set of historical crimes. Until we acknowledge our equal complicity in making the injustice we see around the world, we cannot create a diversity that will gives us the equal justice for which anyone with a heart and conscience should aspire.

Making racism colorblind
One of the writers I admire most in the world, one of those writers who constantly reminds me of just how powerful the written word can be, is Nigerian author Wole Soyinka. There are many things to admire about his work, from his densely but eloquently written plays to his poignant memoirs of life in Nigeria, but what I want to offer here from his vast repertoire is a simple quote: "I don't care about the color of the foot pressing on my neck, I just want to remove it."[4] In other words, oppression is oppression, and the "color" of the oppression is completely irrelevant. Color is not the issue, oppression is. Only the most cretinous of idiots would find the idea of being beaten and trampled underfoot acceptable, as long as it was done by one's own kind. *Sure I'm being beaten to a pulp, but at least I am being beaten by someone who "looks like me."* Really? The idea of happy slaves, of trying to divide the world into "bad" oppression (oppression done by outsiders) and "good" oppression (oppression done by insiders which somehow isn't oppression) is absurd to an extreme. Wole Soyinka's point here, paraphrased accordingly, is this: all slaves are miserable, full stop. Humans oppress humans—if you are quibbling about color, then you are wasting everyone's time.

Too much of the rhetoric that is generated in discussions of diversity focuses on dominant or "white" racism, to the point where

---

4 "Tackle the Monster of Zimbabwe, Says Soyinka," *Star* [South Africa] (July 21, 2005), p. 3

there are those who argue that no other forms of racism can exist (since only dominant groups can be truly racist), or that other forms of racism are "reverse" racism (meaning they are somehow different or more innocuous forms of racism). If racism exists among non-dominant communities, it is somehow a derivative by-product of the oppressive and racist environment, created by their oppressors, in which they are forced to live. I would never suggest that racism does not exist in America. But following Wole Soyinka, I would say that looking for the color of racism is not the project we should be working on. It is a distraction at best. Racism exists in America, to be sure, but it is also as diverse as America: it is present among all communities and it is equally real and equally corrosive in all contexts. The project we should be working on is to eliminate racism, wherever it occurs and in whatever color or form it appears.

Two examples
In January 2016, an advertisement for a cosmetics company made its debut that attributed success to having lighter skin, featuring an actress using the product next to one in blackface, and ended with the statement: "Just being white, you will win." The advertisement was quickly withdrawn after an instantaneous outcry of racism, and an apology was offered by the cosmetics company. At this point, you might be wanting to grab me by the ear and tell me: "*See*, this is they kind of thing we're talking about—white racism is real and it is everywhere." Thanks for the message, but there's only one problem with your comment. The advertisement was made in Thailand by a Thai cosmetics company.

If your first response is to start looking for reasons why the very thing you just called racist is now somehow not racist, then you've just started down the path of yet another "happy slave" narrative (and remember, that phrase comes from the example with

Liberating the Enclave

which I started this chapter, and also involved Thai culture). So let's see what reasons someone could come up with to try to argue that what appears to be racist is somehow now not racist because it doesn't involve white people.

First, I said there was an outcry about how racist the ad was. Who made that outcry? Other Thai people, that's who. It turns out that skin-color-based prejudice isn't just a thing in America. In Thailand, for instance, there is a long history (long as in pre-dating the arrival of Europeans) of associating lighter skin color with higher status, and conversely, of associating darker skin color with lower status. The dominant ethnic group in Thailand (yes, Thailand has diversity, too) tends to look down on and discriminate against other non-dominant minority groups whom they perceive to be darker-skinned (such as indigenous hill-tribe and minority groups, or the Cambodian and Indian communities in Thailand). If you're thinking that this is merely just prejudice and not racism (because only white people can be racist), then you would have a hard time explaining why Thai social media lit up with comments from Thai people that this was *definitely racist*. So if Thai people see it as racist, then clearly people in Thailand can be racist. And if people in Thailand can be racist, then people of Thai heritage can be racist. And if people of Thai heritage can be racist, then Thai-Americans can also be racist. And if Thai-Americans can be racist, then clearly not just white people can be racist. Anyone can be racist.

Oh, but wait, you might say. Clearly this is the result of colonialism. Clearly this is yet another sad chapter in the way that white imperialists forced their racism onto subjugated peoples and made them become racist. In this way, what looks like Thai racism is really Thai people being colonized victims of white racism. It's a noble effort, I'll admit, but there's one glaring problem in your argument. *Thailand was never colonized by any European power.*

These types of examples are far more common than self-styled advocates of diversity would have us think.[5] Their occurrence is either denied entirely, or else written off as an example of how white colonizers forced their racism onto other cultures against their will. In 2012, for instance, the cover of the Filipino version of *FHM* magazine featured a light-skinned Filipina model (Bela Padilla) standing in front of darker-skinned models in the background (some of whom were also Filipinas, just covered in black make-up to look darker) with the caption "Stepping Out of the Shadows."[6] Racist? Absolutely. The outcry was fierce and quick, especially on social media, and eventually the editors pulled the cover out of circulation. But according to the *Racism = Prejudice + Power* crowd, we either cannot acknowledge this racism, because it didn't involve white people, or we have to interpret it as an example of how people like Bela Padilla, who had no regrets about the cover and did not see the problem, were forced to be racist by white colonizers and so aren't responsible for their racism.

Speaking of blackface—and let's return to the United States for this second example—stop me if you've heard this one. A man walks into a Halloween party dressed in blackface. There's no punch-line to that because it's not a joke. The question is, when it happens, is it always racist? *Of course it is*, you shout emphatically. Why, it's an outrage that I even had to ask. Okay, so here's where I tell you that the man in question is Terry Rambler. Why would that matter? It matters because Terry Rambler is a Native American, from the San Carlos Apache Tribe in Arizona. To make things

---

5 For a similar ad in Malaysia, see Fahima Abdulrahman, "The 'blackface' ad that got Malaysia talking," *BBC News* (June 30, 2017) at http://www.bbc.com/news/av/magazine-40447395/the-blackface-ad-that-got-malaysia-talking

6 See Kate Springer, "'Racist' Filipino Magazine Cover Axed after Online Outrage," *Time* (March 1, 2012) at http://newsfeed.time.com/2012/03/01/racist-filipino-magazine-cover-axed-after-online-outrage/

worse, he was also an ardent proponent of the campaign to force the Washington Redskins to change their mascot because—you guessed it—the Redskin mascot was and still is considered offensive and racist to Native Americans.⁷ Like the Thai cosmetics company, Terry Rambler offered an apology and said he hadn't meant to offend anyone.

If you are struggling to find a way to see this as anything other than racism, since a Native American was involved, and if you cannot bring yourself to utter the phrase *Native American racism*, then hopefully you can see the problem. When we hear a story about white racism, we tend to think of it as typical, almost expected. When we hear of racism by non-whites, however, we immediately think it must somehow be an aberration, an exception, a mistake, something to be explained as anything other than racist. In 2007, for example, when Indian cricket fans mocked cricketer Andrew Symonds, who is of Afro-Caribbean descent and at the time was playing on the Australian team during a match in Mumbai, by making monkey gestures at him, Indian cricket authorities initially tried to explain it away as a "cultural misunderstanding."⁸ Australian officials, however, saw it for what it was and called out the Indian fans for their behavior, and eventually four Indian spectators were arrested and charged with racial abuse. If you are trying to find some other way to view this incident—a legacy of white colonialism, a cultural misunderstanding, or anything other than Indians being racist—then this is precisely why our efforts to end

---

7 Miriam Wasser, "San Carlos Apache Chairman Offends Many with "Blackface" Halloween Costume," *Phoenix New Times* (November 5, 2015) at http://www.phoenixnewtimes.com/news/san-carlos-apache-chairman-offends-many-with-blackface-halloween-costume-7802016

8 "Indian fans face racism charges," *BBC News* (October 18, 2007) at http://news.bbc.co.uk/2/hi/south_asia/7050264.stm

racism haven't worked. Racism shouldn't get a pass depending on the color of the racist. It's ugly in every color.

I know there are those who would argue that white racism is the most important problem right now and therefore we should deal with that racism first—the other forms of racism, if they exist at all, can wait. I'm not convinced of that, and I can't see any legitimate reason to wait. To let other forms of racism continue and fester while we focus only on one will let too much injustice seep through. As I have said, to argue that one form of racism is worse than another is a bit like trying to argue that one genocide is worse than another. There are no degrees of genocide. Genocide, like racism, is always wrong and always horrible. Would we really be willing to let one genocide happen because there was another, "more important" genocide we wanted to deal with first? I shudder to think that anyone would find that acceptable.

White racism certainly exists and it is certainly a problem, and not a word of what I have said here should be construed as an effort to ignore or excuse white racism, or to claim that white people are somehow being victimized. But white racism is only one part of racism in America, and if we are serious about trying to end racism, then we need to spend less time fighting about the color of racism and more time focusing on the racism itself. Racism comes in all colors, and it's just ugly, always. Only three things we can do with racism: rethink it, reject it, end it.

CHAPTER 2

HERITAGE AND THE STRANGE NOTION OF PRIDE

In March 2001, Johannes Rau, then president of Germany, was giving an interview on German television when he mentioned that while he could be *pleased* and grateful to be German, it was not something of which he nor any other German person could or should be *proud*. Predictably, a firestorm of controversy erupted in which Germans of all ilks and shapes began falling over themselves to show just how proud they were to be German.[9] Some even asked whether Mr. Rau should be allowed to stay on as president. I mean, what kind of president is not proud of his country? Only the Greens—ah, one can always trust the Greens on these things—showed their support for the president's position. I suppose there is a case to be made for feeling reluctant to be proud to be German, given the last century or so of German history, but that was not really the point that Johannes Rau was making. He was making a much deeper and more philosophical point: how

---

9 Bernd Hops, "Debatte um Nationalstolz: Die Stunde der Patrioten," *Der Tagesspiel* (March 19, 2001) at http://www.tagesspiegel.de/politik/debatte-um-nationalstolz-die-stunde-der-patrioten/212332.html

could anyone be proud of something they did not accomplish or choose on their own? After all, to be born in Germany, to have one's birth take place within the legal boundaries of the nation-state of Germany, was simply sheer cosmic luck or random chance. To be proud to be German in that sense would be like being proud to win the lottery or to be born into a wealthy family—there is no effort or skill involved, only luck. Thus, one could be pleased or grateful or even thankful to be German, but pride was something reserved only for the things that one accomplished through one's own efforts.

On this point at least, I think Johannes Rau deserves credit for publicly questioning the link between pride and identity. Much of human history, and not just the German version, reveals an unfortunate correlation between pride and violence; the downside of identity pride is that those who are so proud can only boast of their pride if other people from other groups are left to feel shamed or humiliated, or at least less proud, for not being part of the "chosen" group. Sometimes it is national identity, sometimes it is ethnic, sometimes it is religious, but all sorts of evidence shows that when people feel proud about something, they want to make sure that others who do not share their identity cannot experience the same pride. Aside from the link to violence, there is also the link to ignorance. Pride, especially excessive pride, tends to exert its gravitational pull in the direction of blindness, and so people who are taught or who teach themselves to be proud of their identity are usually unable to accept any information that calls that pride into question. Incidentally, it is this type of identity-based doltishness that gives us the whole ignominious library of dreadfully inane ethnic pride narratives, which mimic so much of the happy slave narratives we saw in the last chapter. The whole thing is an unfortunate mess, all the more because so much of diversity has hitherto been designed to make us feel so proud of who we are. Yet when we focus so excessively on ourselves, we forget about others, and diversity fails. So if diversity is teaching pride, diversity is also failing itself.

Inculcating narcissism through heritage learning
One of things I often do during the semester is to change the screen saver picture on my computer each week, drawing on the large collection of photographs I have accumulated over the years from my various research trips to different parts of the world. Before I begin the slide shows I use to support my lectures, I will usually ask the students in my courses if they can identify the country or place portrayed in the screen saver photograph. During one semester, I happened to post a picture from South Korea that showed the characteristic colors and architectural styles of a Korean palace, and one of my Korean-American students was able to identify it immediately. He then proceeded to describe South Korea, nodding his head in admiration as he looked at the photograph, as "the best country in the world." I then pursued the conversation a bit further and asked why he felt that South Korea was the best country in the world. His response was that he had been there for a study-abroad program for one semester and had a great time with his Korean family and friends. When I asked how many other countries he had been to in the world, in order to make this assessment that South Korea was the best country in the world, the answer was quite astonishing: aside from being born and raised in America, South Korea was the only other country he had been to. As I pondered the breathtaking narcissism of his response, next to him were two other Korean-American students, who immediately did some quick high-fives, one of whom proclaimed quite audibly to the others, "Korean pride!"

Earlier I discussed some of the liabilities of programs that are designed for students to study abroad, liabilities that serve to undermine the premise of diversity due to the fact that students tend to seek out opportunities that reflect their own heritage rather than something truly different and foreign (which it seems to me is the whole point of studying abroad). Here I want to address the larger phenomenon of heritage and along with it the idea of "heritage learning," which is both a formal part of university education and also a path that many individual students pursue, some as a life-long project. Heritage learning at the university, and at other levels of education in the United States, is a central part of current diversity policy whereby increasingly large amounts of resources are set aside to provide opportunities, in the form of classes and other academic activities, for students to learn about their own culture. While these sorts of possibilities have always existed in the educational system of the United States, heritage learning takes this a step beyond in that the programs are set up specifically to attract individuals from a specific heritage to learn about their own cultures, usually in the company of students from their own group. Sometimes whole schools are set up for this; for instance, a school that emphasizes Chinese language and culture might be set up to allow children of Chinese heritage to immerse themselves in their own culture while learning the same general educational materials that all American students must learn. Heritage learning is considered by most current advocates of diversity to be an integral and positive part of diversity. As I see it, however, and based on my own experience with heritage learning, it is quite the opposite. It is mostly an exercise in narcissism, and often, it is a gateway to ethnic pride and chauvinism.

Most people do not understand how heritage learning works against diversity because most people do not get the chance to see how heritage learning works. With me, being in the formal educational environment and being someone who has spent his professional career immersed in other cultures, I have seen how heritage learning is packaged and presented and how students experience the opportunity of heritage learning. Since the example I cited above from my class involved Korean-American students, and since I have spent a fair amount of time living and working in South Korea, I can use this as but one example of how heritage learning works and how it works in the opposite direction of what diversity should be.

The first thing that heritage learning does wrong is that it rewards people for choosing non-diverse actions, something especially unfortunate considering that heritage learning is supposed to expand diversity. If you are in an institution of higher education, where the options of what you can study are mind-bogglingly diverse, and your choice is to say, "I want to learn about myself and things already familiar to me, in the company of people who are just like me and from the same group," then you have taken one huge step in the *opposite* direction of diversity. The second thing that heritage learning does wrong is that it creates what might be called a "homeland narrative," which floats the arrogant boat of pride on an ocean of cultural fiction. When I taught in an international summer program at a university in Seoul, for instance, the director of the program made it clear that one of the major intentions of the summer program, which incidentally is a study abroad program, was to bring back "Koreans born in America" (they did not want to say Korean-American) so they could establish a sense of belonging and pride in their homeland. I found the whole idea very strange, especially for a program calling itself an *international* summer program, but not as strange as watching Korean-American students imbibe this message and inhale the intoxicating vapors of their newly-minted "homeland." This narcissistic reaction to the idea of a foreign homeland is not unique to Korean-Americans, but it helps to clarify how a Korean-American student could smile with delight and proclaim South Korea to be the best country in the world, though he had no other international experience and though he was unaware of the contradiction that he was saying this while sitting in a seat in a classroom at an American university. The stark reality is this: for him, and for all Korean-Americans,

South Korea is just another foreign country, one among many. But heritage learning teaches instead a narrow-minded attachment to a fictive homeland. If heritage learning encourages us to prefer self over other, sameness over difference, then heritage learning cannot be reconciled with the task of diversity. We have to choose one or the other. In the end, one of them has to go.

The deleterious effect of heritage learning on identity and diversity, especially in institutions of education, is something I see nearly every day of my professional life. As I pointed out earlier, one of the disturbing trends I notice in my courses is that when I offer an assignment in which students are allowed to pick any topic they want, anything at all, more often than not what students choose is something that is far more self than other—usually something to do with their heritage or homeland, real or imagined. In the specific class I referred to earlier, where my student claimed that South Korea was the best country in the world, all three of the students sitting in the cluster (all were Korean-American) eventually came to my office hours to discuss possible topics for their papers, and all of them started with the same idea: "I want to do something on Korea." But it isn't just the narcissistic choice of Korea that surfaces nearly every time. It is also the way that choices on anything relating to Korea are filtered. If the topic drifts toward Korean-Americans in the United States, the desire will be to write a narrative of victimization (the "America is racist" narrative) or a Korean-American success story (the "celebrate my community" narrative). Any hint of a different narrative—Korean-American racism in America, Korean racism in Korea, Korean patriarchy and the status of women in Korean culture—these are quickly rejected as possibilities, since they cannot be reconciled with the narcissism offered by heritage learning, which is designed to promote only positive, "beautiful heritage" images through carefully crafted and conveniently edited narratives.

Here is a more specific example of how this works, with slightly more detail to illustrate the point of how heritage learning and heritage pride put blinders on the learning process that ultimately result in the degradation of diversity. One of the courses I teach at UC Berkeley is a course on international human rights, and one semester a Korean-American student came to office hours to talk to me about his research paper topic, which, as in many of my other courses, can be on any topic of the student's own choosing, so long as it addresses the themes of the course. The conversation started, as it often does, with the student expressing an interest in wanting to write about "something Korean." That was a bit too broad, I pointed out, and so I pushed the inquiry further about what sort of things "Korean" attracted his interest. He then said he wanted to write a paper to show that the treatment of Korean-Americans in the United States amounted to a human rights violation. When I asked him which specific human rights had been violated, he wasn't sure (actually he had no idea). When I asked him who was responsible for these alleged human rights violations, he said, and I quote exactly, "Americans." When I told him that this implied that Korean-Americans were not Americans, or, if they were Americans, they were somehow exploiting themselves, he laughed nervously and changed his answer to "the government."

We then returned to the question of which specific human rights had been violated, at which point he took his narrative back to the 1940s and the 1930s and then to the nineteenth century, at which point I stopped him. In the world of human rights, I reminded him, there are two things that are necessary to prove a human rights violation: one, the human rights violation must be specifically detailed, and two, it must have taken place at a time when the relevant human right in question was actually in force as human rights law. None of the examples he offered satisfied either condition. I then pointed out that while discrimination is without doubt one of the more sordid and ugly chapters of the complex narrative that makes up American history, the discrimination of the past took place before human rights principles were in force and as for the discrimination that takes place in the present, after human rights principles had come into legal force, these would not amount to a systematic human rights violation—not even close. I could tell from his face that frustration was setting in.

I then told him there was another option he could pursue as a topic, if he was convinced he wanted to write about something Korean. I then told him that he would have a much stronger case if he wrote about the discrimination against minorities and migrant workers in South Korea, and even showed him the webpage for the National Human Rights Commission of South Korea, showing that by far the largest number of human rights cases in South Korea were about discrimination and racism against minorities, refugees, and migrant workers. At that point, however, he became very uncomfortable, since this topic introduced the possibility that Koreans could be the perpetrators of the same sort of injustice that he was convinced only happened *to* Koreans and *in* America. That topic was immediately rejected, and he left convinced that he could find a way to show that Korean-Americans were victims of human rights abuses in America. The pride of heritage had made it impossible to consider Korea as anything other than a utopian homeland, and so as a result, if there were human rights problems to be found where Koreans were involved, it had to be somewhere else. In America, for instance.

Torching diversity
Of course, Korean-Americans are not the only demographic group to engage in narcissistic reflection over their own heritage. Back in 2008, for example, during the build-up that preceded the hosting of the Olympics by China, news emerged that San Francisco was going to be the only American city that would host the running of

the Olympic torch. Almost immediately, news also surfaced that the route of the torch in San Francisco was to be kept secret to avoid any "unpleasant scenes" created by protesters who were upset for many reasons, such as the fact that a country with such a poor human rights record had been allowed to host the Olympics in the first place. Back at UC Berkeley, many Chinese student groups on campus—which included both Chinese-American and Chinese students—sprang into action and organized caravans to San Francisco in an effort to line the streets of the torch route (parts of which had by now been leaked to the press) to show support and pride for China. This of course generated a certain amount of controversy, as did the decision by then-mayor Gavin Newsom to try to keep the route secret and without prior notice to shift the location of the closing part of the ceremony to San Francisco International Airport, in order to foil any possible protests. In the days that followed, I had a number of conversations in my classes about this, and was surprised to hear just how many students of Chinese heritage stated that they wanted to show their support for China simply because of their heritage. And it wasn't just students who felt this way. According to one native San Franciscan of Chinese heritage, "I'm here to show my pride. I've wanted for 30 or 40 years for China to stand up."[10] For China to host the Olympics, I heard over and over again, was a great thing, something that all Chinese people around the world, including Chinese-Americans, should be proud of. Somehow, whatever problems and whatever faults and whatever forms of oppression and violence occurred in China—these were to be glossed over and covered up under the warm and fuzzy blanket of heritage pride.

---

10 Riya Bhattacharjee, "East Bay Tibetans, Chinese Clash over S. F. Olympic Torch Relay," *The Berkeley Daily Planet* (April 11, 2008) at http://www.berkeley-dailyplanet.com/issue/2008-04-11/article/29697

Back to heritage learning

I should point out that it is not just students who seem to cultivate if not celebrate this trend toward utilizing heritage learning as a means to foster community solidarity and pride. When I was on a committee for faculty research and curriculum development grants a few years back, I read a proposal that asked for a sizeable amount of funding to rewrite the Tagalog language curriculum so that it would appeal directly to students of Filipino heritage and help them to appreciate and celebrate their culture. The argument behind the request for funding was that the overwhelming majority of students who signed up for the language classes in Tagalog were either originally from the Philippines or else were American-born children from families that had immigrated from the Philippines, and thus were part of the Fil-Am (Filipino-American) community. Since nearly all the students in the language classes were Filipino, by birth or by heritage, the grant application claimed that the curriculum should be re-written to appeal to members of the Filipino community in order to strengthen the community and the heritage that created it. On the committee, I argued strongly against awarding the grant. My point was this: the problem was not that the curriculum as currently structured does not meet the needs and interests of the Filipino heritage students, but rather from a diversity standpoint the curriculum as currently structured does not attract enough *non*-Filipino students. The curriculum should be re-written not to attract more Filipino heritage students, but instead to attract more non-Filipinos. Had the grant requested funding to diversify the Tagalog-language classes by introducing creative ways to bring non-Filipino heritage students into the classroom, I would have wholeheartedly supported the grant. But as it was written, it seemed little more than an exercise in narcissistic heritage-centric thinking that leads to the type of identity-based involution I discussed earlier, another example of how our current diversity mindset leads to a distinct lack of diversity.

There are even heritage-centered language classes that are separated from the regular foreign-language curriculum. These language courses are designed *only* for students of a particular heritage, and are special and separate classes for those who grew up hearing a language due to a heritage-based connection to the language. Such students are not necessarily fluent in the language, or else never learned that language in a formal environment, but are too familiar with the language to start with a beginning class. Thus, for instance, Chinese-America students can take separate heritage classes to learn Mandarin. From a pedagogical standpoint, there is some justification for offering classes to students who are already familiar with the language they want to study, since it would give them an unfair advantage over students who are taking the same language out of interest but for whom the language is entirely unfamiliar. But from a diversity standpoint, the whole enterprise is a disaster: it creates an enclave of heritage students—say, Chinese-Americans (in the case of Mandarin language learning)—who separate out from the other classes and who go through the whole progression of language classes as a separate community. They share and celebrate their heritage with each other, immersed in an environment of sameness, rather than sharing that heritage, as diversity requires, in the company of others.

If I were to redesign the curriculum of American universities in this regard, a redesign based on what diversity should be and not on the festival of narcissism it currently is, I would first make the foreign language requirement non-negotiable (all students must take at least two years of a foreign language) and then, and here is the most important part, I would exclude from the list of languages a student can study *any language that has any relation to their cultural or ethnic heritage*. A Chinese-American student could still study Mandarin, if they want to, but it would not fulfill the foreign language requirement. They would have to take Mandarin in addition to another language. The point is to take students out of their cultural comfort zone, where they are surrounded mostly by people of the same heritage, and put them in an environment where they have to struggle with true cultural difference. A Chinese-American student studying Swahili or Finnish does far more for diversity than letting them self-segregate into Chinese heritage-learning language classes.

Heritage and diversity

I suppose there is a natural urge to understand our heritage. After all, we all come from somewhere and that seems to be at least one interesting chapter in the story that we tell ourselves about who we are. The problem with heritage pride and heritage learning, as I see it, is that it confuses what is only one chapter of a long and complex narrative with the entirety of the story. Heritage pride and heritage learning ask us to stop reading just when we started the book, and we end up with an incomplete image of ourselves, of who we are and what else we could be. If diversity asks us to move in different directions, then heritage pride tells us to move in the same. Heritage pride and heritage learning tell us to seek out our own kind and be proud of who we are, but that pride blinds us to the reality that our heritage is not everything we are but only a small part of it. *Diversity is not about who we are; it is about who others are and about how understanding other people changes the way we see ourselves.* Once we are lured by the siren song of heritage, particularly as the vision of all that we are and by the pride we think we should feel about being what we are, we become far less interested in the stories of others. *That is their story, not mine.* This is why heritage is not a part of diversity, but rather its opposite.

In the long and complex narrative that diversity writes for us and that we write for diversity, heritage is at least a part of that narrative, so my point is not to suggest that we ought to forget or deny our heritage. It is the naturalness with which we begin to link heritage and pride that concerns me, for it is precisely that pride that produces the distortions in how we see ourselves among others. Once we develop pride in our heritage, we become far less likely to accept any negative moments of reality that pop up in the narrative. They either get glossed over, rewritten, or attributed to outsiders. Heritage narratives all too often become narratives of collective victimization designed to attribute the unpleasant elements that occur within them to outsiders, foreigners, and other allegedly oppressive forces. Yes, sometimes, indeed often, that has happened in history—no one is fool enough to deny that. But the interlinked narratives of pride and victimization create a degree of truculence in the politics of identity that make mutual understanding far less likely, hence undermining the task and function of diversity.

Imagine for instance if the United States decided to revamp the entire history curriculum to claim that slavery never happened, or if it did, that it was forced upon the United States by outsiders, say, Britain as the oppressive, colonial power. The justification for this rewritten history would be that slavery makes many Americans feel ashamed, or makes America look bad, and what America really needs is more pride, so we should just airbrush out all of the unpleasant events and moments and leave behind a narrative that boosts and cultivates American pride. I can only imagine the outrage that would occur in the United States over this, and the bewilderment that would happen in Britain, suddenly finding itself the villainous cause of all that is wrong in America. And yet, on a smaller scale, this is exactly what heritage narratives do. They encourage us to question the actions of others, and not to question the actions of ourselves. If pride-soaked buffoonery is the end goal of diversity, then hooray for everything since we are well on the way to one fantastically bizarre masquerade party in which no one is who they appear to be. But if well-tempered and well-crafted diversity is our goal, then we are going to need a truckload of erasers, a giant vat of ink, and a boatload of editors (not sure if editors come in boatloads), because the history of *everything* has to be rewritten and the airbrushing removed. Rule number one? For every word we read in our own narrative, we need to read a word in another's.

Pride and victimization

Many of the problems I have highlighted in this chapter are produced by the dramatic clash of two conceptual tectonic plates that seem perennially to grind together: pride and victimization. Identity-based groups often claim that the reason they need to write a revised and edited version of their own story is that their culture or their identity has been systematically distorted by the narratives about them written by others. The distorted narratives written by outsiders create a sentiment of victimization, so the new and unblemished story has to be written as a pride-inducing corrective to replace the old version written by "outsiders." The problem with these types of narratives is that they don't correct anything. They simply replace one distortion with another. False pride cultivated by insiders is just as destructive to diversity as the disparaging inaccuracies attributed by outsiders. Replacing one with the other does nothing for diversity.

Lost in all of this is the cost of writing histories that are designed to restore or to cultivate pride of any sort, whether that pride is cultural, ethnic, or any other variety. Conveniently excised from these types of histories are all of the practices and events and traditions that would undermine that sense of pride, so that we end up either with false histories (buttressing false pride), or with unjustifiable interpretations of inconvenient truths that would otherwise blemish that history. The oppression carried out by one's own group is expunged from the record, and replaced by narratives of lamentation whereby outsiders are identified as the "true oppressors." Think about it: there has been a disturbing amount of oppression in human history, but can you name a single cultural narrative that confesses a role in that oppression? No—oppression is always something that others do.

At no point does anyone ask the question of why we need cultural or ethnic pride in the first place. Does it really play a role in diversity? If we know that the wok is a great and efficient instrument with which to cook, does this really boost the pride of all Chinese-Americans? If Chinese-Americans do not cook with a wok, are they betraying their heritage? And if we celebrate the wok, should we neutralize the pride generated by it by pointing out the less flattering traditions of the same culture such as foot-binding? Sure, you invented the wok, we might say, but you also had foot-binding so the two cancel each other out. Sorry, no pride for you. And does it really mean anything for members of an ethnic group to say "we" invented the wok (for instance)? Is there really any substance to the idea of collective cultural credit for anything? These types of things tend to leave us with a diversity that is based on general aggregate characteristics that emphasize the group over the individual, and at some point diversity has to be brought back to the individual level. Without bringing diversity to the individual level, we always run the risk of inculcating group-think, which as I have already pointed out, is the very death-knell of diversity itself.

DNA in culture
It has become increasingly easy in recent years for pretty much anyone to get a DNA test to find out their genetic composition, broken down neatly in percentages of cultural heritage. By now, most people have seen at least one of the ads or commercials in which a person has a whole new sense of self because they somehow didn't know they were "part Caribbean" or that they now had some cultural element in them that changed entirely how they saw themselves. Most famously, perhaps, is the Ancestry.com ad in which a person who spent his whole life "being German" found out that he

was really 52% Scots-Irish, and so as the ad states, he "traded his lederhosen for a kilt."[11]

The whole idea that DNA is our one true cultural destiny makes me extraordinarily nervous, and I'll have more to say about genetics later in this book. But the idea that my whole sense of self should change based on a DNA test makes no sense. If I were adopted into an Indian family at birth, for instance, wouldn't I grow up culturally Indian? That wouldn't show up in my DNA test, but why would that matter anyway? Even stranger is the fact that in the example above, it is the majority DNA component that determines the culture of the person—52% is barely over half, and yet suddenly it's time for kilts and bagpipes.

Part of my discomfort with the DNA as cultural destiny is that it plays into another growing trend that has emerged out of the dysfunction of diversity, and that is the debate over cultural appropriation. "STOP TRYING TO BE OTHER CULTURES!" screamed one website I came across devoted to protesting cultural appropriation. We're one step away from being asked to take DNA tests so we know which culture we can legitimately be, with the additional requirement that we can only be one culture. It's either lederhosen or kilts—no kilterhosen. All other alternatives are apparently off limits, lest someone mistakenly feel pride in a culture that is not genetically theirs. Those who think they are somehow strengthening diversity by resisting and unmasking acts of cultural appropriation, however, are doing diversity an extraordinary disfavor. As it turns out, diversity cannot work properly *without* cultural appropriation.[12]

---

11 See, for instance, the video and some additional commentary from the blog of the History Department of Saint Anselm College, at https://saintanselmhistory.wordpress.com/2017/02/22/ancestry-com-lederhosen-and-genetics/

12 For a more detailed version of this argument, see D. C. Zook, "Culture is a beautiful thing to appropriate," *Medium* (September 29, 2017) at https://medium.com/@zookkini/culture-is-a-beautiful-thing-to-appropriate-812b955052cf

Misappropriating culture
I look on with concern and consternation at the recent hullaballoo to denounce and oppose this thing called cultural appropriation. It's a poor choice of words at work here anyway, for what these critics and activists really mean is cultural *misappropriation*. To appropriate something is to take something and make it one's own in an integral way. To dress appropriately, for instance, is to dress in a way that is right and respectful. To misappropriate something is to take it in a way that is outside of or antithetical to its original purpose and context. Any rugby fan knows that New Zealand's national rugby team, the All Blacks, perform a *haka* before each match. If you've ever seen it (and if you haven't you should definitely look for it), you'll notice that both indigenous Maori and non-indigenous kiwis perform the *haka* together. Are the non-indigenous players therefore "appropriating" the *haka*? Yes, they are, and it's a good thing, too. The team actually has a *haka* coach, who ensures that the player-performers understand the meaning and importance of the *haka*. The important thing isn't the ethnic or cultural identity of the performer of the *haka*. It's whether the *haka* has been performed with appropriate cultural respect and understanding.

Culture, you see, is not a limited or scarce commodity. There's a bottomless well there, with plenty of cultural water for everyone. The outcry over cultural appropriation assumes that only people born within a certain culture can participate in it, own it, and be proud of it. It's a movement that asks us to stick to our own cultural kind and turn our backs on cultural others. To evoke some of the language from the recent presidential campaign in the US, here is what I would say to the self-appointed guardians of culture who are trying to stamp out cultural appropriation: you can't make culture great again by building a wall around it.

The nay-sayers of cultural appropriation make it out to be an inherently villainous thing, and they also (and inexplicably) make it out to be a white thing. The whole argument is based on the misguided belief that culture is destiny. The culture you were born with is who you are meant to be, which links directly back to my previous concerns about the "DNA as cultural destiny" approach. The implication is that you have no business looking at someone else's culture—it's not yours, and you can't have it. So stick to your own kind.

In May 2017, for instance, a scandal of sorts erupted in Portland, Oregon, when a food cart serving breakfast burritos was shamed into shutting down after information surfaced that the two women who set up the food cart had traveled to Puerto Nuevo, Mexico to learn how to make the perfect tortilla.[13] In their words, they "picked the brains of every tortilla lady" in that town, apparently using badly-spoken Spanish at that, and then brought their knowledge back to set up a food cart serving burritos wrapped in what they hoped would be the best tortilla in Portland. An uproar ensued over Portland's so-called "appropriation problem," with someone even setting up a public Google doc to list and presumably "out" all white-owned restaurants that were serving dishes outside their defined cultural domain. Interestingly, one of the businesses singled out for egregious acts of appropriation was Voodoo Doughnut, apparently because they took their name from and are therefore profiting from a religion that—and I note this with great irony—itself blended together and therefore appropriated different sets of cultural practices and religious beliefs.

I also note with concern that the whole controversy seemed to single out white business owners, as if somehow, had the two women in question been Asian or black, for instance, the appropriation would have been acceptable or not even seen as cultural appropriation. This isn't an isolated incident either. In March 2016,

---

13 See Tim Carman, "Should white chefs sell burritos? A Portland food cart's revealing controversy," *The Washington Post* (May 26, 2017) at https://www.washingtonpost.com/news/food/wp/2017/05/26/should-white-chefs-sell-burritos-a-portland-restaurants-revealing-controversy/

a black female student at San Francisco State University called out and confronted a white male student simply because he had dreadlocks. A video taken of the confrontation quickly went viral, with the black student telling the white student he had no right to wear dreadlocks because it wasn't his culture. Yet another act of resistance against (white) cultural appropriation, right? Only people like Bob Marley should be allowed to have dreadlocks, right? If you answered yes to that question, then you've only got one problem: Bob Marley was half-white. By the logic of the opponents of cultural appropriation (or lack thereof), Bob Marley should have been allowed to wear dreadlocks, but only on one side of his head.

We need to be able to differentiate between cultural appropriation and cultural misappropriation. The distinction is crucial, because yes, it does happen that cultural theft and exploitation can occur in ways that denigrate other cultures. I'm not sure two white women traveling to Mexico amounted to a loss of culture in Mexico. And at least the two women tried to interact with and learn from another culture (though I'm not sure why they had to travel to Mexico for that, since there are dozens of videos on YouTube showing how to make the perfect tortilla—and last time I checked, you didn't have to be Mexican to watch those videos). The fact is, most of the boisterous opponents of cultural appropriation are too mired in and enamored with their own cultures to bother to learn about others, and learning about others, as I have said repeatedly, is actually an essential part of diversity.

If I really wanted to go straight to the button-pushing part when it comes to cultural appropriation, which apparently I do, I'd bring up the N-word. I don't have to argue that the use of the N-word in black communities is cultural appropriation, because that has been common knowledge for a long, long time. Black communities, the argument goes, appropriated a word from the white community that was used in a derogatory, racist way, and then in turn transformed it and adopted it within the black community as their own, with an entirely different meaning. But remember, the opponents of cultural appropriation did not say you should not take from other cultures unless you can get something positive out of it. No, the opponents have said you should not and cannot take anything from any culture that is not your own. So if the opponents are correct, we have to ask the question: isn't it time the black community gave the N-word back?

The answer to that question, of course, is a resounding no. And the reason the answer is no is because the opponents of cultural appropriation simply have no idea what they're talking about.

To take a less extreme example, consider a swim in the San Francisco Bay. I have a good friend who swims in the brutally cold waters of the bay on a regular basis, and from time to time he invites me to go along for a swim. As I make my way through the frigid water, one of the things that keeps me going is the knowledge that after I finish, I know there's a sauna in the clubhouse after I'm done. Now, *sauna* is a Finnish word and the sauna is a product of Finnish culture, and I'm not Finnish. So according to the opponents of cultural appropriation, it would actually make sense if a Finnish person ran into the sauna, grabbed me, and threw me out, telling me in no uncertain terms: "Stop trying to be other cultures!" But that makes no sense to me, and it shouldn't make any sense to anyone. The world would be a much poorer and more divided place, culturally speaking, if that's the direction diversity took us.

The US Supreme Court made it clear in its decision in *Grutter* (discussed in Part 1 of this series) that the end result of diversity was to be one thing: an integrated society in America. Integration itself relies necessarily on assimilation, and assimilation is not possible without cultural assimilation. I have also argued that diversity is an intercultural process, designed to cultivate intercultural understanding. Intercultural understanding would similarly not be possible without some degree of cultural appropriation.

The opponents of cultural assimilation want to build a society of walled-off enclaves, and as I earlier made clear, a society composed of enclaves is the opposite of diversity.

For me, in terms of what makes a person who they are, cultural heritage is a place to start, not a place to finish. If we build walls around our cultures to keep outsiders out and insiders in, then we all lose something in the process. We are prevented from seeing how others see the world, prevented from seeing other ways to be who we are. How can I learn to walk in the shoes of another if the path is forever closed to me? We retreat to an extreme form of cultural fundamentalism, without realizing that in knowing nothing of other cultures, we really know nothing of our own. *Diversity simply cannot work without cultural appropriation; indeed, it requires it in order to thrive.*

CHAPTER 3

HEROINE ADDICTION

Not all narratives are about identity-driven distortions drawn from elements of ethnicity or race or other facets of the complex category of heritage. Some, for instance, relate to an entirely different aspect of identity that so far has not been moved to center stage in the theater of insightful scrutiny: gender. Gender is an interesting character to move to center stage right now, for it provides a moment of delightful consternation whereby gender simultaneously interrupts and emulates all of the other elements of identity we have discussed so far. Gender interrupts by creating confusion in the narratives that often construct the self-portraits of identity-based groups. Just as an identity-group—doesn't matter which one—is putting the finishing touches on its unblemished narrative, along comes gender to ask why all the central figures in the narrative are men. One might even point out the irony, prevalent in so many identity-group self-portraits, that a narrative that continuously laments the group's mistreatment at the hands of outsiders simultaneously glosses over its own mistreatment of women by insiders. To lament to the outside world and to ignore in the inside world is to dabble in nonsense of the highest order. Unless the groups in question are aspiring to be known as the

Hypocrites, then the self-portrait narrative must address the relentless interruptions that undermine and complicate the integrity of the image. Gender arranges for this quite nicely, I might add.

Where the irony thickens into a bitter and dyspeptic stew, however, is when those very interruptive uprisings begin to take on the same characteristics of the airbrushed self-portraits they so plaintively denounce. The narrative of gender might complicate the narcissistically distorted self-portraits of so many groups, but only at the cost of emulating those very same mistakes, deceptions, and distortions of what they seek to resist or alter. With the various narratives through which women, for instance, try to rewrite the pre-existing narratives and rework the traditional templates that compose the self-portraits that so many identity groups, if not every identity group, seek to inscribe on the walls of diversity's edifice, history literally repeats itself ad nauseam. In the gender-based, gynocentric (female-centered) narratives that make up women's history, we discover rather quickly that we have two types of characters, or perhaps caricatures, that dominate the orthodoxy of feminist unorthodoxy: gynocentric narratives can only be good stories of good women, or stories of how men turned good women bad. Gynocentric narratives here transform into an endless litany of heroines, some who resisted the dominance of gender-based outsiders (also known as men), and some who stoically endured their oppressed status in ways that always and necessarily inspire. Stories that show women willfully exploiting other women or other people or other groups are either airbrushed out or explained as aberrations created by that wily pack of mendacious fiends—aka, men. In other words, the gender-based narratives penned by women show a strong and pronounced predilection for heroines, leading to what I like to call *heroine addiction*.

Now, as many readers recover from what must seem a loquaciously heretical rant, or return from a quick search for a flame source with which to burn this book—accompanied as it always is by the struggle with a guilty conscience that tells you that burning books is wrong (also, please note that burning an e-reader or tablet computer on which you might be reading this is not an effective or environmentally-friendly form of protest)—allow me at least to illustrate how this preference for heroines manifests itself in a variety of everyday settings. Every April at UC Berkeley, for example, the campus plays host to Genocide Awareness Week, organized primarily by the Armenian student groups on campus to commemorate the Armenian genocide but also to cover and discuss all genocides. I am sometimes invited to give a talk during the week, an invitation which I am always honored to receive and happy to accept. At one of these events, I gave a talk comparing the Armenian genocide with the Cambodian genocide to make the point that all genocides happen in different ways and for different reasons (too many people think that all genocides are the same and differ only in size). After my talk, as is the usual practice, the floor was opened to questions from the audience. The first question I received from the audience was from a student who identified herself as a senior with a major in Gender and Women's Studies. Her question was as simple as it was disconcerting: "It seems like genocide is something that men do. Do you think if women were in control of the United Nations, we wouldn't have the problem of genocide?" Seriously, this was the question.

The question itself is emblematic of all of the problems that exist in our current practices of diversity, practices that teach members of any particular identity group, women included, to see the world with themselves at the center and to see that center as perfect and unblemished and worthy of pride. If only my group were at the center, they say, then the world would be a beautiful and perfect place. So how did I respond to the question? I immediately brought up the case of Pauline Nyiramasuhuko, the former Minister for Family Welfare and the Advancement of Women in Rwanda who also has the dubious and disturbing distinction of being the first woman convicted of genocide at the International Criminal Tribunal for Rwanda (in June 2011). Among the many horrible things she for which she was convicted, she ordered the ethnic Hutu men under her control to rape as many ethnic Tutsi women as possible, preferably after killing their own children in front of them. In another incident, she ordered the men over whom she held command to pour gasoline on a group of Tutsi women and burn them alive. The student, however, was unconvinced. These and other such counterexamples were summarily dismissed by the student as "exceptions." In her mind, women were inherently good and could only do good and peaceful things. Anything that did not fit that image, such as the orchestration of the mass slaughter of children and mass rape of women *by a woman*, was merely an "exception" to the beautiful, gynocentric rule. Women were heroines, always.

Light through the thicket
Before I go any further into this discussion of gender and the role it plays in diversity, I should say two things. *First*, I want to state that I know this discussion will make many people uncomfortable. Diversity is supposed to afford us the "robust exchange of ideas," yet as I have pointed out, and this chapter is in many ways emblematic of this, what our current practice of diversity usually does is shut down the discussion before it starts. Diversity works not as a facilitator, but rather as a censor. You can disagree with every sentence in this chapter, if you like, but let's at least have a discussion about these issues. *Second*, I want to declare in no uncertain terms that nothing in this chapter is meant to trivialize or deny the pain and suffering that women have experienced throughout history and into the present due specifically to their gender. My point here is to point out how the distorted discussion of gender in the context of diversity actually ends up disempowering women, even as it claims to empower them.

To return to the question-and-answer exchange moment between the student and myself, I know it would be easy to dismiss it as the idiosyncratic rant of one misguided or perhaps overly idealistic Berkeley student. But the reality is that I encounter this viewpoint frequently and consistently in venue after venue. The idea that a man who commits violence is man acting like a man, but a woman who commits violence is an "exception" from the peaceful feminine norm is an idea that needs to be put to rest—the sooner the better. It is often said, for instance, almost to the point of being cliché, that women hold up half the sky. The suggestion embedded in the phrase is that women are half of the world's population and hence deserve to be recognized for their equal contributions. Without women, the sky would collapse and fall. But note how the powerful filter of gender-based narcissism precludes the possibility that this could be anything other than a positive contribution. If women hold up half the sky, would they not also hold up half of racism? If women hold up half the sky, would they not also hold up half of genocide? If women hold up half the sky, would they not also hold up half of patriarchy?

If you find yourself bristling at even the mere suggestion that women could be complicit in any of these things, then you are right smack dab in the middle of the pickly thicket. Now, a thicket of pickles might not be the easiest thing to imagine, but then again, neither is a theory or a history that keeps churning up an endless supply of heroines. Something seems amiss. Something seems unnatural. For starters, I could rattle off an endless stream of anecdotes and experiences that churn up anything but inspiring heroines. When I first lived in India, for instance, I employed a woman to help with various things for part of each day. I had never hired anyone in that capacity before, and I will confess it felt a bit strange to me. She was an extraordinarily kind and honest and hard-working woman, and I made sure to pay her a good and fair wage and to give her two days each week plus all holidays off, and also gave her an extra stipend to cover her children's school expenses. When I hired her, she was already working at several other houses in the neighborhood, and not even one week had gone by before a woman from a neighboring house came to my flat to shout at me for treating a low-status woman like she was anything more than trash on the street. If I paid my domestic assistant a living wage and gave her days off (I later found out that the other households never gave her any days off), this would apparently create an unacceptable situation. She made this quite clear in words that will forever stay with me: "Soon she will think she is a decent woman!" Sometimes when women open their mouth to speak, what comes out is every bit as ugly as what men say. In the uglier moments of humanity, gender often seems surprisingly irrelevant.

Consider alternatively the conversation I had during a roundtable on the horrific violence that accompanied the collapse of the former Yugoslavia. The roundtable brought together academics, diplomats, and other professionals along with several people from the region who were in some way involved directly with the violence. At one point, the discussion turned to the role of gender in the war, an especially important topic since it was in this conflict that for the first time mass rape was recognized as a war crime (as opposed to being a "tragedy of war"). A woman who was present offered this assessment of how things happened: "It was the men's duty to fight, but it was the women's duty to make them fight." When someone else asked her to clarify how women carry out this alleged duty to make men fight, the woman offered as an example the fact that no woman in her village would have anything to do with any man who talked of peace or refused to fight. A man who did not act "like a man" was shunned by the women. It was an interesting moment when it became clear that each gender was constructing the other in a mutual and intertwined fashion.

Before I continue, I'm going to pause for a moment and check in with you (yes, you, the person reading this). I am quite sure at this point that many a reader is right now searching for ways to reinterpret these anecdotes and examples or to reject them outright.

What is interesting to note is that if you are one of the people doing that, chances are pretty much 100% that you are doing that reinterpreting or rejecting *only* in relation to the actions and words of the women and *not* the men. Men who rape and kill are doing what men do. Nothing made them do that—it's just what they are. Nothing to explain. But women who rape and kill, women who discriminate, or women who seem to be complicit in the actions of men, well, something else *has* to be involved, right?[14] Something *has* to be explained, and explained in a way that turns women back into heroines. Garden-variety feminism tells us that men construct their own dominant roles and then use their patriarchal power to force women into subordinate roles that the men have constructed for them. A Serbian man who fights in an ethnic militia is just a man. A woman who admits she was equally complicit in making the man fight "isn't herself." Instead, she is indirectly displaying her oppression under patriarchy, forced as she was by men into a role not of her own choosing. Men make wars, and women suffer through them. That's the story diversity gives us in relation to gender. I think the truth is far more complex than this. I also think the truth is far more ugly. If there is a silver lining to all of this, it is, as I will demonstrate, that ugly is empowering.

Of monologues and perorations
In a general sense, one could argue that the two anecdotes I have just offered are exceptions. Just as the student at the genocide

---

14 I know there are many people who will simply reject the idea of "women who rape" or "women who kill" as absurd impossibilities, but it happens far more frequently than most people think. See, for example, these stories: "Tennessee family sues after female janitor charged with raping boy," *BBC News* (April 27, 2017) at http://www.bbc.com/news/world-us-canada-39735902 and also "Nurse shoots Texas mother dead and steals her baby," *BBC News* (April 19, 2012) at http://www.bbc.com/news/world-us-canada-17759886

conference insisted that any evidence that showed women to be complicit in genocide *had* to be an exception, many of the proponents of feminist history argue that exceptions must not be allowed to undermine or obfuscate the general truth of the narrative that consists of a long and ever-expanding litany of newly discovered female heroines who had hitherto been silenced and stifled at the hands of patriarchal scribes. But in my experience and in my reading and in pretty much everything I do and see, I have been unable to suppress a growing awareness that these non-heroic exceptions exist in such copious amounts that they stop being the exceptions and they become the rule. To stock the pantry of women's history with so many heroines takes just as much selective censorship and convenient distortion as it does to stock the pantry of men's history with heroes. And just so I am perfectly clear what I am getting at here, let me state what I think the rule is, once we accept that the female exceptions are not really exceptions at all. *If human history had been matriarchal rather patriarchal, the world today would look pretty much exactly the same as it does now, with the possible exception of a nascent men's liberation movement.*

No doubt it is difficult to imagine a world in which *The Vagina Monologues* is replaced by *The Penis Perorations* as the most well-known gender-based piece of subversive and liberationist theater. But just because it is difficult to imagine does not mean it isn't a worthwhile enterprise to try. Diversity after all is designed to make us see things from a different perspective, one other than our own and other than the one with which we are familiar and comfortable, and a project like this one certainly fits the bill for that. Indeed, one of the things that gets lost in concatenating an endless stream of heroine stories one to another is the sheer diversity of gendered experience. It takes just as much social pressure to get women to adopt patriarchal norms as it does to get them to adopt matriarchal ones—it is not a question of the artificial versus the natural—and so the heroines whose stories get celebrated and promoted may not speak for anything other than one specific part of women's history. It's part of the story, but not the whole story. For diversity to work, we need the whole story.

The problem with equality

Setting aside for the moment the question of whether feminism as a school of thought is inherently radical or whether radical feminism is a more extreme version of mainstream feminism—and to make a point, any movement that has to tell me it's radical most likely isn't—we have the more interesting question in the context of a discussion of gender-based narratives of whether it is possible for a woman to be enslaved by her own emancipation. The stereotypical narrative revolves around the argument that patriarchy is the social construction that forced women into the kitchen and into domestic servitude, and therefore liberation involves taking the woman out of the kitchen and making her fight the hegemonic social force of patriarchy. Putting a woman into the kitchen is enslavement; taking the woman out of the kitchen is liberation. Supposedly. And the liberated woman, so the argument concludes, is *woman as woman should be.* In reality, however, both images of a woman, the one in the kitchen and the one out of it, are normative constructions. That is, it takes just as much normative power to put a woman into the kitchen as it does to take her out. The emancipated image is also an aspirational model, one created by an alternative ideology. We have no real way of knowing which one is natural and liberated and which one is artificial and oppressed. To become an emancipated woman requires the same conformist pressure as it does to become a woman who bakes cookies.

What the entire debate, if it is a debate, misses, is that the experience of gender is itself diverse. There are many different ways to be a woman, just as there are many different ways to be a man. To the extent that a woman has a choice as to what type of woman she wants to be, we can speak of liberation. But if a woman chooses not to conform to or chooses a path other than feminist liberation, in the sense that liberation is constructed by feminism, then she is not necessarily enslaved and oppressed, for she has in fact made a choice. If feminism does not allow or accept these other choices, that is, if feminism does not tolerate the resistance of women to the normativity of feminist liberation, then feminism is suppressing diversity within the category of gender. Feminism, not patriarchy, becomes the oppressor.

Positive equality and negative
The pattern I refer to as *heroine addiction* stems from the generative foundation of feminist history, which was to write an empowered history that corrected or resisted the negative depictions of women that were replete in male-written, patriarchal texts. This was the origin of the idea that the whole point of feminist, gynocentric narratives was to offer positive images of women (and negative ones of men where possible), images that showed women doing everything that men did and doing it just as well if not better. Negative depictions of women were to be rejected, either because they jeopardized or questioned the nascent feminist project or because they might confirm at least some of the depictions offered in patriarchal narratives, which had to be proven wrong on all counts. But the way I see it, this is a furtively fragile and flagrantly flawed fount for female empowerment. We end up with a situation akin to totalitarian regimes, where news agencies are required to report only the good and suppress the bad (or we end up like a certain democratic country whose leader accepts only the good news and dismisses all else as fake news). Patriarchal histories never had an agenda to show men as only good and virtuous actors, so they could be heroes or villains or anything in between. That gave men as historical actors a full range of choices and possible outcomes, meaning they had both positive agency (the ability to do good) and negative agency (the ability to do bad). By restricting

women-centric narratives only to those that show positive agency, feminist histories deny full agency and choice to women and the result is in fact a general and persistent sense of *disempowerment*. A narrative of genuine gender equality must inscribe full agency to women, meaning that depictions of negative actions and other non-heroine narratives are actually an essential component of full equality. Negative equality is just as important as positive equality.

There are numerous examples of how the lack of negative equality for women leads to odd and unproductive results. I remember reading a book review once for a book on psychopathology and violent crime. The author of the book had decided to be democratic and diverse by alternating his use of the third person pronoun between *he* and *she* throughout the book. The book reviewer, who was a woman, took exception to this, noting that it was disconcerting to see sentences such as "she killed…" or "she murdered…" In the case of negative things such as murder and psychopathology, apparently it is preferable to leave gender equality out of the picture and let men take on their proper roles as violent, murderous bastards. Similarly, an article that appeared in a top-rated academic feminist journal on the topic of feminism and vegetarianism—many feminists advocate vegetarianism because meat is associated with patriarchy and manhood—tried to argue that since meat-eating is linked to heart disease and heart disease mostly affects men, feminists should therefore eschew vegetarianism as it is something that might help keep men alive.[15] I wish I were making this up. Is this article radical, you might ask? Sure is—radically stupid, which probably isn't the kind of radicalism that's going to help women or, quite frankly, anyone.

The predilection for heroine stories also runs into some awkward terrain when and if we combine the narratives of women's

---

15 Kathryn Paxton George, "Should Feminists Be Vegetarians?" *Signs* 19/2 (1994): 405-434

history with that of other identity groups, especially non-dominant ones. Aboriginal and indigenous groups in Australia and New Zealand, for instance, are deeply hierarchical and patriarchal, to the point that if they *weren't* indigenous, feminist critics round the world would be denouncing them as positively medieval, or negatively medieval, as it were. In September 2008, for instance, mega-publishing house Harper Collins issued a public apology for including a section in the Australian version of *The Daring Book for Girls* that showed a girl playing the didgeridoo. Aboriginal activists made it clear that women are not allowed to play the didgeridoo, as its intrinsic ceremonial and ritual power can only be handled by men and never by women.[16] More controversially, in 2002 a North Queensland judge (a female judge, I should add) ruled in an Australian court that the rape of a 15-year old aboriginal girl by a 50-year old male tribal elder wasn't really rape because it was a customary and traditional practice and therefore not morally wrong, at least by indigenous standards.[17] Indeed, the girl's parents had offered their daughter to the elder in exchange for a share of his government allowance. Nor is that case unique.[18] And of course, anyone who has seen Niki Caro's movie *Whale Rider*, itself based on the eponymous book by Witi Ihimaera, knows of the strong discriminatory pressure of patriarchy prevalent in Maori communities in New Zealand, in this case, in the refusal of the local *iwi*

---

16 "Aborigines complain Daring Book for Girls breaks taboos by urging girls to play the didgeridoo," *The Daily Mail* (September 3, 2008) at http://www.dailymail.co.uk/news/article-1052236/Aborigines-complain-Daring-Book-For-Girls-breaks-taboos-urging-girls-play-didgeridoo.html

17 Sonia Shah, "Judge Rules Rape of Aboriginal Girl 'Traditional'," *Women's eNews* (November 29, 2002) at http://womensenews.org/2002/11/judge-rules-rape-aboriginal-girl-traditional/

18 "Rape case ruling shocks Australia," *BBC News* (December 10, 2007) at http://news.bbc.co.uk/2/hi/asia-pacific/7136269.stm

(tribe) chief to admit that a woman could ever be capable of any sort of leadership in the local community.

What I find most disturbing if not appalling in cases like these is the extent to which so-called feminist scholars who continuously denounce the culture of patriarchy will suddenly bow down to the great and unswayable god (goddess?) of culture and go silent. Much like the happy slaves narratives I discussed in an earlier chapter, here feminists are happy to let women be oppressed by men in indigenous cultures because they are being oppressed indigenously. There is a reluctance to criticize aboriginal or any other non-dominant cultures for the pervasive practice of patriarchy because it undermines the hagiographical belief that patriarchy is something that stems from dominance, and therefore only dominant people in dominant cultures can be genuinely responsible for the manipulations of patriarchy that have pilfered women's autonomous potential for centuries, if not millennia. If we find the same manipulations in non-dominant groups—and I think anyone who's not a corpse would be able to see that clearly—then it calls into question everything we think we know (but don't actually know) about the link between patriarchy, gender, and power. Non-dominant groups are supposed to find a presumed sympathy among each other in their universal struggles against various forms of unbridled and unjust power, sort of like a Justice League of identity-based activists, and so evidence that this might be based on a fundamental misunderstanding of, well, pretty much everything in human history tends to get brushed under the historical rug. This is all the more sad and ironic considering that intellectuals, especially those who self-anoint themselves as radicals, are supposed to be open to directing their critical lens at all that needs a critical viewing. In this, I think, feminist history has failed its own constituency, and failed it spectacularly.

From herstory to mythtory
In the world of diversity-based thinking, it doesn't take a genius to understand why incorporating the voices of women into the narrative that society collectively tells itself is an important endeavor. Diversity requires us to tell our own stories as much as it requires us to listen to the stories of others. Several of the problems associated with social diversity, such as the ones I have discussed throughout this book, reveal themselves in the weaving of this collective chronicle. They reveal themselves, for instance, in the way that many identity-based groups are attracted more and more to the telling of their own stories, so much so that they forget to listen to the stories of others and instead are perennially seduced by the sound of their own beautiful story. Blemishes become inconvenient and embarrassing, so over time, to make the beautiful story increasingly and unceasingly beautiful, those blemishes are conveniently erased or attributed to others whose job it becomes to bear the blame and guilt. In the part of the diversity narrative that deals with gender, the term that has been used by many a writer to talk about this specific part of the narrative is the rather bizarre rhetorical concoction called *herstory*. The idea behind herstory is that the canonical narratives of all social groups, both of dominant groups and of non-dominant, were written by men, which of course puts the *his* in history. Herstory was thus meant as a corrective to those narratives. Herstory is thus the story of how, from a woman's point of view, women subverted the control of patriarchy and revealed a new and altered truth that had hitherto remain occluded by the clever craftiness of power-perverted men.

From a slightly different perspective, it is easy to see again where the tendency toward heroine addiction—the predilection for heroines in feminist narratives—comes from. For if feminist history is meant to be a corrective to all the negative images etched into the narrative by male writers, fulsomely exuberant as they are in their patriarchal bias, then feminist history must by its very nature search for those figures that undermine, challenge, and disprove the existing patriarchal narrative. Women who lend credence to any part of that patriarchal narrative, whether in whole or in part, are to be quietly marginalized or actively censored out or written off as exceptions, leaving only an immaculate lineage of women who have resisted and struggled against and endured the unbearable weight of male oppression. Yet the temptation to airbrush out all of the unpleasantries and infelicities of the narrative of women's history in order to sing the heroine's chorus does not necessarily give us a better or more complete history, and it does not give us a corrective or even an alternative to patriarchy. If the orthodoxy of history is really a biased narrative of patriarchy that was designed to make male dominance look natural and ineluctable, then one could argue—and many have—that *his*tory is really just a grand historical project to serve the power of men. But if *her*story is a narrative designed to serve the power of women, the result only shows that if we had herstory rather than history, it would be (and is) just as biased and distorted as what we already have. Much as history highlights the accomplishments of men, herstory highlights the accomplishments of women, thereby ending up doing the same thing that it claims to oppose. Herstory is therefore *not* a corrective, but merely a complementary distortion. Same history, in other words, just with different distortions. For all the talk of heroines and resistance, we really end up with an emulation of the dominant narrative. Imitation as flattery. Rather than history and herstory, we end up instead with endless incantations of *myth*tory.

An example from India

To understand how these endless variations of heroine stories give us just more mythology—not better mythology, but just more of the same with different names—we can take a look at an example taken from a relative obscure tome about a woman from India that most people have never heard of, even in India. The savvy reader might suddenly proclaim that using a relatively obscure tome would make my example an exceptional one that proves a rule to the contrary, but an academic book that is relatively obscure and about a topic no one has ever really heard of *is* the rule, so the example will hold up well under whatever scrutiny the reader wants to offer. So, here we go.

In the 1880s, in the midst of a number of reform movements that had emerged with the rise of nationalist and anti-colonial sentiment in India, a woman from the Marathi-speaking region of India penned a tract—the only known writing of any substance from this woman—that took up many issues of social reform in colonial India, including the topic of gender relations in Indian society. The woman's name was Tarabai Shinde, and her tract appeared just over a century later in English translation, alongside a lengthy academic essay written by scholar Rosalind O'Hanlon, that set Tarabai Shinde's tract in proper historical context. The book was published by Oxford University Press in 1994 with the title *A Comparison between Women and Men*. The academic essay that introduces the book goes out of its way to position Indian women in the nineteenth century as upstarts and rebels, secular heretics that caused men to tremble in fear at the possible loss of their manly privilege, and then concludes with an observation about Tarabai Shinde herself, which was that she had "her own clear sense of a vanished Indian warrior and courtly culture, where some women at least had commanded power and wealth on their own terms."[19]

What makes that point particularly interesting is that it reveals the flawed premise of the whole enterprise: when Tarabai Shinde

---

19 Rosalind O'Hanlon, *A Comparison Between Women and Men: Tarabai Shinde and the Critique of Gender Relations in Colonial India* (Oxford: Oxford University Press, 1994), p. 47

remembers the evocatively wonderful past, before the arrival of the patriarchal white male British colonizers, she envisions herself as one of the elites, leading a life of cultural richness and leisure. This kind of pre-colonial nostalgia is an incorrigibly elitist phenomenon, and it has always perturbed me that the celebration of this self-indulgent nostalgia has remained the pastime of both academics and activists alike. Moreover, it is as much a truism of colonial as it is of pre-colonial times that one cannot have elites without having non-elites. Tarabai Shinde's "critique" of gender relations completely glosses over any critique of unjust and exploitative social relations in Indian society, so when Tarabai Shinde remembers women as having their own say in the household, she is thinking of a woman in an elite household run by servants. If Tarabai Shinde imagines herself engaged in a vibrant discussion of Sanskrit texts in a luxurious pre-colonial parlor with other women, it is a dream made possible only by the reality that it is entirely dependent upon the drudgery and work of other non-elite women, ones who must spend their time cleaning the house and removing the elite feces from the elite toilet bucket of the elite household. Those women did not have their own say, and for them, pre-colonial nostalgia is in very short supply—a luxury they can neither afford nor desire.

But nostalgia is not the key issue here. The key issue here is that we have a booklet written by a woman in nineteenth-century India, and this booklet is translated and presented to us as a tract that will provide an insouciant and ribald critique of gender relations. The heroine-author is going to shake things up and show us a perspective that has been absent from all those patriarchal texts in circulation. Is the voice different from the voice of patriarchy? To a certain extent, it is. But it is also an ugly and ignorant voice, just as ugly and ignorant as the voice of patriarchy. In reality, it is not all that different from what men write: the radical heroines of matriarchy, much like the heroes of patriarchy, more often than not disappoint. Nothing is shaken. Nothing is really even stirred. Yawn.

Consider, for instance, that Tarabai Shinde, a woman who seems keenly aware and genuinely upset at the gendered hierarchy that prevents her from experiencing elitist leisure to its fullest potential, has almost no awareness of how the hierarchies of the caste system generate lifetimes and generations of unjustifiable misery and shattered lives, particularly for those at the bottom of the caste hierarchy. Indeed, she excoriates her fellow upper-caste elites for confusing or abandoning the rules of caste-based status due to the influence of British rule and the new opportunities provided by the colonial administration. Consider this quote, for instance, where she is lamenting how her fellow elites no longer know how to tie a turban properly to show their proper (elite) status in society: "Ten or twenty years ago, who'd have wound such tatty old strips of cloth round their heads like that, apart from Telugu folk or people in mourning?" Here we have not only a caste and status-based critique of men who no longer know how to embrace and exude their exalted place in the upper echelons of society, but also a bit or racism as well. "Telugu folk" refers to the Telugu speakers who were found mostly in what is today the states of Andhra Pradesh and Telangana in India, and to make the comparison that a Marathi man who cannot tie his turban like a proper elite is somehow like one of the Telugu folk is an extraordinarily offensive insult to any Telugu-speaking person. What we have here is *not* someone whose putatively rebellious voice makes her a heroine in the Great Struggle against patriarchy, but rather someone who is just one more myopically racist individual (and if we can't speak of race here we can at least speak of extreme social discrimination) whose story adds to an already sad litany of voices of people who cannot understand the suffering of others. Women can be as indifferent as men to the suffering of others.

Keep in mind also that though this booklet of Tarabai Shinde is presented as a critique of gender relations in colonial India, it is not a critique of colonial India itself or even of British rule. Indeed, much of Tarabai Shinde's booklet praises British rule and the "critique" of gender relations consists mostly of emasculating remarks against Indian men for not being as good or as enlightened as British men. Here for instance is one more example of the tone of the text, referring to the accomplishments of British rule:

> These people put an end to [the revolts and rebellions] and spent crores of rupees giving you education. They brought all sorts of arts and skills, all kinds of laws and regulation; they set up offices and courts and protected everyone in peace and comfort. (p. 96)

In sum, "This [British] government has done so much to promote your happiness." Tarabai Shinde then pleads for British intervention in order to restore women to their rightful place in society. As for the other part of the "critique," the one against Indian men, it rests on a few faulty principles. In looking for an explanation as to how patriarchy managed to dupe women into accepting an inferior position, we get this: "Women are so covetous and gullible by nature they'll believe anything they're told." (p. 110) This means that men are tricksters who find an easy target in women, which leads to conclusions such as this: in describing the presumed wickedness of women, Tarabai Shinde states that "wickedness starts off with you [men] and you alone," followed by the claim that "if there's an image of every wickedness it's really you men." (p. 111, 117) In other words, Indian men are wicked and take advantage of "covetous and gullible" women by making them accept patriarchy, a situation that apparently can only be reversed by the enlightened intervention of the British colonial rulers. Herstory has spoken, but it sounds an awful lot like history.

Why liberation is human, not gendered
Again, it would be easy to dismiss this example as an aberration or an exception, an obscure nineteenth-century text that perhaps not many people have ever read, in the past or in the present. But the same problems surface pretty much anywhere one looks. The current state of gender-based critiques, even the so-called radical ones, all of which inform so much diversity policy and practice, start appearing like so many fingers plugging up so many holes in so many dikes until they can no longer hold together and the deluge washes away the intellectual detritus that now forms the ruins of a once-hyped phenomenon. If we consider the collective corpus of contemporary Vietnamese writer Duong Thu Huong, for instance, which in my humble opinion is one of the greatest collections of contemporary fiction to grace our contemporary world, we meet a long line of female characters who suffer relentlessly, sometimes quietly and sometimes restively, at the hands of a cluster of cultural values that place women in impossible positions and burden them with impossible expectations. Duong's work can be read as an extended critique of all the things that encumber women and weigh them down in a morass of corrosive constraints and attribute to them layers of undeserved turpitude.[20] Nothing is sacred in Duong's critique: certainly patriarchy is given its fair share of invective and ridicule, but so too are culture, religion, and ideology in equal measure. Indeed, anything that promotes group-based conformity is held up to scrutiny and then showered with obloquy. What Duong's work shows is that little or nothing is accomplished by simply erasing one layer of oppression, as attached as that layer often is to so many others, or by simply throwing off a single chain. So if women are as constrained by patriarchy

---

20 For anyone wishing to delve into Duong Thu Huong's works (which I highly recommend), I would suggest starting with *Paradise of the Blind* (1988) and *No Man's Land* (2002).

as they are by the values of Vietnamese culture, are we to strive to liberate women from patriarchy, or from culture, or both?

Diversity tells us that we are to celebrate all the different cultures in equal measure, but Duong's work shows clearly that there is little to be celebrated in the damage wrought by (in this case) Vietnamese culture on the aspirations of Vietnamese women. Her work raises interesting and provocative questions. Is a Vietnamese woman who walks away from her culture a heroine, or a traitor to her culture? Or is a Vietnamese heroine a woman who accepts her cultural constraints (because culture is always beautiful, according to diversity) and then endures her situation as best she can? Neither diversity nor feminism, at least as we currently have them, can help us answer those questions. For lack of a better word, they are useless in this moment. Clearly, we need something more and something different.

Domesticating violence

The distortive gravity of mythtory—and mythtory comes in many forms but here we are focusing on gender-related examples—is something that needs to be recognized and remedied if gender-related issues are to play a constructive role in the refashioning of diversity. Normatively, for instance, when we hear the word "domestic violence," we tend immediately to think of a man engaging in violence against a woman. The distortive gravity of gender-based mythtory induces us to think of this as the essential representation of what domestic violence is—bad men inflicting harm on innocent women—and anything that does not fit this model is written-off as an exception or an aberration. And indeed, there is sadly no shortage of examples for that sort of violence, and all of it is condemnable and contemptible. Yet the prevalence of female-on-male domestic violence has also been extensively documented—one particularly informative study is Philip Cook's book *Abused Men: The Hidden Side of Domestic Violence*

(2009)—though it is often hidden or removed from discussions on domestic violence because it confuses more simplistic notions of victimhood and also undermines the heroine-saturated narratives of feminist mythtory.[21] There is also considerable documentation of same-sex (female-on-female, male-on-male) abusive relationships, but these too are often swept aside in favor of a hopelessly and uselessly one-sided narrative that not only takes us away from the information we need to know, but actively compromises the entire validity of gender-based elements of diversity policy and practice.

At some point, particularly if we want diversity to work effectively for all of us, we need to recognize that the exceptions are not exceptions at all: they are all part of a normative pattern. How many examples will it take, one wonders, before the same activist minds that seek to change others are willing to be changed themselves? A study carried out in 2006 by the Family Research Laboratory at the University of New Hampshire investigated the claim that violent and abusive actions in relationships were carried out almost exclusively by men, and after pouring through data collected from over 13,000 respondents in 32 different countries, the conclusions showed that reality worked to the contrary: the two most common patterns were *mutual violence* (both male and female were equally violent) followed by *female-initiated violence* against a male partner.[22] Violence initiated by the male partner alone, contrary to all expectations, was found to be the *least* common pattern of all.

---

21 See also "Male domestic violence deaths become focus in Cornwall," *BBC News* (January 23, 2016) at http://www.bbc.com/news/av/uk-england-cornwall-35377666/male-domestic-violence-deaths-become-focus-in-cornwall

22 Murray A. Straus, "Dominance and Symmetry in Partner Violence By Male and Female University Students in 32 Nations," Family Research Laboratory, University of New Hampshire (2006)

In my own research on human trafficking in Southeast Asia, I have found over and over again that women play just as contributive a role to this sad and traumatic trade as do men, and I have grown increasingly tired of explanations that want so desperately to believe that these women were "made bad" by the men who started the trade. Why does no one ever ask who made these men bad? At some point, the blindness and myopia of so many happy slave narratives has to give way to the acidic grit of reality; sure, the happy slave narratives allow us to walk around in a morphine-like euphoria that makes us feel good about ourselves among others, but as any addict knows, eventually the morphine wears off and the pain of reality returns. Moreover, all forms of addiction end in one of two ways: either in death, or in the ruinous crash of withdrawal. Neither of those seems a good platform for diversity.

One can understand and be empathetic towards the original impulse of feminist narratives: to inscribe the agency of women into an historical narrative written largely by the hands of patriarchal scribes. But there is a sad irony in repeating and mimicking the mistakes of the forces against which one purports to rebel. What justice do we get if in the task of showing agency for women, we show only the agency that results in good and positive actions? What justice do we get if in the task of showing gender equality, we show only equality of positive actions? Women and men can be equal in many things—they can be equally creative, it is true, but they can be equally violent as well. Both show equality, yet we smile at the first comparison, and only bristle at the second. So when in the name of diversity we end up with a narrative in which feminist authors erase the bad women in the exact same way that patriarchal authors erase the good, we end up not with radical voices of resistance and opposition, but with more nonsensical monotony that takes us nowhere toward the goals of justice that we so often profess.

Therein lies the fault of so much rhetoric and rubric over gender-based diversity. It is drawn so narcissistically towards self-directed gender-praising that the goal of justice recedes from view. If patriarchy is bad history, then the matriarchy of herstory must be good, right? But this argument loses sight of the fact that both patriarchy and matriarchy are predicated on invented and unjustifiable hierarchies: in either version, one group appoints themselves to rule, and others must accept that they will be ruled over. It takes just as much distortive violence to convince women that they should be ruled by men as it does to convince men that they should be ruled by women. We don't need to be liberated from patriarchy to experience the benevolence of matriarchy. We need to be liberated from ideas such as patriarchy *and* matriarchy to move towards something that works for men and women and everyone in between. That, it seems to me is the true task of diversity.

Diversity, consistency, and equality
If diversity is supposed to lead us toward an integrated and inclusive society, and if diversity is also supposed to lead to the "robust exchange of ideas," then it means we have to be able to approach any person and any category with a consistent and consistently equal perspective. In fact it is the opposite that has usually happened, which is why diversity is failing us. In the latter stages of the 2016 presidential campaign, for instance, consider how differently the two candidates were viewed. If you said, for instance, that Donald Trump is unfit to be president, or that his policies make little sense, or that he makes little sense, then anyone who heard you would accept that you are questioning or opposing his policies and perspectives. To put it simply, you could disagree with Donald Trump. But now look what happens if you did the same thing with Hillary Clinton. After having eight years of people claiming that anyone who questioned or opposed Barack Obama, even on just

one point, was "clearly" a racist, now we heard that anyone who disagrees with Hillary is doing so not because they might disagree with or oppose her policies, but simply because she is a woman. How's that for the robust exchange of ideas? When November 2016 rolled around, we had this caricature of democracy offered to us: either (1) vote for Hillary Clinton, or (2) you hate women. Thanks, diversity.

Are there people who don't like Obama because they are racists? Of course there are. And yes, there are also people that wouldn't vote for Hillary because she's a woman. But it is dreadfully simplistic to claim that these are the only ways to see it, to claim that any opposition to a woman is misogynistic, or any questioning of a black person is racism. Diversity is supposed to expand our conversations, yet here its proponents are using diversity to stifle democracy, and to shut down the robust exchange of ideas.

It is an insult to Hillary Clinton and to women in general to claim that any opposition to Hillary stemmed from some visceral patriarchal urge to suppress women. If I question Hillary Clinton, or any of her policies, it is because I am treating her with absolute equality. I am questioning her and holding her to the same standard that I would hold any other person, regardless of gender. The gender element of diversity is trying to push for positive equality only, which means we can only praise women and see them as heroines. *Negative equality*, which allows me to criticize and question her actions as I would with anyone else, is censored out and shouted down. If I call Donald Trump an imbecile, everyone knows it's because I think he's an imbecile. If I call Hillary Clinton an imbecile, suddenly it's because I'm a misogynistic patriarch who can't handle an intelligent and strong woman. Hillary Clinton is placed beyond question—she is a heroine, always a heroine. Supposedly diversity demands equality for women, but then it insists upon unequal treatment when it comes to anything negative.

The unexpected empowerment of negative equality
Pop quiz: which candidate in the 2016 presidential elections promoted rape culture? Easy question, right? *Of course* it was Donald Trump. But actually it's a trick question, because the reality is this: *both* candidates promoted rape culture. That's right. Donald Trump and Hillary Clinton both promoted rape culture. Now let me explain how.

The Donald Trump version pretty much everyone knows. As part of the October surprise tradition in American politics, in which candidates or parties strategically release the worst information they have on their opponent one month before the election, in October 2016 a video of a conversation between Donald Trump and TV personality Billy Bush was released that centered on a lewd and degrading conversation they had about women. In the recording, which was made in 2005, Donald Trump could clearly be heard saying that as a man with power and as a star and celebrity, he could do pretty much anything he wanted to women, including—and here is the infamous quote—"grab them by the pussy." Billy Bush did not challenge Donald Trump and his laughter seemed to make him complicit in Trump's remarks. Trump dismissed the remarks as so-called "locker-room talk," the kind of conversations men supposedly have in private that relate to some kind of male-bonding ritual. After Donald Trump won the election, of course, opposition galvanized against a president who could so callously refer to women in such a disparaging, sexist way, leading to huge "women against Trump" protest marches across the country, complete with symbolic pink knitted caps and the very quotable counter-phrase "pussy grabs back."

So far, so bad, you say. But what about the Hillary Clinton part? How could I say such an outrageous thing? It can't possibly be true, right? (Note again, for the record, that many of you probably had no problem accepting that a man could promote rape culture, but even the mere suggestion that a woman could do the same made you start looking for ways to refute or reject the possibility before you even hear the evidence. This in spite of starting this chapter with the unsettling story of Pauline Nyiramasuhuko, which shows very clearly that it is more than just a possibility. It is also a reality.)

So, Hillary Clinton. For that part of the story, we have to go back to a different presidential campaign, the one in which Bill Clinton was running for the presidency in 1992. When first one woman, then another, and then many others came forward with accusations that Bill Clinton had engaged in various inappropriate acts that amounted to sexual harassment and sexual assault, it threatened to derail his campaign and end his bid for the presidency. At that point, Hillary Clinton, along with top aide and deputy chair of the Clinton campaign, Betsey Wright, put together a task force with one specific goal: to discredit and destroy each of Bill Clinton's accusers and stamp out—and this was a phrase coined by self-described feminist Betsey Wright herself—"bimbo eruptions." Note that the goal was not to investigate the allegations first to see if they were true. The goal was to silence the accusers, to have their stories dismissed as "fake news" before we even knew fake news was a thing. Yes, in the 2016 campaign, as accusers came forward about Trump, Hillary Clinton said that "every survivor of sexual assault deserves to be heard," and yes, people can change for the better over time. But having never repudiated her comments and approach in the 1992 campaign, the comments in 2016 seemed to imply we should hear the stories of survivors of sexual assault only when it is convenient for our political agendas. By actively suppressing the stories of those survivors back in 1992, she did her part to promote rape culture.

So now let's stop to assess the situation. If you are thinking that I just attacked and degraded Hillary Clinton, look again. Did I really? All I did was point out that two people, both of whom were presidential candidates, played an equal role in promoting rape culture. It just so happens that one of those persons was a man, and one was a woman. And again, I wonder how many people reading that had no problem hearing that a man could promote rape culture. That's just what men do, right? But a woman? There must be some mistake, you say. There has to be a way to turn the woman into a heroine. If you are thinking the latter, then quite frankly, there's your problem.

Let me re-write verbatim a sentence I just wrote, only this time italicizing a word you may have glossed over the first time: "All I did was point out that two people, both of whom were presidential candidates, played an *equal* role in promoting rape culture." Do you see it? What I just did was recognize the very thing that so much feminism and herstory have campaigned for and demanded for so long: absolute gender equality. So why is this so hard to accept? The answer is simple: because it isn't the kind of equality that reconciles with heroine addiction. It is *negative equality*, in that I have shown clearly that men and women have an equal capacity to do equally negative things. You might think that in doing so I am trying to make women look bad. I'm not, and in fact I am doing the opposite. In accepting negative equality along with positive equality (men and women have the equal capacity to do good things) we end up restoring full agency to women, an agency that was taken from them when heroine addiction became the norm. The quest for diversity in gender had led us to a blind spot that actually disempowered women even as it claimed to empower them, namely by only allowing them to make good and heroic decisions. Just as in an earlier chapter I showed how so many people distort diversity and race to argue that only whites can be racist, here diversity and gender conspired to do the same so that people can believe that only men can be bad.

By recalibrating our understanding of diversity, by understanding that *anyone* can be racist and *anyone* can do bad things, we end up with a far better chance at justice, equality, and liberation than we ever had previously.[23] Consider, for instance, the different outcomes that are associated with each of the candidates from the 2016 elections. For his role in laughing alongside Donald Trump and not opposing him or "doing the right thing," Billy Bush was punished by being immediately fired from his position and sent into professional exile. For her part in actively discrediting and destroying the stories of victims of sexual assault, Hillary Clinton was punished... by being praised as a feminist icon and glass-ceiling-shattering superhero who should be president of the United States. Anyone on any side of the political divide should be able to see how disturbingly problematic this is. And yet we still wonder why we don't have more gender-based justice in this country?

Towards rehab

As we have seen, the same arguments apply to groups from many different categories of identity—not just race and ethnicity and culture, but also gender. The same argument is made here, too: because all of our dominant narratives were written by dominant males, women have to write their own histories, or herstories, in which the disparagement of women by men is replaced with an endless narrative of heroines who just as often end up disparaging men. Living in Berkeley, I tend to see an endless streams of cars with the rather cliché bumper sticker that proclaims, "Well-Behaved Women Seldom Make History." *Oh, those rebellious women, refusing to be put down by men. Heroines, all of them.* Except that the bumper

---

23 For anyone still having difficulty letting go of the women-as-eternal-heroines idea, there's an endless stream of evidence to be found in even a brief online search. For starters, there's this: Pete Thomas, "Videotape showing women abusing seals on San Diego beach causes uproar over access," *GrindTV* (March 20, 2013) at https://www.grindtv.com/wildlife/videotape-showing-women-abusing-seals-on-san-diego-beach-causes-uproar-over-access/

sticker holds true for any category of identity—well-behaved men, and well-behaved people in general, rarely make history. There is nothing special or exceptional about the category of women in this regard. Indeed, history as we know it is usually a story of the least representative people from any identity-based group. Also, the implied subtext to the statement is that women who are misbehaving are somehow overthrowing patriarchy. The messier truth is that the rules imposed on women come as much from other women as they do from other men. Women are just as often misbehaving against other women.

If you know anything about the horrible atrocities that are referred to as "honor killings"—though trust me, no honor is involved—then you'll know that quite often women are involved in the decision to kill a daughter or a wife due to some perceived insult to the honor of the family. That's not *always* the case, but it's not something that should be brushed under the rug as a "by-product of patriarchy." The same holds true for the nauseating moral outrage of human sex trafficking. In many of the countries in Southeast Asia where I have worked, the share of the trafficking industry that is *run by women* is upwards of 70%. Those aren't heroines. They are women who are doing horrible things to other people. If we want to recognize the agency of women in history, we have to recognize not just the successes but also the mistakes. Equality means noting the good along with the bad.

Must a woman be a heroine to have her story noted? Must a woman misbehave to be a heroine, and are there limits to that misbehavior? If she misbehaves and becomes a psychopathic killer, is she still a heroine? And more fundamentally, do women always speak in a different voice? What if herstory turns out to sound exactly like history (as I think it does)? Somewhere in the midst of all of this, the diversity of being a woman gets lost. Some women will no doubt misbehave, just as some men are wont to do, but other women might not misbehave at all and yet still will leave a profound impact on the lives of so many other people. Women who behave well are not necessarily failures or collaborators with patriarchy, and women who misbehave might just be insufferable idiots. Diversity requires us to tell the stories of all of them.

When empowerment gets ugly
One very recent example of how the narrative of *heroine addiction* has become normatively orthodox comes to us from Sweden. Sweden's biggest music festival is called Bravalla, and it is normally quite the celebration of music. But due to a number of sexual assaults at the 2017 event, Sweden announced that they would cancel the event for 2018 and perhaps even cancel it for good. Swedish comedian Emma Knyckare took this one step further and announced that instead Sweden should offer a "man-free" music festival, one where only non-men were allowed to attend, and that such an event should be held each year "until all men have learned how to behave."[24]

At this point, I imagine many a reader is thinking what a great idea this is—a world without men would be like a world without injustice, right? A veritable utopia for women. But let's unpack this one layer at a time to see how what looks like an act of "resistance," or an act of female empowerment, is actually quite the opposite.

First, we'll start with the assumption that I'm quite sure almost everyone made when they read the phrase "sexual assault." The assumption is this: men carried out attacks against women, which is the definition of sexual assault, right? It also nicely fits the heroine addiction narrative, which puts women in the position of heroically fighting back against bad men. Yet, watch what happens when we take a closer look. I'll start by asking a question: what percentage

---

24 "Efter Bråvalla: Emma Knyckare satser på mansfri festival," *Aftonbladet* (July 3, 2017) at http://www.aftonbladet.se/nojesbladet/musik/rockbjornen/a/3nPpX/efter-bravalla-emma-knyckare-satsar-pa-mansfri-festival

of sexual assault victims are men? You're probably guessing maybe 0%? Certainly less than 1%, and even that might seem a bit uncomfortable. Well, hold on to your hat, because according to the National Crime Victimization Survey, the actual number, at least in the United States, is 38%. Clearly, that's not equal to the victimization rate of women, but we're pushing almost 4 out of 10 here. That means that if I told you there were ten sexual assaults at the Bravalla festival, the reality is this: four of those assaults might have been against men. My guess is that you didn't even entertain that thought at all.

If you're shaking your head in consternation at this point, wondering how you've never heard this before, let me add a few more details. One of the reasons this information might be unfamiliar is that for many years, the very definition of sexual assault was itself gendered. The FBI definition, for example, contained the language "carnal knowledge of a female forcibly and against her will."[25] In other words, it was legally impossible for a man to be raped. The second reason why you've probably never heard of this is because of the social stigma against men who have been victims of sexual assault. Women also have to battle social stigma when it comes to sexual assault—only an idiot would deny that. But men do, too, and it's a different sort of stigma, one that keeps the numbers on this statistic consistently under-reported.[26] The third reason you might never have heard of this is because it *challenges nearly every assumption we have* about gender-based crimes and *challenges the heroine addiction narratives* that have been the focus of so much

---

25 Conor Friedersdorf, "The Understudied Female Sexual Predator," *The Atlantic* (November 28, 2016) at https://www.theatlantic.com/science/archive/2016/11/the-understudied-female-sexual-predator/503492/

26 Hanna Rosin, "When Men are Raped," *Slate* (April 29, 2014) at http://www.slate.com/articles/double_x/doublex/2014/04/male_rape_in_america_a_new_study_reveals_that_men_are_sexually_assaulted.html

of this chapter. To admit that men could be victims, and even more than that, that men could be victims of violent sexual crimes perpetrated by women, that the #MeToo campaign should be more gender-inclusive, is something that requires us to rethink nearly everything we thought was "true" about gender-based crimes. And since the whole project of this book is to get us to rethink everything, well, that's why I'm bringing it up now.

Now, let's return to the claim that what Sweden needs is a man-free festival for as many years as it takes "until all men have learned how to behave." If you're not seeing yet why this is an extraordinarily disturbing claim to make, then you are still under the spell of the normative orthodoxies of heroine addiction narratives. The best way to shake this complacency is to take the same idea and translate it into a parallel context—that usually makes things painfully clear. On New Year's Eve (*Silvesternacht*) at the end of 2015, for example, over 1,000 women were sexually assaulted in several different cities in Germany, including Köln and Hamburg. When it became clear that the overwhelming majority of suspects were asylum-seekers from the Middle East and North Africa, authorities at first tried to downplay the assaults out of fear of stirring up anti-immigrant feelings. But the outcry from women and women's rights groups was far too loud to ignore, and eventually the investigations were made public.[27] But now think of how things might have turned out had these German cities subsequently issued the following statement: All public holidays in Germany would be immigrant-free "until all immigrants have learned how to behave." Or, to push the button a little further, since those arrested for the attacks were almost all Muslim immigrants and asylum-seekers:

---

27 Georg Mascalo and Britta von der Heide, "1200 Frauen wurden Opfer von Silvester-Gewalt," *Süddeutsche Zeitung* (July 10, 2016) at http://www.sueddeutsche.de/politik/uebergriffe-in-koeln-frauen-wurden-opfer-von-silvester-gewalt-1.3072064

All holidays in Germany would be Muslim-free "until all Muslims learned how to behave." You're probably thinking how horribly racist that sounds, and how ridiculously unfair it would be to hold *all* immigrants responsible for what *some* immigrants did, or *all* Muslims responsible for what *some* Muslims did. Seeing it yet?

Keep in mind for this comparison that over 1,000 sexual assaults occurred in the New Year's Eve attacks and over 2,000 perpetrators were listed in the subsequent investigations. At the Bravalla festival, there were 27 reported sexual assaults. Admittedly, that's 27 too many. But if you're going to ban all men from a music festival for the actions of 27 reprehensible male miscreants, then you'd better also applaud when Germany holds all immigrants responsible for what 2,000 immigrants did. And why stop there? How about after 9/11 in the United States, George W. Bush made the announcement that no Muslims would be allowed out in public "until all Muslims learned how to behave"? Does it make you want to scream, shout, throw up, and wail just thinking about it? How could anyone hold all Muslims responsible for what a few Muslims did? Yet when a comedian in Sweden wants to do the same in an open hate-fest against men, people stand aside and some even applaud. This is why we need to end the long reign of heroine addiction. At the end of the day, heroine addiction is ugly and filled with hate.

Diversity should first and foremost be about justice that works for all of us. We can't hold all Muslims accountable for what some Muslims do, and we can't hold all immigrants responsible for what some immigrants do, and we most assuredly cannot hold all men accountable for what some men do. I agree that there should be am absolute zero-tolerance approach to sexual assault, whether the victim is male, female, transgender, or any other category of identity. But zero-tolerance should not translate into *intolerance*, especially given the fact that intolerance is the acid that dissolves the heart of diversity.

Better diversity, better feminism
The reason that feminism has not given us a better diversity is that feminism argued itself into an ideological corner, largely due to its ever-expanding addiction to heroines. Feminism from its early days packaged itself as a "radical critique" of the forces deemed responsible for the social oppression of women, and quite frankly, in its early days it was exactly that. But over time—and this isn't unique to feminism—the so-called radical critique began to ossify into brittleness, dismissing anything that didn't agree with it as "non-radical" and thus part of the oppressive establishment. Anything that critiques the critique is wrong, and so the ideology becomes unable to consider alternative ideas and becomes its own orthodoxy. It is no longer radical and no longer a critique. The result is the retreat into euphoric smugness and an inability to stomach any criticism or any negative comments. Hence, heroine addiction.

Since diversity is supposed to introduce us to new ideas—note again that I said *supposed to*, even if our current version isn't doing that—it means that we need to be able to offer new perspectives of others and also listen to new perspectives about ourselves. In the case of feminism, it means that diversity ought to be able to craft a new, more inclusive, and better feminism. Feminism itself needs to diversify. (I would love to see more male and transgender faculty in Women's Studies departments.) That's the feminism I subscribe to, the one I will perennially endorse. You can't generate respect for women or shatter glass ceilings by telling only the good stories and censoring out the bad ones. You can't drool with excitement over Hillary Clinton shattering the glass ceiling (which is debatable anyway), and then go silent over someone like Frauke Petry, the former head of Germany's ultra-conservative *Alternative für Deutschland*. She rose to the position of leadership of her party, after pursuing an advanced degree in chemistry and starting her own business, and did so through her own hard work.

She shattered a glass ceiling. It doesn't mean you have to accept or endorse the values of the party she leads, but you can still recognize her story for what it is: an intelligent and independent woman who worked hard and achieved success through her own efforts. Unfortunately, since contemporary feminism fancies itself a radical movement of the political left, stories of successful women of the political right are often censored out and pushed aside, much like feminists claim patriarchy did to women.[28] It is interesting to note, to my mind at least, how many of the far-right parties in Europe are or have been led by women. Yet their stories won't show up in feminist histories, because those women were not well-behaved according to the rules of feminism. They can't be heroines. All of which violates rule #1 of the playbook on how to build a successful movement for justice: you cannot oppose something and replicate it at the same time.

Some girls want to be a part of history, and other girls, in the immortal words of Cyndi Lauper, just want to have fun. Women might speak in a different voice, but only sometimes is it because they are women. Sometimes it is because they are just different people, and their gender is irrelevant. Men, too, speak in different voices—yes, masculinity is as diverse as femininity. Not every male voice is patriarchal, and not every female voice is feminist. Men contradict women, women contradict men, and just as often they contradict themselves. And sometimes there is no contradiction at all. Diversity is a wonderful cacophony: the minute we try to give it unity—here it is patriarchal, there it is feminist—we erase the multitude of voices and thereby limit and suppress diversity. It isn't the difference between a grand symphony and a three-chord rock anthem, since both of those can be wonderfully expressive in their

---

28 See D. C. Zook, "About that glass ceiling: why having women in power doesn't bring power to women," *Medium* (September 15, 2017) at https://medium.com/@zookkini/about-that-glass-ceiling-acf459426c1

own way. It's the difference between anything that is recognized as creatively musical, which is the diversity we want, and some inebriated idiot sitting in a park belting out an off-key rendition of "Stairway to Heaven" while incessantly pounding his bongo drum. If that's the soundtrack of our diversity revolution, then we are all incessantly screwed.

CHAPTER 4

LGBTQI+ AND ITS DISCONTENTS

Homosexuality is a relative latecomer to the debate on diversity. Part of the reason for this is that during the time when other sorts of identities were collectively creating the idea of diversity, the issue of homosexuality created an undesirable complication. Would a black gay man enter the diversity debate as a black man or as a gay man? Could he be both? Or should he be neither? When the vocal trio of Three Dog Night, for instance, sang of how "the child is black, the child is white" and "together they grow to see the light" in the song "Black and White" (1972), there was no corresponding lyric for the "child is gay" and "the child is straight" and "together they grow to face the hate."[29] A few years later, when the Tom Robinson Band released the gay liberation song "Glad to Be Gay" (1978)—one of the first of its kind—BBC Radio 1 refused to play the track, in spite of its popularity. In the Woody Allen film *Bananas* (1971), Fielding Mellish, the character played by Woody Allen, asks a judge to declare a mistrial by pointing out: "Do you

---

29 The song was actually written in 1954 by David Arkin and Earl Robinson. Before Three Dog Night turned it into a pop-oriented song, it had been performed by a number of other artists, including Pete Seeger in 1956.

realize there's not a single homosexual on that jury?" When the judge replies that there is, Fielding Mellish is intrigued: "Oh, really, which one? Is it the big guy on the end?" What is significant about the scene is that Fielding Mellish cannot tell which person is gay. It was a part of one's identity that, unlike skin color, for example, could be hidden away, in the closet, as it were, and so in the ever-expanding civil rights movement, which subsequently paved the way for the era of diversity, it was difficult to deal with homosexuality because it seemed, well, a bit mercurial. One minute it was there, and the next it wasn't. It was easier to deal with visible and tangible expressions of identity: black, white, brown, female, and so forth. Color? Gender?—Yes. Sexual orientation?—No. Not yet.

The other reason it is a latecomer is because it has only been accepted—partially accepted, I should say—as a separate identity of its own substantive merit quite recently. Well into the early 1990s, two decades after the Stonewall riots of 1969 that announced the start of the gay liberation movement, homosexuality was treated as something of an identity accessory: "so-and-so is black, but did you know he is also gay?" Gayness was something you had on the side—it was not who you were, but a minor quirk that made you different and made you *queer*. It has only been quite recently that the idea of "coming out" was seen as an affirmative act of one's identity and an act that was accepted (or partially accepted) by a non-gay public. Optimists would point to the popularity of the demeanor "metrosexual" as a sign that gayness was now mainstream. Less optimistic observers would point to the ongoing controversy over same-sex marriage (yes, it's still there, in spite of the victory) and horrible incidents such as the fatal beating of Matthew Shepard in Wyoming in 1998 as clear indicators that we are still a long way from mainstreaming gayness.

Although there have been considerable gains made in the past few years in terms of bringing gay identities out of the closet and into the public, the inclusion of sexual orientation in discussions of diversity still creates a great deal of discomfort and unease. Is the gay community a separate community? Or is it dispersed among all the other already-existing communities? If we accept gay identity as its own, separate identity as a sexual minority, will the gay community want to be included in affirmative action programs? The latter question creates tensions because the distribution of the benefits of diversity programs such as affirmative action are hotly contested and any newcomer that stands to compete for those benefits means that other beneficiaries may have to accept a smaller slice of the diversity pie (since they are now shared with more people). But not all of the tension regarding the role and position of homosexuality in the debate on diversity is generated by the reluctance and lethargy of others to accept gay selves in the midst of non-gay others. Some of the tension is generated by the way that gay identity has been packaged and presented to those others. For some, the victory of gay rights creates a pyrrhic victory for diversity: the inclusion of one community generates questions of exclusion by others. For others, including gay rights in the civil rights stream of diversity talk is nothing other than a win-win situation—more diversity, and more rights. In more ways than one, however, sexual orientation as a facet of identity is literally not like the others, which means it will either be a tremendous asset to diversity that forces the rather stale dialog out of its current endless loop of race-ethnicity-gender discussions, or it will be an unexpected liability that reveals the fragility of diversity as policy and practice, one that threatens to bring the whole structure down along with it. Which outcome will we get? The answer in a moment. First, we need some more information.

I need to say up front that I have absolutely no issue with homosexuality being a fundamental part of a person's existence. If you are thinking in this moment—well, that's an odd disclaimer to make—then you are first of all correct and second of all tapping into the limitations of our current dialog on diversity. The sad fact is, in the discussion of sexual orientation in the context of diversity, our present state of affairs allows only one of two positions: either accept all aspects of sexual orientation and LGBTQI+ existence without question, or, if you even begin to ask questions or think critically, then please admit you are a hate-filled, alt-right, conservative Christian homophobe whose views can be immediately disregarded. What concerns me—and sadly I know that even expressing concern sets me up as a target of invective, but fortunately I don't care—is that the short-run feel-good moments in which advocates of gay rights and LGBTQI+ identity have thumbed their noses at others with a take-this-or-else-you-are-a-bigoted-homophobe will end up creating long-run problems for the whole enterprise of diversity. Truth be told, I see trouble ahead—unless the dialog opens and changes direction.

It's really a question of creating a better foundation for a diversity that seamlessly incorporates sexual orientation and LGBTQI+ identity. If you had to choose, for instance, between resentment or respect as a foundation, which would you choose? If you answered resentment, then clearly—you are a fool. Respect is the better and necessary answer in this case, but the ugly reality we now have, though no one wants to talk about it, is this: what appears as acceptance of LGBTQI+ identity is actually a barely concealed grimace masked under a thin veil of resentment if not disdain. It's not because there is still so much homophobic hate waiting to be outed and destroyed, but rather it is because anyone with questions is shouted down and sent off stage without an answer. Remember, diversity is about *ourselves among others*—and that never works without dialog. And so with LGBTQI+ issues, it seems to me, we have another variant of how diversity fails, even when it appears to succeed.

Who's afraid of being gay?
If I were ever called upon to compile a dictionary of overused words, one word that I would certainly include would be *homophobia* (for what it's worth I would also include the word *literally*). One might think that homophobia is pretty much the same thing as something like Islamophobia, only with sexual orientation substituted for religion, but the fact of the matter is that homophobia is its own peculiar type of phobia and so warrants its own exploratory moment. In the rhetorical universe that gravitates around diversity, we have a problem. Any statement that questions or queries any aspect of sexual orientation or homosexuality is immediately and automatically labeled "homophobic," and so what we end up with is a situation where those seeking information or understanding, or those who want to voice any critical thought, often end up in the same frustrating position. Either they must accept homosexuality and LGBTQI+ perspectives in their entirety and without question, or they must admit that they have an extreme and irrational fear of them, which is by definition what a phobia is. Curiosity is apparently frowned upon, unless of course it is bi-curiosity, although even that is now frowned upon, since the idea of being "bi-curious" (as in, being intrigued by and open to bisexual encounters) implies that choice is possible in sexual orientation, which no longer fits with current orthodoxies. Put simply: to ask questions of LGBTQI+ identity is to hate it or to fear it, or both. This is extraordinarily problematic in relation to diversity: diversity should provide answers to questions, yet accusations of homophobia stop us from even asking them.

What makes homophobia different as one of the many phobias invoked in discussions on diversity is that it is part of a larger historical process whereby the very aspect of identity itself—being gay—has required a sustained and arduous struggle simply to be recognized as a valid category of existence. No one has ever had to struggle, for instance, to convince the world that Islam is an actual religion, or that being Muslim is a meaningful state of existence. No one has ever said "so-and-so has Muslim tendencies" or questioned the "religious preferences" of Muslims or anyone else of a religious inclination (although discussions of Scientology tend to spiral out of control quickly). As a result, part of the ongoing conversation in which homophobia is frequently invoked is about establishing the legitimacy of gay identity or queerness (or any other similar term) as a fundamental aspect of a person's identity.

There are a number of ways in which those who advocate homosexuality as an essential and integral part of a person's identity use the idea of homophobia to argue that sexual orientation is an immutable characteristic. Please note that I am not questioning whether it *is* an immutable characteristic; I am focusing instead on the way the argument is made. Take for example the oft-heard claim that those who oppose homosexuality and all things related to it (such as same-sex marriage) are most likely doing so because they are secretly gay themselves. The more a person opposes homosexuality, the more likely it is that such a person is homosexual themselves—or so the argument goes. So why does a person who is already homosexual so vociferously oppose homosexuality? Because that person is afraid of their homosexual urges and afraid to express or act upon them, and might also be jealous of those homosexuals who have bravely come out of the closet. The end result is a self-directed homophobic hatred that reveals more about the pathology of the accuser than the status of the accused. This is reflected in the rather smug celebration of stories such as the Larry Craig scandal of 2007, when the conservative Republican senator was caught (allegedly) soliciting gay sex in the men's restroom of the Minneapolis-St. Paul airport.

But there are a number of serious flaws with this approach. One can see the deliciously attractive and almost mischievous intent in the articulation of this position: those who support homosexuality are good and right, and those who oppose it are probably gay themselves but are afraid to admit it. No matter what, gay identity is right and gay identity always wins. But there is a dangerous illogicality in the argument that actually ends up short-circuiting the kind of fruitful discussion we need to address and remedy the concerns that many people actually have about homosexuality. The illogicality is generated by the premise of the argument: that those who oppose or denounce homosexuality do so because they actually are homosexual themselves. If this were even remotely true, think of what it would mean for other forms of opposition. If I oppose and denounce racism, is it because I am secretly a racist myself? If I oppose and denounce fascism, is it because I am secretly a fascist myself? If I oppose and denounce intolerance, is it because I am secretly intolerant myself? And indeed, if I am Islamophobic, is it because I actually want to convert to Islam? These types of arguments do nothing to further the type of understanding required for diversity to succeed. There is a self-congratulatory smugness to them, of course, in so far as they seem to say "you only oppose me because you know I am right," but in delegitimizing any line of inquiry that seeks knowledge and understanding, we end up with a lot of smugness but no real understanding, and without understanding, we cannot have any sort of meaningful diversity. Invoking homophobia every time someone has a question or a critical comment does not create tolerance or acceptance. It creates frustration and resentment.

Another way that homophobia is invoked to "prove" the idea that homosexuality is an intrinsic part of one's identity can be seen in the unrelenting opposition to the idea that homosexuality is or ever could be a choice. Again, I am not introducing the idea that it *is* a choice—I am simply talking about the way the argument is made and the way that the word homophobia is invoked. Not that long ago, we spoke in terms of "sexual *preference*" or "lifestyle *choices*" in relation to homosexuality, but since both of these terms implied that choice was involved, and since the idea that choice was involved could lead one to argue that homosexuals need to accept the consequences of their presumably wrong choice (as opponents would see it), these ideas were scrapped in favor of the term *sexual orientation*. The idea behind sexual orientation is that it is something that is hard-wired into a person's existence, it is something that is immutable and intrinsic. It is not a product of choice and therefore it is something that cannot be changed or questioned. Sexual orientation is like race or ethnicity or skin color: it cannot be changed and hence discrimination toward people who are gay would be like discrimination toward people with a certain skin color, which is always and everywhere wrong and certainly against the fundamental principles of diversity. In the words of the well-known Lady Gaga song, a person who is gay is "born this way" and society simply has to accept it. Otherwise, society is bigoted, intolerant, and of course, homophobic.

Again, this is not an argument that convinces so much as it cajoles. It complicates and obfuscates more than it clarifies or edifies. Take, for instance, one of the pillars of reasoning that is often used to support this argument: given the severe discrimination that homosexuals have faced in society, up to and including murderous violence, why would anyone choose to be gay? It could not possibly be a matter of choice, the argument goes, since no one would ever choose an identity that is fraught with so much difficulty and persecution. Really? There is an interesting irony embedded in this line of reasoning in that the best example for why this argument fails to hold up under scrutiny just so happens to be the arch-nemesis of much of the gay rights platform: Christianity. In the early years of the Christian community, Christians were routinely persecuted, martyred, and quite literally fed to the lions, and yet—miracle of miracles—more and more people continued to choose to join the new religion, regardless of how difficult or risky the choice may have been. If the argument that homosexuality could not possibly be a choice since no one would choose an identity that created so much difficulty and risk were correct, then Christianity would not exist. And as far as I know, no one has yet tried to explain this apparent historical anomaly by claiming that therefore those people must have been born Christian, though many a Christian might claim that they were "born again this way," to paraphrase and corrupt Lady Gaga's line. People make unpopular choices all the time, in the past and in the present, and without doubt will do so in the future as well.

Fitting into our gay genes
While we are on the topic, we may as well discuss another brick in the foundation of the homosexuality-is-innate line of reasoning, the one that no one wants to bring up because it just generates so much vituperous heat. Yep, it's time to discuss the idea that sexual orientation is genetic. Sometimes this is attributed to what has become known as the "gay gene." To a certain extent, this is something of the El Dorado of gay identity: to be able to prove definitively that a person was born this way *genetically* would be to put homosexuality beyond the realm of scrutiny. It just *is*, and no one can do anything about it except accept it.[30] Yet I worry about this nearly obsessive search for the hitherto elusive gay gene, not because I believe it will never be found, but rather because I am concerned about the consequences if it *is*. Rather than be the irrefutable proof that homosexuality is intrinsic and indelible in the very genetic make up of a person, rather than be the fait accompli discovery that silences any further debate about whether society should accept homosexuality without question, I fear that it will open a whole new and disturbing chapter in the ongoing debate

---

30 See Ed Yong, "No, Scientists Have Not Found the 'Gay Gene'," *The Atlantic* (October 10, 2015) at https://www.theatlantic.com/science/archive/2015/10/no-scientists-have-not-found-the-gay-gene/410059/

over homosexuality, gay rights, marriage equality, and any and all things related.

For one thing, the discovery of a gay gene has tremendous potential to become a bioethical nightmare. Suppose a gay gene is discovered. What role will it play in the context of the entire genomic composition of a person? Will the gay gene mean that a person is gay, as in either you have it and are gay or you don't and are straight, or will it mean that a person is *predisposed* to homosexuality but might not become gay unless a number of other environmental and medical factors come into play?[31] If it is the latter, then I can all but guarantee there will be a mad rush by some in the medical community first to create programs to discover which environmental and social factors cause the gene to manifest itself and then by others to create programs to ensure that the factors that cause the predisposition to homosexuality are mitigated or minimized, so that persons with the gay gene might live "normal" heterosexual lives. Even then, if it is the former, where the presence of the gay gene means that a person is and always will be gay, I can envision all sorts of gene therapy programs that would allow a gay person the option to remove their gayness genetically, which rather paradoxically would make remaining gay completely a matter of choice.

I can also see a future of prenatal tests to screen for homosexuality, or, should gene therapy reach such a degree of sophistication (as some think it will), parents might ask that the gay gene be implanted so that they may "contribute to diversity" by having a gay child. (For anyone who thinks that last idea is preposterous—I live in Berkeley, and I can guarantee there would be a steady supply of people thronging to that trend.) And what if a child is "made gay"

---

[31] As has been argued frequently in articles such as: "Womb environment 'makes men gay'," *BBC News* (June 27, 2006) at http://news.bbc.co.uk/2/hi/5120004.stm?ls

by the parents through the implantation of a gay gene—would the child have a right to sue the parents for creating a destiny not of her or his own choosing? If the child wanted to reverse the decision and have the gay gene removed through gene therapy, against the wishes of the parents, would the child have to wait until she or he reached the age of eighteen, creating a life that is gay as a child but straight as an adult?

And of course at some point, since we talked about genetic tests and cultural heritage in a previous chapter, there will be a person who has lived his or her entire life as a straight person and will then decide to have a DNA test done, only to discover that he or she has the gay gene. That is, a person who genetically *should* have been homosexual turned out to live quite comfortably as a straight person. Just as with the example of the person who "traded his lederhosen for a kilt" after discovering his different heritage through a DNA test, would a person who discovered he had the gay gene "trade his straight spouse for a gay one"? Or what if a gay person had a DNA test and discovered they *lacked* the gay gene? Would that imply they were gay by choice? Would that imply that the gay gene is all but irrelevant, an over-hyped phenomenon that tried but ultimately failed to establish homosexuality as something inherent to and immutable in a person's identity? And don't forget the final possibility that if we do discover the gay gene, no doubt there will be talk of finally finding a "cure." Sorry to say, but the discovery of a gay gene will not solve anything. It will open far more painful doors than it will close.

But if the gay gene might not be the definitive result that many hope it will be, what about other arguments that homosexuality is somehow hard-wired into a person's identity, perhaps not genetically, but in some other part of a person's biological composition? Perhaps it is somehow etched into the structure of the brain at birth (or before birth), for instance. There have been studies using brain scans that purportedly show that people who are gay think in fundamentally different ways from those who are straight. If homosexuality is not genetic, then perhaps it is hard-wired into a person's brain, something that a simple brain scan can reveal plainly and clearly.[32] Such an idea would fit with the trend in recent years to prove in one way or another that homosexuality is the inevitable and unavoidable result of a number of elements working together, some of them genetic and biological, and some of them environmental and behavioral. Simon LeVay, for instance, in his book *Gay, Straight, and the Reason Why: The Science of Sexual Orientation* (2012), argues that sexual orientation is largely the product of a complex interplay of biological and genetic elements that were already set in motion before birth. Similarly, Jacques Balthazart, in his work on *The Biology of Homosexuality* (2011), details the role and influence of genetic and endocrinal factors to argue that there is little room for choice with regard for sexual orientation. The idea here is to mobilize science (amusing that science is seen as somehow irrefutable) behind the idea that sexual orientation is a naturally occurring phenomenon and not something that can be "cured" or "fixed" or altered or questioned—and definitely never chosen. The only problem that would remain is the irrational social phobia—irrational because science shows us that it cannot be changed—toward sexual orientation: aka, homophobia.

I wish I could celebrate all of these scientific contributions, but I will admit that they all leave me with a feeling of unease and discomfort. When "science" tells us there is *little* room for individual choice, it means that there is at least *some* room for choice. And once again, that little bit of room will soon become an issue of intense focus as the elusive key to being able to predict whether a person will or will not become homosexual. No scientific study

---

32 See, for instance, "Scans see 'gay brain differences'," *BBC News* (June 16, 2008) at http://news.bbc.co.uk/2/hi/health/7456588.stm

has been able to show definitively that homosexuality is the result of biological, genetic, or endocrinal processes that leave *no room* for choice, and as long as there is some room, no matter how little that room may be, it means that some element of choice, or at least some malleable variable, is involved. Simon LeVay documents how the hormonal levels of animals have been manipulated in various experiments and that those hormonal manipulations have induced "straight" animals to become attracted to same-sex partners. In other words, homosexuality can occur in anyone if her or his hormonal composition is just so concocted. My concern here is that if hormonal manipulation can turn straight animals gay, then certainly the converse must also be is true: hormonal manipulation can turn gay animals straight. If the same can be done to humans, then again, I can easily see hormone therapy becoming an option to eliminate and "cure," or alternatively induce, gay identity, or to alter sexual orientation in some specific way. Far from showing that homosexuality and sexual orientation are biologically and genetically determined and therefore beyond question, most of these studies actually open up new possibilities for discrimination and new opportunities for scientists and others to influence and alter sexual orientation at any point in a person's life cycle.

LGBTQI+ as a state of mind
Next I will turn my attention to the many studies have been carried out using brain scans in an attempt to show that homosexuality, if not genetically determined, is at least hard-wired into the structure of the brain in a way that leaves little or perhaps no room for choice. A study conducted by the prestigious Karolinska Institute and published in 2008 in the *Proceedings of the National Academy of Sciences* argued that there was a clear and distinct brain asymmetry present in homosexual brains that was not present in heterosexual

brains.[33] The brains of lesbians, for instance, were found to be more like those of heterosexual men, while the brains of gay men were found to be more like those of heterosexual women. The authors of the study concluded that sexual orientation was therefore already set in place in the womb and gay people were clearly born gay—case closed. I have no problem with the research itself, but what does concern me is what the conclusions say about social perceptions of gayness. The brain scan studies are intended to undermine the prevalence of discrimination against homosexuality, including homophobia, by showing that it is a naturally occurring phenomenon, hard-wired into the brain, and unchangeable. But the results, even as they are confirmed by other studies based on brain scans, can actually have the opposite effect by entrenching and reinforcing stereotypes about homosexuality. If the brains of gay men resemble the brains of heterosexual women, and if a gay man therefore thinks like a woman, then shouldn't gay men be effeminate if they are "truly" gay? And if the brains of lesbians resemble the brains of heterosexual men, and a lesbian thinks like a man, then shouldn't lesbians who are "butch" be seen as somehow the only proper and authentic manifestation of lesbianism? And what of men-hating lesbians—should they be somehow seen as lesbians who engage in a form of self-loathing, since they hate the very people they (or whose brains) most closely resemble, the very men whose way of thinking most closely resembles their own? While the intentions of the scientific community may be to settle many of the debates regarding homosexuality by offering evidence of the absence or near-absence of choice, I am concerned that however well-intentioned these studies may be they will open

---

33 Ivanka Savic-Berglund and Per Lindström, "PET and MRI show differences in cerebral asymmetry and functional connectivity between homo- and heterosexual subjects," *PNAS* (online early edition), 16-20 June 2008 (abstract at http://www.pnas.org/content/early/2008/06/13/0801566105.abstract)

up far more complicated questions and take the debate on sexual orientation into more divisive and more contested conceptual terrains. We also have the added problem that raising questions is usually dismissed as homophobic, so we'll end up with more questions, and less tolerance for finding answers.

While I am on the topic, there is one other very important caveat that is in order here. I just cited a brain scan study, for instance, from the Karolinska Institute showing that the brain patterns of homosexual men and women were fundamentally different from their heterosexual counterparts, thereby "proving" that homosexuality is innate and unalterable. The Karolinska Institute, I should mention, was also one of many scientific institutions that was involved in research several decades ago that allegedly "proved" that individuals with a specific chromosomal variation—dubbed "XYY Syndrome"—were slow learners and genetically predetermined to veer toward deviance, violence, and criminality. All of that research has since been thoroughly discredited, but when it was all the rage in the scientific community in the 1960s and early 1970s, people believed it just as fervently as people believe now that brain scans and gene samples show that sexual orientation is inherent in the biological composition of particular persons. The damage and misinformation of XYY Syndrome lingered for decades, so it is worthwhile to ask what would happen if all of the current brain scans and genetic studies hoping to prove that homosexuality is biologically inherent also become discredited in a few decades.

Note again that I am not trying to imply that sexual orientation is *not* inherent in the individual. What I *am* trying to imply is that the belief in the gay gene is based upon a parallel belief in the near-papal infallibility of scientific research, and trust me on this, science is hardly infallible (and most scientists would agree). I am concerned for what will happen if research on the biological innateness of homosexuality goes the way of XYY Syndrome research. If the whole argument for why diversity needs to create new space for gay rights and other related issues is based upon the scientific evidence that homosexuality is innate and unalterable, then what happens if science in the end cannot prove that at all? Do we just take the claim on faith? Or do we need alternative ways of viewing homosexuality that take us past the argument that it is innate but still provide shared space in the newly-evolving dialog on diversity? It seems to me we need something new here, but once again, with our currently impoverished views on diversity and homosexuality, we can't even start that conversation—too many censors jump in to shut it down before it starts. Suggesting a change in the way we speak of homosexuality is considered homophobic.

Censoring diversity

The mania to find some sort of definitive and irrefutable proof that homosexuality is never chosen and always innate has already created a rather disturbing and paradoxical result, at least as it has been presented by current advocates of gay rights and same-sex marriage: *censorship*. Diversity, when and if it works correctly, is supposed to open up discourse and discussion, the "robust exchange of ideas" that diversity supposedly promises, so that we can articulate our own thoughts and questions on difference and on how we are to view ourselves among others. Yet when "Sex and the City" actress Cynthia Nixon made a comment in an interview for *The New York Times Magazine* in January 2013 to the effect that being gay was a conscious choice she had made, the outcry was loud, quick, and merciless. She was immediately criticized and strongly encouraged to revise *her own words and her own opinion of herself* to make it clear that no choice was actually involved. Suddenly, she was bisexual—but not by choice—and the only thing she had chosen was to be in an exclusively gay relationship.

My point here is to note how the gay rights movement has itself moved in the direction of censoring out diversity within the gay community as a tactic to secure the rights of diversity. It troubles me deeply when the procurement of rights and the protections they generate do so at the cost of eroding other rights, in this case of freedom of thought and freedom of speech. Why is it so threatening for a gay person to be gay by choice? Why can't there be a diversity of ways to be gay—some by choice, some by birth? Apparently, while those who are gay by birth are encouraged to self-liberate by coming out of the closet, any gay person who feels they may be gay by choice is shoved back into the closet and silenced by having a rights-filled sock shoved down their throat. Any version of diversity that relies upon the stifling of alternative possibilities will always and inevitably collapse. In other words, if gayness is to become a part of diversity, then gayness itself must include diversity.

One of the central reasons for why gay rights advocates demand conformity to the idea that homosexuality is biologically innate is that one of the strongest pillars supporting the gay rights movement is the claim that "being gay" is analogous to other permanent markers of identity that generate strong rights protections: race, ethnicity, gender, and so forth. Central to the argument for same-sex marriage, for instance, is the idea that same-sex marriage is akin to what interracial marriage was a few decades ago. The bigoted opposition to the idea that two persons from different races could marry was found to be legally indefensible, and the arguments made against interracial marriage—that it was unnatural and deviant, for instance—one by one fell under the weight of legal scrutiny. In *Loving v. Virginia* (1967), the US Supreme Court struck down all existing legislation that banned interracial marriage, most of it based on laws designed to oppose and prevent miscegenation as an abomination and a crime against nature (based on what was once considered to be compelling scientific research, I might add). By making the argument that "being gay" is like "being black" (or any other identity category regarded legally as inherent to the person), advocates of same-sex marriage have argued—successfully—that similar legislation preventing the marriage of homosexuals should also be struck down. This is why it has become of paramount importance to find evidence that shows that homosexuality is biologically determinative and not a personal choice. This evidence would make homosexuality just as much a marker of identity as race or ethnicity, and would make it a protected category for all civil rights-based initiatives, including marriage equality and affirmative action programs.[34] Since so much is riding on the idea that homosexuality cannot be chosen, any alternatives to this idea are quickly censored and relegated to the realm of the absurd and impossible.

The rush to deny the possibility that a diversity of homosexualities could exist with regard to choice (some choose, some don't) also creates other strange moments and tensions among groups traditionally associated with gay rights advocacy. Consider for instance the rather awkwardly-worded category of "men who have sex with men." One might think that we already have a word for men who have sex with men, which is gay, but men who have sex with men in this case are in fact *not* gay, according to gay rights activists, and here is why. Men who have sex with men are men who are straight—or at least do not identify as gay—but who *choose* to have sex with other men, presumably for pleasure (and not out of boredom, confusion, or poor vision). Since these men also participate in heterosexual relationships—married men who have sex with other men on a habitual but not exclusive basis, for example—they cannot be considered gay because it would imply that gayness could somehow be a choice. Even though these men engage in intimate acts with other men just as gay men do, they are not considered innately gay precisely to deny the existence of

---

[34] Conor Friedersdorf, "Why Gay-Marriage Opponents Should Not Be Treated Like Racists," *The Atlantic* (April 10, 2014) at https://www.theatlantic.com/politics/archive/2014/04/why-gay-marriage-opponents-should-not-be-treated-like-racists/360446/

choice in sexual orientation. So apparently it is possible to choose to engage in gay sex without being gay, even though we have no way to distinguish between a person who is heterosexual and has chosen to add gay sex to his intimate repertoire and a person who is homosexual but who tries to pass as straight by existing in a heterosexual relationship and occasionally expresses his "true" desire by having sex with other men. Are men who have sex with men therefore bisexual? Again, the answer is no, since a "true" bisexual would not be able to choose (as Cynthia Nixon was told), whereas men who have sex with men choose to engage in gay sex without being gay, and so they are excluded from that category as well. So if a man chooses to have sex with another man, then realizes he wants to continue to do so exclusively, the only option we now have would be to claim that the man "must have the gay gene," since otherwise choice might have been involved. And that is something the censors just won't allow.

Interesting side note here: there is at present no search for a *bisexual* gene. I wonder, too, if soon we will have more brain scan studies, trying to identify the cranial and cerebral differences between gay men, lesbians, men who have sex with men, men who have sex with women though they ought to be having sex with men, men who have sex with men though they ought to be having sex with women, women who are attracted to men who have sex with men while dressed as a woman, and so forth. There is something unsettling in all of this, and not just the part about the manic overreliance on science. For anyone who knows anything about history, and about the link between the brain and behavior—anyone who has seen Quentin Tarantino's movie *Django Unchained* will know where this is going—I might just ask, in my best Orwellian accent: Phrenology anyone?[35]

---

35 For more on phrenology, see Erika Janik, "The Shape of Your Head and the Shape of Your Mind," *The Atlantic* (January 6, 2014) at https://www.

Understanding and misunderstanding the LGBTQI+ community
For those who don't know, the "LGBTQI+" community comprises Lesbian, Gay, Bisexual, Transgender, Queer, Intersex, and All Other Related Things (the "+"). Though it is presented as a community, it is really an unstable and confused descriptive label. The L and G, for instance, refer to sexual orientation. The B is something that involves orientation and preference, and as I said, it is kept out of genetic discussions because no one is quite sure where it fits (they just know it's not G or L). The T part has nothing to do with sexual orientation but is rather a category of gender identity, one that actually questions whether the genes we are born with really determine who we are. The T category actually opens up the possibility that a person born with the gay gene might nevertheless feel very strongly that they are straight, which renders the whole gay gene quest somewhat moot.[36] The Q category is an unstable category within an unstable alliance of identities. People who are G or L or B, for instance, may or may not identify as Q, while a person who identifies as Q may or may not identify as L or G or B. The I part, which is frequently left out (leading to charges of discrimination and erasure by the LGBTQ community against I persons), refers to persons who identify neither as male nor female, though there is usually an association with gender anatomy that differentiates it from the T category. Lastly, "+" category is an all-inclusive one that comprises any other identity that might exist

---

theatlantic.com/health/archive/2014/01/the-shape-of-your-head-and-the-shape-of-your-mind/282578/

36 For comparison, see Susan Donaldson James, "Twin Boys, One Transgender, Become Brother and Sister," *ABC News* (December 13, 2011) at http://abcnews.go.com/Health/identical-twin-boys-transgender-brother-sister/story?id=15142268#.TulV3xyq9_0

that is somehow different from the dominant category of male or female heterosexual (also referred to as cis-gender).

The LGBTQI+ category is predicated on the claim that all identities that are not part of the dominant, normative cis-gender and heterosexual group are pretty much the same in terms of culture and experience. The idea that a collection of people who are gay, lesbian, bisexual, transgender, queer, intersex, and all other non-cis-gender identities somehow share so much in common as to be part of the same community is way too much shoving of very different square pegs into non-diverse round holes and not enough let everyone find their own hole. If you are about to tell me that I just don't "get it," then let me offer a quote from transgender media personality Domino Presley: "Gays do not understand straights, straights don't understand gays, gays don't understand lesbians, lesbians just don't give a fu*k and NO ONE understands bisexuals." (Blog post of July 23, 2014, slight edit to the F-bomb is mine.) Her words, not mine. In other words, as I have said repeatedly, the biggest flaw in our approach to diversity is that almost no one tries to "get" anyone else because they are to busy admiring their own visage in the undiverse mirror. It isn't just dominant communities who don't "get" the others. It's too many groups not caring about anything outside their own narcissism. Added to that is the fact that the identities in the LGBTQI+ category may not represent a community at all, though there is tremendous normative pressure from within the community not to question it and, of course, not to leave.

Feminist transphobia and other unexpected results
Let's explore these categories a bit more to see how diversity takes us sometimes to unexpected results. We'll start with the category of transgender. The LGBTQI+ label, as we have seen, separates transgender persons from gay persons. So how, then, should we view a male-to-female transgender person who engages exclusively

in relationships with other men? Still simply as transgender? Or, if the person identifies as a woman, as a heterosexual woman? There are also male-to-female transgender persons who have sex exclusively with other women. Does this also means that the transgender person is now a lesbian? You can see how sexual identities and sexual orientations are clearly not the same thing.

To push this just a bit further, however, let's suppose that the male-to-female transgender person who is in an exclusive relationship with another woman identifies as a lesbian. A lesbian relationship is defined as a relationship between two women, so that would mean that the male-to-female transgender identifies as a woman. So far, so good, you might say. But wait a minute, now a new critical voice has entered the arena, one that supposedly is a radical voice of support for diversity, and one we already met in a previous chapter. Enter the feminist voice that rejects quite vehemently the possibility that a male-to-female transgender person could ever be considered a "true" woman. For many feminists, only a person born with the "right" genitalia can be a real woman and a real feminist—transgender women can call themselves whatever they like, say these so-called radicals, but they can't be women, they can't be a she, and they certainly can't be a feminist.[37] It's not even that they have to sit at the back of the gendered bus—they aren't even allowed to get on the bus at all. The radical voice of diversity now becomes the radical voice of discrimination, creating a situation where a voice from one non-dominant group that claims systematic discrimination from society (women) discriminates against and denies the identity of another (transgender). This

---

37 Kelsie Brynn Jones, "Trans-Exclusionary Radical Feminism: What Exactly Is It, and Why Does It Hurt?" *Huffington Post* (August 2, 2014) at http://www.huffingtonpost.com/kelsie-brynn-jones/transexclusionary-radical-terf_b_5632332.html?ncid=txtlnkusaolp00000592

specific phenomenon is something called "feminist transphobia."[38] One wonders how many times we have to see things like this before we finally admit that racism, discrimination, hatred, and phobia are not things that only dominant groups can possess or exert.

The clash of diversities

Different types of diversity often get muddled and confused in the long-winded tirades of advocacy from one direction or other. In the advocacy for LGBTQI+ rights and the inclusion of LGBTQI+ identities into society, for instance, other forms of diversity are often overlooked or denied, both from within or without. Every year, in major cities across the United States, for example, members of various ethnic communities stage parades and pageants and spectacles to affirm their presence and celebrate pride in their culture. In many of these parades, which by definition are designed to boost awareness of and support for diversity, minority cultural groups often refuse to allow gay or lesbian (or any part of LGBTQI+) members of the group to march in the parade, as if sexual orientation nullifies one's cultural orientation, or at least one has to take absolute precedence over the other. There is an ongoing annual drama in New York and San Francisco in the South Asian community, for instance, as to whether or not gay South Asians should be allowed to march in the South Asian parade. In 2009, the advocacy group SALGA (South Asian Lesbian and Gay Association) was denied the right to march in the India Day Parade, ironically in the same year that India's Supreme Court decriminalized homosexuality. The same sort of exclusion occurred in the St. Patrick's Day parade in New York City in 2012. The argument put forward by the parade organizers was that the parade was a celebration of *culture*, and not

---

38 Sarah Seltzer, "The Disturbing Trend of Second-Wave Feminist Transphobia," *Flavorwire* (October 27, 2015) at http://flavorwire.com/544701/the-disturbing-trend-of-second-wave-feminist-transphobia

one of *sexual orientation* (which requires a separate parade). I have often asked non-LGBTQI+ South Asian friends about this issue and many of them try to argue that this is not actually "discrimination." The idea seems to be that LGBTQI+ is a "Western" thing that does not exist in traditional Indian culture, and so excluding LQBTQI+ South Asians is really just a way of preserving traditional culture from Western influence. The absurdity comes in waves when one thinks this argument through, but it is not unique to the South Asian community. President Ahmadinejad of Iran also argued at an appearance at Columbia University in September 2007 that there was no discrimination against gays in Iran because Iran has no gay people. Apparently, gayness is a foreign and Western thing, and thus causes immediate loss of culture for persons of non-Western cultural heritage.

As absurd as the argument sounds, this is precisely the peculiar and peculiarly disturbing strain of reasoning that created the idea that the entire movement against LGBTQI+ rights and marriage equality in the United States was composed of people who are white, Christian, and (mostly) male. To be sure, much of the opposition to LGBTQI+ rights and marriage equality has been underwritten by conservative religious groups, particularly but not exclusively the Mormon and Catholic churches. But not only are there many members of these churches that are not men and not white, but also, hidden from view in the entire discussion were the other religious groups that also supported a ban on same-sex marriage, groups that would certainly be characterized as non-dominant minorities of one sort or other in any discussion on diversity. The discussions of views on same-sex marriage from Hispanics, Latinos, African-Americans, Filipinos, Muslims, Hindus, and other groups remained decidedly off the record, largely because it complicates and compromises the idea that the opposition to marriage equality was a "last-stand of the old white conservative male order" or a "whitelash" in the face of a new progressive diversity. It would also have undermined the tenuous alliance between LGBTQI+ rights and marriage equality proponents on the one hand and other minority groups on the other based on the analogy that "being gay" was like "being an ethnic, racial, cultural, or religious minority." The fact is, many minority communities are deeply divided on the issues of LGBTQI+ rights and marriage equality, some on the same religious grounds that are mistakenly attributed to white (male) Christians, and yet the discussion of this issue is shut down before it starts, ironically in the name of diversity.

Lost moments of diversity
What we need to remember in these moments is the whole point of diversity: to understand what is different from ourselves. With the securing of marriage equality in the United States, for instance, there was a great deal of in-your-face celebration, especially against white male conservative Christians, as if to say "you and you alone are the enemy." Just because a court's decision says "I got what I wanted and now you have to accept it, so get over it" does not mean that we have a viable and constructive moment for diversity. To procure marriage equality through a court decision might be a *legal* victory, but it is not a social one, nor is it a cultural or religious one. Having same-sex partners shouting diatribes of hate at practitioners of religion on one side, and having practitioners of religion shout hateful slogans right back on the other, gives us another configuration of separate but equal: two groups with equal rights who exist together but live in two separate and irreconcilable Americas. That, to my mind, is not diversity. It generates no understanding and it cultivates no respect. It just sits there and festers.

Securing identity-based rights through the courts without engaging in a wider arena of social and cultural dialogue will give us at best a society suffused with resignation, or more likely, resentment. We far too often forget that religion is also an integral part of diversity in America. To demand recognition of and respect for one's own identity, while simultaneously denying that recognition and respect to another, is sheer hypocrisy. A better approach, it seems to me, would be to open up an inclusive dialog that engages in deep theological debate on the principles of LGBTQI+ rights and marriage equality. It may surprise people to know that each of the Christian denominations, for instance, has a distinctly different theological interpretation of the institution of marriage. The definition of marriage is itself diverse, for theological and conceptual reasons.[39] It might be possible and indeed desirable to introduce arguments for LGBTQI+ rights and marriage equality into theological debates in ways that benefit and enrich both theology and rights-based jurisprudence.

Think, for example, of beliefs regarding judgment and eschatology: even if a Christian opposes same-sex marriage for religious reasons, is it theologically tenable to argue that Christians are obligated to enact and enforce divine judgment on others (for instance, by not baking them a wedding cake)? If homosexuality is a sin, would it not still be preferable to display compassion for the sinners in this world, and leave eschatological judgment of the actions of others to God? Alternatively, can LGBTQI+ rights and marriage equality advocates not understand and find some sympathy with the deeply held beliefs and convictions that practitioners of various religions cultivate?[40] There is certainly as much historical evidence for the divinity of Jesus as there is scientific evidence for the existence of a gay gene, so how is believing in the former "conservative" and "bigoted" while believing in the latter is

---

[39] Rebecca Greenfield, "How Marriage is Defined Around the World," *The Atlantic* (July 26, 2013) at https://www.theatlantic.com/national/archive/2013/07/how-marriage-defined-around-world/312757/

[40] Marjua Estevez, "More and More Latinas Are Finding Refuge in Islam," *Vibe* (September 8, 2016) at https://www.vibe.com/2016/09/growing-number-latinas-convert-islam/

"progressive" and "diverse"? For those who profess a religion, the structures of faith and belief are the things that fundamentally order the world and give meaning to everyday life. Those beliefs are as fundamental to a religious person's life as LGBTQI+ rights are to a member of the LGBTQI+ community. Engaging in those types of discussions just might give us the one desideratum that eludes so many of our endeavors in the world of diversity: mutual understanding and respectful consideration.

Homonormativity and other unmentionable things
One of the buzzwords that is frequently invoked in discussions of gay rights is the idea of "heteronormativity." This is an idea that suggests that heterosexual behavior and thought creates a pervasively normative social pressure that marginalizes and oppresses anything other than heterosexual behavior. In other words, it is the thing that society does, even without being aware of it, that makes homosexuality appear abnormal. Since heteronormativity is produced by the dominance of heterosexual thought and behavior, the movement for LGBTQI+ rights must find a way to expose the dominance of heteronormativity and then engage in acts of resistance against it until it is finally dismantled.[41] Once heteronormativity is unmasked and dismantled, non-hetero behavior will no longer be marginalized and non-hetero persons will no longer be oppressed. Diversity will be enhanced and justice will prevail.

I suppose the logic behind the idea is compelling enough, but as with so many of the various elements that make up the diversity universe, a closer look at the details leaves me with far more questions than answers. For instance, why stop with heteronormativity? Embedded in the whole argument against heteronormativity is the

---

41 On the origins of heterosexuality and heteronormativity, see Jonathan Ned Katz, *The Invention of Heterosexuality* (1995), and Hanne Blank, *Straight: The Surprisingly Short History of Heterosexuality* (2012)

suggestion that the margins of society suffer by the thoughts and actions that emanate from the tyranny of the majority. Since the majority is dominant, then what the majority does must also be tyranny. If that is true, then it seems that anyone interested in diversity and justice should resist anything that the majority believes or does. In essence, all forms of majoritarian normativity should be resisted and dismantled.

Consider in this context exhibit A: the idea of monogamy. Monogamy is certainly one of the strongest socially normative values we have—we have laws against bigamy and polygamy and we tend to view adultery and infidelity as severe moral failings—and yet there is sufficient evidence from fields such as evolutionary psychology, sociology, and neurobiology to suggest that monogamy goes against the natural impulses and hard-wiring of the human brain, especially and perhaps exclusively for the male brain.[42] The evidence that supports this position, which is every bit as credible as the evidence that supports the idea that sexual orientation is also natural and hard-wired, suggests that it is in essence unnatural for people to be faithful to their spouses or their partners and that society should therefore stop expecting them to conform to this socially normative idea.[43] We should no more condemn or criticize a man for being unfaithful to his wife or partner than we should condemn or criticize a man for being gay (and note how normative the word "unfaithful" is). It is simply unrealistic, the argument would go, to think that a person should suppress her or his natural desires to be with another person, and so society should stop its oppressive normativity and just let people do what they want, without consequence and without any judgment or reproach. Whatever desires are hard-wired into our brains must be

---

42 Eric Anderson, *The Monogamy Gap* (2012)

43 For more on this, watch "The Science of Cheating," *YouTube* (October 29, 2015) at https://www.youtube.com/watch?v=mqQf4Sg1g9w

allowed to manifest themselves, and social expectations need to be overruled, by the courts if necessary.

If we are going to rally support to resist the idea of heternormativity, why not do the same and resist monogamonormativity? Think of the words we use to label people who dare to express their polyamorous inclinations—adultery (the great scarlet letter), cheating, and so forth. Those who don't follow society's monogamous norm must be labeled as lewd and perverse. During the movement for marriage equality, activists went out of their way to argue that same-sex marriage would in no way open up the possibility for things like bigamy and polygamy, arguing that an LGBTQI+ person is born that way whereas a bigamist is not. But there is just as much evidence that we are hard-wired to be polyamorous as we are to have a particular sexual orientation.[44] Besides, what can we do for a person who is bisexual who wants to get married? Must that person choose only one gender for their spouse, and then have to suppress their in-born desire to be with someone from another gender (or else commit what would legally be a lifetime of adultery)? (Technically asking a bisexual person to commit to one gender would be like asking a gay man to commit to being straight.)

Incidentally, if you haven't looked up why bigamy is illegal in the United States, it's actually quite interesting and very relevant to our discussion. The marriage equality argument broke down the heteronormative idea that marriage should be based on one *man* marrying one *woman*. Those who defended traditional marriage in the courts did so on the grounds of religion, morality, and tradition, all three of which were tossed out by the Supreme Court as having no relevance in decisions of law. So why are we not also

---

44 Melissa Hogenboom, "Polyamorous relationships may be the future of love," *BBC News* (June 23, 2016) at http://www.bbc.com/future/story/20160623-polyamorous-relationships-may-be-the-future-of-love

opposing, on the same grounds, the monogamonorative idea that marriage has to between *one* man and *one* woman (or *one* of any gender)? If you answer that it's because bigamy is illegal, you'd be correct, but bigamy is illegal in the same way that same-sex marriage was once illegal. The reasoning for the laws against bigamy (and polygamy) in the United States rests upon three things: religion, morality, and tradition.[45] That's it. Since we have plenty of historical and biological evidence that we are *by nature* polyamorous, and since the Supreme Court tossed out religion, morality, and tradition to pave the way for marriage equality, isn't it time we alter our oppressively normative ideas about monogamy and let consenting adults marry whomever they please and in whatever number they want?[46] Imagine a world in which John is married to Susie, and John chooses to sleep with Ayesha. Susie is devastated because John "cheated." If we overcome our normative beliefs, however, in the same way that we were asked to overcome normative beliefs about "traditional" marriage, we might instead say that John "created love," and as we all know, love wins. Susie just needs to "get over it."

I am of course being a bit puckish about these points, just to have some fun with the usually unquestioned rhetoric that supports the LGBTQI+ rights and marriage equality movements. (If you are feeling uncomfortable with my discussion of bigamy and polygamy, remember, when conservatives said they were uncomfortable with same-sex marriage, liberals ridiculed them relentlessly and ruthlessly.) But I do marvel at the hitherto unnoticed contradiction that exists, particularly in the marriage equality movement, in

---

45 Adam Winkler, "Are Polygamy Bans Unconstitutional?" *Huffington Post* (December 16, 2013) at http://www.huffingtonpost.com/adam-winkler/are-polygamy-bans-unconst_b_4454076.html

46 William Baude, "Is Polygamy Next?" *The New York Times* (July 21, 2015) at https://www.nytimes.com/2015/07/21/opinion/is-polygamy-next.html

which we are told how much we need to resist and fight against this thing called heteronormativity but at the same time need to accept the spectacularly normative idea of marriage itself. The very same normative pressures that encourage straightness and excoriate homosexuality also tell us that being single is abnormal. And if we *are* in a relationship, not too much time should go by before the decision is made to get married. Otherwise, we think, something's wrong, or queer, about that relationship. I know many people who have ended relationships because they hit the two-year mark and there was no proposal: *society says we should be married by now, as is normatively normal, so if you haven't proposed, I'm out.* I also have friends who have been together for forty years, and though they are completely faithful to each other and will no doubt remain together for life, others who know them always doubt the relationship since they never sealed the deal by getting married. Anything less than marriage, society says, is not a complete relationship—there is always some doubt that lingers.

Indeed, though the marriage equality movement was based in part on the denial of benefits to same-sex couples that normally accrue to married couples—lower tax rates for instance (based by the way on the idea that married couples are more responsible members of society, an assumption that also carries through in lower insurance rates, etc.)—no one has yet questioned the normativity built into those ideas. Higher tax rates in essence punish people for choosing to remain single.[47] Everywhere we turn, we are reminded that being single is a problem and that being married is normal, and I find it odd that a movement that champions itself as a bunch of heroic rebels who dare to battle heteronormativity has

---

47 Nancy Leong, "The Other Marriage Discrimination," *Huffington Post* (October 30, 2014) at http://www.huffingtonpost.com/nancy-leong/the-other-marriage-discri_b_5702032.html?ncid=txtlnkusaolp00000592

no problem allowing other forms of normativity to pass through unquestioned.[48] When did progressives become so conservative?

And then there is the specter that haunts the whole movement against heteronormativity, a specter that no one wants to talk about though it is painfully obvious everywhere one looks. This is the specter I call *homonormativity*. Wait, what? Homonormativity? Yes, that's what I said. We have already seen one example of homonormativity in the act of censoring out all of those in the LGBTQI+ community who dared to voice doubts about whether they were born that way. But there are other elements as well—modes of behavior, modes of dress, codes of conduct, and so forth. There are rules to being LGBTQI+ and the LGBTQI+ community has no problem enforcing those normative values on itself.[49] That is, if you are gay but do not act *correctly* gay, as in you are too gay or not gay enough or are gay but try not to act gay—then there are consequences to face from one's gay peers.[50] This is true across the gamut of the LGBTQI+ community as well, where the tyranny of the LGBTQI+ majority marginalizes those who choose to be gay or transgender in their own way. Odd how we continuously bump against this in the world of diversity: groups who claim to be

---

48 Maura Kelly, "Singled Out: Are Unmarried People Discriminated Against?" *The Daily Beast* (February 6, 2012) at http://www.thedailybeast.com/singled-out-are-unmarried-people-discriminated-against

49 Sometimes the LGBTQI+ community seems to discriminate against itself. See Jay Barmann, "SF Institution Trannyshack Changing Name Amid PC Pressure," *SFist* (May 21, 2014) at http://sfist.com/2014/05/21/sf_institution_trannyshack_changing.php

50 Eric Larson, "Internalized Homophobia: The Next Movement After Same-Sex Marriage," *Mashable* (June 25, 2014) at http://mashable.com/2014/06/25/internalized-homophobia-lgbt/#O7gWislWDZqa

victimized or marginalized by society in some way or other usually do the exact same thing *within* their own community.

There is also another peculiarity of homonormativity. The cluster of values and practices that constitute homonormative behavior are only coherent because they identify as the opposite or the social complement of all that is not heteronormative. Yet this relationship of homonormativity and heteronormativity implies that all that is heteronormative can be lumped together in one homogenous category. But since heteronormative society is actually composed of many different groups—different by ethnicity, race, gender, religion, to name just a few—the stance against heteronormativity is a stance that also denies the diversity of society by simplifying the complexities of diverse societies down to one of two identities: heteronormative or homonormative. This simplification creates an artifice that is in fact an untenable caricature of the very diversity that the LGBTQI+ movement claims to promote. Strangely, the battle against heteronormativity causes a reduction of diversity: the rainbow of the gay community fades and leaves us with a uniformly heteronormative gray sky, drizzling down an uninteresting and drab drizzle of plain and undifferentiated rain.

Gay racists and other sordid realities
If I told you the story of my friend and colleague, a recently-divorced Muslim woman who confided in me that she felt she was being sexually harassed by a lesbian coworker, would you even try to believe me? The story is completely true, but my point here is how we have become accustomed to thinking in very normative terms, in spite of all the claims that diversity is somehow breaking those normatively oppressive terms down. The fact of the matter is, if you hear the phrase "sexual harassment," most of us won't follow that question up with anything—we'll just assume it's another piggish heterosexual man and another victimized woman. A lesbian

harassing a straight, Muslim woman by becoming increasingly suggestive in requests for intimacy? No way, we would say. It's just not possible. Diversity won't allow us to think it.

The harassing lesbian is just one of many examples of characters that by the puritanical logic of identity-based justice cannot possibly exist but actually do. Even in the face of overwhelming evidence, there are always those who want to deny the reality right in front of them. Living in a place like Berkeley, I hear people opine out loud that a "gay republican" is either a hypocrite or not actually gay. By definition, apparently, gays have to be democrats and/or liberals (if you think this is an inane suggestion, remember that the *Grutter* decision discussed earlier contained a statement that Cuban-Americans couldn't be Hispanic because they were Republicans). But a gay republican is child's play in the realm of implausible identities. If we are going to entertain the reality of the harassing lesbian, then why not go for something equally outrageous? Could there be, for instance, a gay racist? Considering the previous discussion of how a substantial portion of the gay rights and marriage equality movement is based on convincing the courts and other opponents that "being gay" is like "being black" (or some other racial/ethnic category), a gay racist would seem to be utterly impossible, a perversion of gay identity and an expression of the most absolute sort of hypocrisy. And yet, unlike unicorns and fairies, gay racists really do exist, and I can name one good example quite easily: Pim Fortuyn.

Pim Fortuyn was a Dutch politician and the head of his own political party—Fortuyn's List. He campaigned on a platform of stopping all Muslim immigration into the Netherlands and encouraging rapid and state-coerced assimilation into Dutch culture for all Muslim immigrants who had already come to the Netherlands. He was also an openly gay politician, one whose opposition to Muslims and other non-European immigrants was partly based on *their* opposition to gay rights. Fortuyn was also a Roman Catholic. Yes, here was a far-right politician who was advocating forced assimilation to Dutch culture because Dutch culture was good and tolerant. Yet as tolerant as Dutch culture was, it could not tolerate those who did not tolerate: hate was to be fought with hate (something we have also seen in the debate over same-sex marriage in America). His party was making strident gains among the Dutch electorate, and many analysts thought that his party might win, until his campaign was cut short in a most unexpected way: Pim Fortuyn was assassinated in May 2002 by a fellow Dutchmen, Volkert van der Graaf, who was angered not only by Pim Fortuyn's stance against minorities but also by the fact that Pim Fortuyn openly wore fur. Volkert van der Graaf was, among other things, an animal rights activist.

Of course there are always the detractors who will want to claim that cases like Pim Fortuyn are the exceptions to the rule and cannot in any way be taken as representative of the larger group from which they come (much like feminists like to argue that anti-heroine women are exceptions). But these arguments always lead us back to the problem of homonormativity. For if Pim Fortuyn is an exception to the rule, it means there must be a rule that exists, and where rules exist we will find norms, and where we find norms we will always find normativity. For anyone to claim that Pim Fortuyn was an exception to or non-representative of the LGBTQI+, then we must conclude that either Pim Fortuyn was not gay or that he was gay *in the wrong way.*

Pim Fortuyn was no singular exception. In France, for instance, in spite of Marine Le Pen's promise to end same-sex marriage, many persons in the LGBTQI+ community supported her party, the National Front, and her bid for the presidency in the recent French elections (May 2017). It may seem like a glaring act of hypocrisy, but her LGBTQI+ supporters liked her anti-immigrant stance, especially her anti-Muslim immigrant stance, largely because they felt that Muslims were on the whole intolerant of LGBTQI+ rights.[51]

We don't have to travel to Europe to scour for examples, by the way. There are plenty to find right here in America. A recent report by the Philadelphia Commission on Human Relations (January 2017), for example, documented longstanding and deeply-rooted racism in the part of town known as the Gayborhood. And it wasn't just racism they found. They also found severe discrimination against women and transgender persons. That's right, the LGBTQI+ community discriminated against itself. The Commission incidentally recommended that the residents and business owners of the Gayborhood district undergo diversity training to counter racial bias and also encouraged business owners to hire more diverse (non-gay) employees. Gay persons can also discriminate against straight persons, thereby replicating the very hate they claim to oppose.[52] And of course from a national perspective, let's not forget the recent US presidential election and the Gays for Trump movement.

One wonders how many examples have to be listed before proponents of diversity realize that the problem with diversity isn't the white heterosexual man. People of color can be racist, gays can be racist, the LGBTQI+ community can be intolerant, women can rape men, and so forth. None of these are "exceptions." They are all part of the abysmal rule. Proponents of diversity who think the battle is to shove the white heterosexual man aside and replace

---

51 See Will Clark, "Why gay French men are voting far right," *BBC Newsbeat* (April 19, 2017) at http://www.bbc.co.uk/newsbeat/article/39641822/why-gay-french-men-are-voting-far-right

52 Alan Farnham, "Gay Man Sues Boss for Pro-Gay Bias," *ABC News* (May 10, 2012) at http://abcnews.go.com/Business/gay-man-sues-boss-pro-gay-bias/story?id=16314667#.T6yCwo60nes

him with people from so-called diverse communities (which usually aren't diverse) often wonder out loud why there is still no justice, but the answer is staring them in the face. It's because they misunderstand everything about diversity, and they are fighting the wrong battle. Diversity isn't the struggle to replace whites with non-whites. It's about making *all* of us better people.

Making homosexuality normal
At this point in the discussion, someone will most assuredly jump up and tell me to "stop hating" or at least to stop talking about all these things because anything that makes the LGBTQI+ community look less-than-perfect might jeopardize the movement for LGBTQI+ rights or open the door to more discrimination. And this is where I have a big problem with the way this whole set of issues—LGBTQI+ rights, marriage equality, and anything related—is being presented for validation and consecration. I can no more accept a movement for LGBTQI+ rights that censors out all discussion of blemishes and inconsistencies on the grounds that it stands in the way of what the LGBTQI+ community wants than I can accept a movement for American patriotism that asks me to stop talking about the history of slavery because it undermines the amount of pride an American might have for her or his country. Whether it is American pride or gay pride, we can't base it on a heavily-censored mythology of unblemished actors. Once again, we are back to happy slave narratives and heroine addiction stories. When we simplify what are in reality complex things due to the single-minded end goal of getting something we want—LGBTQI+ rights or marriage equality, for instance—then once the complexities emerge after the acquisition of the end goal we end up with intractable problems, the kind that ultimately undermine the work of diversity. In other words, simplification through censorship is counterproductive, and as I said earlier, censorship emerging out of normativity, and the compromise of democratic rights of

freedom of expression and freedom of thought, are all too high a price to pay for the realization of diversity.

The normativity that is cultivated through simplification does not just occur in the form of censoring out blemishes and inconsistences as exceptions. It comes in other forms as well. Earlier I discussed the mania for proving the existence of a gay gene and stated that the discovery of such a gene would most likely create more problems than it would resolve. This is not the only part of the gay rights and same-sex marriage debate that involves recourse to science to provide what is supposedly irrefutable evidence that homosexuality is an intrinsic part of identity. There is a whole body of scientific literature that is dedicated to documenting the existence and indeed prevalence of homosexual behavior among other species in the wild. Since homosexuality is found in nature, the argument goes, human homosexuality is just a part of a larger natural phenomenon and not an aberration and certainly not *unnatural*. Homosexuality is natural, and all arguments to the contrary should be dismissed. Rights granted, case closed.

But as with the search for a gay gene, this argument actually works against the movement for gay rights and same-sex marriage. There are many things I could mention in this regard—how the argument rather interestingly relies on yet another form of normativity (homosexuality is not an exception but rather part of the natural rule), or how the argument actually creates a compelling parallel argument for animal rights (human behavior is so like the behavior of other species that rights granted to one ought to be granted to the others), but here I will focus on the central claim of the argument to show it actually undermines what it claims to support.

This is the part of the argument that focuses on the idea that homosexuality cannot be unnatural or wrong because it happens prevalently and commonly in nature. Whatever happens in nature among other species, to generalize the argument, should be accepted as *natural* behavior that cannot and should not be inhibited by law. In other words, it is the law that goes against nature, since it asks us to inhibit what is allegedly part of nature.

The fundamental problem with this argument is that it myopically looks at only one form of behavior—sexuality—and conveniently excludes all others. Even then, the existence of homosexuality in nature does not necessarily mean that animals are in fact gay.[53] Homosexuality appeared to be quite prevalent among insects, for instance, until closer research showed that insects are often so eager to copulate that they don't first check the gender of the insect of their desire.[54] Moreover, there are a lot of things that happen prevalently and commonly in nature that are also part of human behavior—murder, rape, incest, polygamy, slavery, genocide, and theft, to name just a few—and yet we have laws against all of them. If we are going to take things that happen in nature as a cue for the laws we create, then we need to do it for all such instances and not just for one. I can't imagine any judge in America that would even countenance the argument of an accused rapist on trial that because rape happens in nature (which it does) it cannot possibly be a crime or even wrong. Killing and mass-violence also happen frequently in nature, so why aren't we trying to get rid of the Geneva Conventions so that warfare can be as brutal as it can naturally be? Animals use their own form of chemical weapons, so why can't we? If we're going to open up the question

---

53 Melissa Hogenboom, "Are there any homosexual animals?" *BBC Earth* (February 6, 2015) at http://www.bbc.com/earth/story/20150206-are-there-any-homosexual-animals

54 Heather Saul, "Billions of insects are having gay sex 'accidentally' say scientists," *The Independent* (October 22, 2013) at http://www.independent.co.uk/news/science/billions-of-insects-are-having-gay-sex-accidentally-say-scientists-8897190.html

of nature, we need to open it up completely, and also to accept the consequences for doing so.

The story of Roy and Silo
Perhaps the most celebrated example of this desire to turn to nature to prove the normalcy of behavior can be found in the story of Roy and Silo, two male chinstrap penguins who, for a time at least, formed a homosexual relationship at Central Park Zoo in the late 1990s. The fact that they were penguins was especially appealing because as we all know (or think we know), penguins are monogamous. Add to this the fact that Roy and Silo appeared to want to raise a little penguin of their own, and you've got the ultimate trifecta of validation: a gay, monogamous family happening as nature intended. The story was so popular among proponents of gay rights that it was even made into a book for children.[55]

Like nearly everything in diversity, however, a closer look reveals a few problems with the way the story was presented. For one, in 2005 Silo ended up pairing with a female partner, so Silo was in fact bisexual while Roy was gay. The family part glossed over the fact that Roy and Silo repeatedly tried to steal eggs from other penguin couples, which is certainly theft if not in fact child theft (both of which happen in nature but are clearly crimes). In a more general sense, too, what we want to believe about penguins, that they are devoted, monogamous, loving bundles of human-like normativity, turns out to be quite inaccurate. Most species of penguins are in fact sexual opportunists, with both male and female penguins quite naturally having sex with others on the side (strengthening the argument that polyamorous relations are as natural as homosexuality). Penguin couples also engage in kidnapping, and

---

55 Some countries banned the book. "Singapore withdraws gay penguin book from libraries," *BBC News* (July 10, 2014) at http://www.bbc.com/news/world-asia-28243356

female penguins often get into violent fights when they are caught in the act. Penguins have also been found sexually abusing and assaulting baby penguins, and on occasion, even attempting sexual relations with dead penguins. Yes, all of that happens in nature. So is all of it therefore *natural*? And are laws against these acts therefore *unnatural*? If all of this is getting quite exasperating, by the way, then all I can say is buckle up, because now we get to take things to a whole new level.

Intermission:
In which I discuss fruit and make people hate me

If anyone has ever paused for a moment and thought, "Hm, I really wish more people hated me," not to worry—I've got you covered. The easiest way to make that happen is to bring up the two most reviled topics in discussions of sexual orientation, topics that will send people into paroxysms of despair and anger before the last syllable has even left your mouth. I have to be very careful here, because my intent is *not* to argue that these two things are necessarily linked with or analogous to homosexuality. As with my earlier discussion of this topic, I am actually more interested in the way the discussion that needs to happen never happens because it gets shouted down or censored out. I am also interested in starting this conversation because it has to be resolved, not dismissed.

Apples and oranges, they say. What are they referring to when they say apples and oranges? They are referring to homosexuality on the one hand, which for now we can assume is an apple, and… take a deep breath…pedophilia and zoophilia (bestiality) on the other, which we can assume are oranges. The dismissive response of apples and oranges is designed with only one end in mind: to shut down the conversation before it starts. It is a conversation not worth having, goes the argument, a hate-filled question that deserves only silence as a response. Indeed, it should not be dignified with any response at all. Apples and oranges cannot be compared—they are so different so as not be related. I am going to weigh in on this a bit more, and the short answer is this: when it comes to the apples and oranges argument, I smell a durian.

I am going to argue instead that we have a case of apples and apples—different kinds of apples to be sure, but still apples. I am, however, going to add an interesting twist, and here is the twist: the problem with the conversation is not that we are told apples and oranges when it should be apples and apples, but rather, that we do not include all of the apples in the conversation in the first place. What do I mean by this? Think for a moment: what do heterosexuality, homosexuality, pedophilia, and zoophilia all have in common? The answer? *They are all sexual orientations.* I didn't say that made them all equal or legal, but at the end of the day, that's what they are. If nothing else, we certainly need to be more careful when we talk about the human right of sexual orientation. The twist here is that we also have to add heterosexuality to the discussion. Those who argue that legalizing same-sex marriage will pave the way for a person to marry her or his platypus, for instance, are wrong if they are making the claim on the grounds that homosexuality is a "perversion" that opens the door to all other perversions. But if we shift the conversation away from the implied argument of homosexuality as a perversion, and instead fill up the apple barrel by adding heterosexuality to the discussion of what is now a large and strange basket of different sexual orientations, then we have a conversation that is an actual conversation rather than an accusation.

What we are in the midst of right now, at least as far as sexual orientation relates to diversity, is the redrawing of one line. This is the line that separates the acceptable sexual orientations from the unacceptable ones. For much of human history, and especially recent human history, and also in many cultures around the world still today, one could arguably say that the line looked like this: heterosexuality was acceptable and normal (the good apple), and homosexuality, pedophilia, and zoophilia were unacceptable and abnormal (the bad apples). Now we are in a moment where that line has been redrawn, shifting homosexuality from a bad apple to a good one. The question is, if we can redraw that line once, why can't we do it again? Arguing apples and oranges to resolve a debate about apples misses the point. We need a better understanding of these apples if we want to answer the question and get to a better diversity. And so, off we go to the market.

The Zoophilia argument
I am going to discuss the two most hated references in this entire array of debates regarding gay rights and same-sex marriage, so it's going to be a rough ride, and I know that. We'll start with zoophilia, more pejoratively known as bestiality. The outrage here stems from the claim by LGBTQI+ activists that comparing homosexuality to bestiality is dehumanizing since it conflates the beautiful and normal sexual desire of one human for another human of the same gender with the perverted and abnormal sexual desire of one human for a non-human animal. As the argument goes, the first is good and positive (an apple) and the second is unnatural and wrong (an orange). Note however that if we include heterosexuality in the comparison it becomes a much more inclusive conversation. But for now, let's revisit an argument that was discussed earlier.

We know from the previous discussion that some have argued that because homosexuality occurs in nature, across a diversity of species, it cannot therefore be considered unnatural or against nature. But we know that cross-species sexual attraction happens in nature as well—there have been clearly-documented episodes of fur seals attempting sex with penguins, for instance—and clearly it also happens among humans, so if we are going to reject zoophilia out of hand as perverse and unnatural while we accept homosexuality as natural and normal (that is, if we redraw that line), then we have to find a way to argue that naturally-occurring homosexuality is right and naturally-occurring cross-species intimacy is wrong.[56] As it turns out, this is actually harder to do than one might think.

Now, at this point I need to make an important clarification. I am well aware that many a conservative commentator has gone down the road of trying to link homosexuality with zoophilia, usually on the grounds that both are unnatural forms of intimacy and so once we endorse one we have to endorse the other. I want to make it very clear here that I am not in any way suggesting that gay intimacy is a gateway to human-animal intimacy or that gay sex is somehow "just like" cross-species intimacy. What I want to focus on instead are the reasons why the animal question strikes us as patently absurd or flagrantly disturbing, and why the question of animals is so far off the radar screen of our concern that we feel it should not even be brought up in the same discussion. It's not just an orange—it's an orange from another planet.

Let's take a moment to look at animals in general, separate from the question of zoophilia. The animal question, as it is often called (as in, the question of the moral and legal status of animals), creates specific challenges for how we justify and perceive our current radar of concern as natural and normal. Forty years ago, the idea of gay rights and marriage equality would have seemed patently absurd and nonsensical to many, even in the context of the civil rights movement. In the present, by comparison, just watch how quickly people roll their eyes when the topic of animal rights

---

56 Matt Walker, "Seals discovered having sex with penguins," *BBC Earth* (November 16, 2014) at http://www.bbc.com/earth/story/20141117-why-seals-have-sex-with-penguins

is introduced into a discussion. Animal rights seem as absurd to us now as gay rights did forty years ago. But why is it that if my neighbor approaches a dog on the street and pounds its head in with a hammer, we are horrified by the psychopathic and senseless brutality of the act, but if the same neighbor hops in his truck and drives to a farm and does the exact same thing to a cow, we nod approvingly and call it dinner. The line of acceptance we currently draw between the dog and the cow, as it turns out, is every bit as arbitrary as the line we have historically drawn between homosexual and heterosexual. The challenge comes in trying to justify why we should redraw one line but not the other.

The challenge therefore lies in how to redraw the lines of normativity in general. The lines provided by heteronormativity create social patterns in which heterosexuality is normal and anything other than heterosexuality—homosexuality, zoophilia, etc.—is abnormal. How then do we carefully redraw the line so that homosexuality becomes normal like heterosexuality but all the other categories remain firmly in the realm of the abnormal? If the methods of argumentation to redraw that line work to the advantage of one category—homosexuality, for instance—then what do we do if they work to the advantage of other categories as well? For the redrawing to work properly and effectively, we have to keep the lines of debate open, no matter how painful or awkward they are. What we cannot do, and what I see happening over and over again, is simply shut down the debate as absurd or dehumanizing—apples and oranges, they say. Time after time, at event after event and debate after debate, when anyone dares to speak up and voice concern over the manner in which lines are being redrawn, without any regard for the potential implications (such as creating a compelling argument to legalize zoophilia), those in the audience simply shout them down and accuse them of homophobic hate speech. Zoophilia is just "wrong" and perverse and unnatural. Apples and oranges. Debate over.

But here is why things are just not that easy. Suppose we consider the argument that homosexuality has been around for pretty much all of human history, and so clearly it is a common and normal thing we must accept. The evidence is certainly compelling that homosexuality has been around for most of human history, but then again, so has zoophilia (there are clear depictions of this even in the earliest human rock drawings, such as at Valcamonica in Italy). Has homosexuality at times been accepted and at other times been persecuted in various cultural and historical environments? Yes, but the same is also true of zoophilia. Does homosexuality exist in nature among other species? Yes, but so does zoophilia. If the best we can come up with is that zoophilia is "just wrong" and "disgusting" and "abhorrent," we are replicating the same rhetorical terrain that the gay rights movements has struggled against with intense frustration. How many times have people rejected gay rights because homosexuality is "just wrong" or "disgusting" or "abhorrent" and so forth? Perhaps those who question zoophilia are just expressing zoophobic hatred? Would we accept the argument that those who are so strongly opposed to intimate relations with other animals only do so because they secretly want to engage in sexual activity with other animals, along the same lines as the argument that those who most strongly oppose gay rights are the ones who are secretly gay themselves? We can't just take a "don't go there" stance and cut off this debate, because any time normative lines get redrawn in any society, it has to be done carefully and convincingly. Otherwise you end up with a fragile revolution, and fragile revolutions rarely last.

No doubt at this point there will be those who find the discussion absurd. Is there really a demand for zoophile rights? Is this really an issue that should concern us? Surprisingly, there is more interest out there than most people care to think. Germany removed its laws against zoophilia only in 1969, thinking them a vestige of the medieval and unenlightened past. But now it may have to reinstate them, what with the rise of "animal brothels" and "erotic zoos" (sadly, not kidding) in Germany and elsewhere and an ever-growing online movement to promote and participate in zoophilia. In 2015, Denmark had to strengthen laws against zoophilia due to a steady rise in animal sex tourism.[57] Apparently, some farms even rent animals out to human consumers for the sole purpose of sexual pleasure.[58] Interestingly, in many places (such as Germany), one of the reasons that many of the laws against zoophilia were taken *off* the books is that the laws that labeled zoophilia a crime against nature were bundled together with laws against sodomy and homosexuality.[59] Zoophilia advocates—yes, there are such people—have protested against the proposed reinstatement of the laws, arguing that to do so is to confuse morality with the law (an argument that turns up frequently in discussions of gay rights and marriage equality). Veterinarians Against Zoophilia—yes, there is such a group—is concerned and alarmed at the rise in popularity of zoophilia and has taken a strong stance against it, not on the grounds that it is inherently unnatural and perverted, but rather

---

57 "Denmark bans bestiality in move against animal sex tourism," *Reuters UK* (April 21, 2015) at https://uk.reuters.com/article/uk-denmark-bestiality/denmark-ans-bestiality-in-move-against-animal-sex-tourism-idUKKBN0NC1Z620150421

58 There is actually a debate in Denmark about the laws banning zoophilia (so definitely not just apples and oranges). See, for instance, Rasmus Brygger, "Danskernes forhold til dyrevelfærd og dyresex er hyklerisk," *Politiken* (March 14, 2015) at https://politiken.dk/debat/arkiv_debattoerer/rasmusbrygger/art 5569418/Danskernes-forhold-til-dyrevelfærd-og-dyresex-er-hyklerisk

59 Germany had to rewrite its laws precisely for this reason. See Christian Rath, "Sex mit Tieren soll verboten werden," *Taz* (November 25, 2012) at http://www.taz.de/Novelle-des-Tierschutzgesetzes/!5078678/

on the grounds that *we should protect animals from human sexual abuse*.

Why the future will be vegetarian

Before I go any further with this, I should stop to answer another common argument that comes up in this discussion, which is that in the case of zoophilia, and very much unlike homosexuality, the animal is not a willing partner and hence it has no comparative parallel to human sexuality, which is based on relations between two *consenting* adults. That is undoubtedly true, but it still creates a rather glaring complication. If zoophilia is wrong because it forces animals into a situation in which they are unwilling participants, then the whole country, if not the whole world, had better be prepared to go vegetarian (if not vegan). As anyone who has seen even a few seconds of footage from a slaughterhouse knows, animals do everything they can to flee the situation, sometimes even breaking their necks in the frantic effort to escape the fate that awaits them. Animals quite clearly do not want to be slaughtered; they are unwilling participants in the process through which humans satisfy their carnivorous cravings. This type of footage is so disturbing, by the way, that the US government is currently considering legislation from meat industry lobbyists that would ban activists and journalists from taking or releasing any such footage without first receiving express permission from slaughterhouse owners and meat industry executives.

Hunting and fishing would have to go, too, unless we can provide some sort of evidence that the animals willingly participate in these acts (which of course we can't). And no one could possibly argue that on the one hand it would wrong to engage in sexual relations with animals but on the other acceptable to kill them, since the animal is an equally unwilling partner in both. In other words, even if we break the link between zoophilia and heterosexuality and homosexuality by arguing that zoophilia is legally different because it involves an unwilling participant, then we end up in a situation where LGBTQI+ rights are in the clear but our food and recreation choices must be completely changed. Heterosexuals and homosexuals have a right to marry, but animals have a right to live.

If you think I've gone off the deep end with this, here's an actual court case on this very issue that shows it's really a question of when, not if, the precedent of marriage equality will open up a vegetarian future. In February 2016, a case was brought before the Federal Constitutional Court (*Bundesverfassungsgericht*) in Karlsruhe, Germany, involving two defendants (a man and a woman) who argued that Germany's ban on zoophilia was discriminatory and therefore invalid.[60] The two defendants argued that (1) they had always been sexually attracted to animals (in essence, they were born that way); (2) there was nothing inherently wrong with inter-species sexual intimacy because again, it happens in nature; and (3) the German state was violating their right to privacy and sexual self-determination. The court ruled against the defendants, but in doing so either wittingly or unwittingly created a legal basis for animal rights. Animals, the court said, have an intrinsic right against forced or unwanted sexual relations. Since they did not and could not give their consent to the two defendants, their actions could not be legally permissible.

The court also made a few other points, one being that there was an overwhelming public interest in preventing zoophilia as it would disturb or offend fellow citizens. You might be tempted to add that zoophilia is also just unnatural and perverted, so case closed. But "offending the public interest" is a weak argument at best, and has been used in the past in laws against homosexuality

---

[60] The court's ruling (in German) can be accessed from the official website for the Bundesverfassungsgericht at http://www.bundesverfassungsgericht.de/SharedDocs/Entscheidungen/DE/2015/12/rk20151208_1bvr186414.html

(as it was in Germany), so it won't hold up under scrutiny. The same is true for calling something "perverted"—it has no specific legal meaning and has failed to hold up in courts when challenged. "Unnatural" in the legal sense can mean one of two things: (1) it does not happen in nature, or (2) the act cannot result in its natural intention, which in this case is procreation. The first does not apply as there are multiple instances documenting cross-species intimacy in nature (as mentioned previously). The second does not apply either, because that very argument was struck down both in Germany and in the US Supreme Court in cases involving gay rights and marriage equality. When opponents of gay rights and marriage equality argued that gay sex could not result in procreation and was therefore "unnatural" (and therefore should be illegal), the courts invalidated the argument by pointing out this would make heterosexual relations where one or both partners were unable to procreate (sterility, for example) both unnatural and illegal.

On a side note, when the German magazine *Der Spiegel* reported on the German case, it referred to the two defendants as "sodomites," which just so happens to be the word that has formerly been used to refer, pejoratively of course, to homosexuals.[61] Remember, Germany's legal efforts to ban zoophilia first required that laws banning homosexuality and zoophilia be unlinked, since the original laws had assumed that both were perverted and unnatural sexual orientations. It is interesting and perhaps a little unsettling that a magazine like *Der Spiegel* would invoke language that seems to relink them.

---

61 "Verfassungsrichter bestätigen Verbot von Sex mit Tieren," *Spiegel Online* (February 18, 2016) at http://www.spiegel.de/panorama/justiz/bundesverfassungsgericht-bestaetigt-verbot-von-sex-mit-tieren-a-1078075.html

The result of all this is that the only part of the ruling in Germany that gives us any firm legal grounding to prevent the redrawing of the sexual orientation line so that it normalizes zoophilia is the part that says animals have an intrinsic right against sexual relations without their consent. But if they have that right, then surely they also have a right not be killed without their consent. Otherwise we would have a situation where rape (sex without consent) is illegal but slaughter (killing without consent) is not, which is a contradiction in legal logic. If you're thinking that this would make it illegal for animals to kill and eat each other, it wouldn't—the laws in Germany on this issue, as in America, only apply to human interaction with other species (to change that, we would have to give legal standing to animals, which would actually strengthen animal rights). So the rights that animals have in Germany in this case protect them specifically from unwanted actions from humans. In other words, we can keep zoophilia as an illegal sexual orientation for now, but it is only a matter of time before another court case comes along to press the issue further. Eventually we will end up with the choice of either accepting zoophilia as a valid sexual orientation, on par with heterosexuality and homosexuality, or else we will have to stop eating meat. Oh, and if you think we'd at least still be able to eat fish, there's definitely a big *no* to that. Recent studies have shown clearly that fish have the same complex emotional lives of other animals, including primates, and so the laws would protect them as well.[62] So I'll go on record with a rather intriguing prediction (and do quote me on this if you like): marriage equality will necessarily create a vegetarian future.

---

62 "Fish Have Feelings, Too: The Inner Lives of Our 'Underwater Cousins,'" *NPR: Fresh Air* (June 20, 2016) at http://www.npr.org/sections/thesalt/2016/06/20/482468094/fish-have-feelings-too-the-inner-lives-of-our-underwater-cousins

More fun with the law
The law in the United States on this issue is equally vexing. It is not just by coincidence that so many states in America are now frantically trying to pass anti-zoophilia legislation. You might think that all of them already have such laws on the books, but it turns out that as I write twenty states lack any such legislation. There is also no federal law against zoophilia, with the interesting exception of military law (10 USCA § 92), although recent events with marriage equality have set things in motion to remedy the situation and create a federal law to deal specifically with zoophilia. As with Germany, there has been a steady increase in recent years in zoophilia in the United States (if you don't believe me, just go online and do a simple Google search—but please be warned that what you find might be really unsettling).[63] Meanwhile, other states have struggled to cover these gaps in their state-level protective legislation. It took Florida *three* tries to pass a piece of anti-zoophilia legislation in 2011, apparently because legislators had a hard time with the wording of the legislation (animal cruelty laws usually stumble trying to find ways to differentiate between killing a kitten, which society says is horrible, and killing a calf, which society says is veal).[64] As with Germany, what appears to be simple redrawing of one line opens up the realization of how arbitrary and close those other lines actually are.

Even then, the law still has bizarre loopholes. In 2012, Eric Antunes was arrested in Florida for having oral sex with a dog

---

[63] See, for example, Michelle Broder Van Dyke, "Woman Reveals She Had a Sexual Relationship with a Dolphin," *BuzzFeed News* (June 10, 2014) at https://www.buzzfeed.com/mbvd/woman-reveals-she-had-a-sexual-relationship-with-a-dolphin?utm_term=.ba7wGG0bkN#.ym7XmmOGLD

[64] Jason Linkins, "Florida Lawmakers Poised to Make Third Attempt to Ban Bestiality," *Huffington Post* (March 25, 2011) at http://www.huffingtonpost.com/2011/03/25/florida-lawmakers-bestiality-ban-third-try_n_840694.html

but could not actually be charged with a violation of the new anti-zoophilia legislation because—taking a page from the Bill Clinton handbook that says oral sex isn't really sex—the law does not explicitly forbid oral sex with an animal.[65] That pales by comparison to the case of Carlos Romero, who is challenging the constitutionality of his arrest for having sex with his pet miniature donkey based on the very same legal elements that constitute gay rights and marriage equality. Indeed, his attorneys are specifically tying his case to marriage equality and gay rights cases. Among other things, Romero is claiming that (1) the act was a private act between a man and his donkey; (2) prosecutors have no way to prove that the donkey was an unwilling participant (as in, did not consent); (3) the case violates the equal protection clause of the Fourteenth Amendment of the US Constitution. Romero's attorneys have stated that laws against zoophilia are based upon religious and moral principles from past traditions that have no place in present-day law: "The personal morals of the majority, whether based on religion or traditions, cannot be used as a reason to deprive a person of their personal liberties."[66] His attorneys are also relying upon the US Supreme Court case of *Lawrence v. Texas* (2003), which overturned existing state legislation against sodomy on the grounds that those laws violated a person's right to privacy.

Incidentally, there is a whole other side-note to the Florida anti-zoophilia legislation fiasco that ought to be mentioned here,

---

65 Ryan Gorman and Erik Ortiz, "Florida man won't be charged in bestiality case because of law loophole," *NY Daily News* (June 22, 2012) at http://www.nydailynews.com/news/national/florida-man-won-charged-bestiality-case-law-loophole-article-1.1100381

66 Kyle Munzenrieder, "Man Busted for Sex with Mini-Donkey Will Challenge Florida's Anti-Bestiality Law," *Miami New Times* (December 13, 2012) at http://blogs.miaminewtimes.com/riptide/2012/12/man_busted_for_sex_acts_with_m.php

since it highlights just why these things—no matter how bizarre or unrelated they may appear—need to be discussed in the open and in detail. Among other things, law in general requires clarity and consistency to be effective. For a brief moment after the Florida anti-zoophilia legislation passed, a handful of legal bloggers rather mischievously pointed out that Florida had inadvertently banned all sex in Florida, since the law banned sex between humans and animals, and humans, it turns out, are also animals. Though it is not a part of the anti-zoophiia legislation itself, Florida does elsewhere in its legal code define what an animal is, but I'm not sure it helps. Here is what Florida law says, and no, I am not kidding: "the word "animal" shall be held to include every living dumb creature." (Chapter 828.02) If that's the way it's defined, all I can say is, I know an awful lot of people who are animals.

Animal is the new queer
In spite of what must look like an endless stream of red herrings, we have to remember that there is a serious legal issue lurking behind all of this. Most people dismiss the very idea of zoophilia on the grounds that there is a firm boundary line between humans and every other nonhuman species. Florida's definition of animals as "every living dumb creature" is based upon the notion, no longer scientifically valid (not even close), that only humans have the capacity for speech and communication. Nonhuman animals just make nonsensical or meaningless noises, or so the argument goes. Florida law stumbled for the same reason that laws banning same-sex marriage faltered: at the end of the day, the lines that drawn to separate are indefensible. So there actually is a reason to put zoophilia in the same discussion as homosexuality, beyond just the fact that both are sexual orientations (as is heterosexuality). But what links homosexuality and zoophilia is that both of them are based upon a set of boundaries that are slowly being redrawn. Do you find zoophilia *disgusting*? Perhaps so, but many

people found and still find homosexuality disgusting. The courts, however, have made it clear that disgust has no basis in maintaining normative boundaries. Is the prohibition of zoophilia based upon religion or tradition? Perhaps so, but the law has made it clear that tradition and religion have no suasion in supporting lines that separate and discriminate. So if we are left only with the final argument that zoophilia creates an unwilling victim, which is pretty much all we have, then the other lines that we draw that say this animal is cute but that animal is food will have to fall soon as well. Animal is the new queer.

If you are still not convinced that there is a link between redrawing normative lines for sexual orientation and redrawing lines for cross-species interaction (including intimacy), consider this. In April 2013, New Zealand joined the small but growing list of nations to legalize same-sex marriage, a move that many people within New Zealand and elsewhere celebrated as a victory for gay rights, human rights, and human dignity in general. New Zealand was praised as a progressive country, and indeed, it *has* been a progressive country in terms of granting rights to an ever-expanding number of communities. So yes, New Zealand did recognize the right of same-sex couples to marry. But this decision was made a full twelve years *after* New Zealand became the first country to grant human rights to (some) nonhuman species, which they did in 1999. New Zealand argued that the normative line that separated humans from primates was not an absolute divide or a legally justifiable separation. Similarly, in Spain, where same-sex marriage became legal in 2005, human rights were granted to the so-called great apes just three years later in 2008. Spain cited reasons that mirrored those offered by New Zealand—that the line separating humans and nonhuman primates was just as arbitrary and indefensible as the line that separates homosexual from heterosexual.

More recently, in the United States, acrimonious debate has broken out over the decision of a slaughterhouse in New Mexico to slaughter horses in order to sell the meat to suppliers in Europe. Speaking of arbitrary lines, horses in Europe are considered food whereas in the United States they are considered beautiful creatures (but note how we consider cows "dumb" to make a distinction between cows and horses, making it easier to slaughter the former). Many activists even issued death threats against the owners of the slaughterhouse.[67] The legal question behind the debates is simple: are horses pets (entitled to be protected) or are they livestock (entitled to be slaughtered)? Once again we come across identity-based lines that once seemed obvious and natural but now seem arbitrary and indefensible, in this case the line we draw between pets and livestock. If livestock are put in the same category as pets, meat will essentially become illegal, and conversely, if pets are seen as livestock, then they can be killed and eaten with impunity.

But wait, there's more. In 2012, at a conference of the American Association for the Advancement of Science held in Vancouver, four scientists initiated a movement to reclassify cetaceans (dolphins and whales) as nonhuman persons.[68] Similarly, in December 2013, the Nonhuman Rights Project filed writs of habeus corpus in New York to argue that chimpanzees possessed legal personhood, which would recognize the right to their own individual autonomy and would prevent them from being encaged or exploited.[69] It is not a coincidence that the lines being redrawn for different species

---

67 Jeri Clausing, "NM slaughterhouse ground zero in horse debate," *Yahoo! News* (April 23, 2013) at http://news.yahoo.com/nm-slaughterhouse-ground-zero-horse-debate-071837115.html

68 "Dolphins deserve same rights as humans, say scientists," *BBC News* (February 21, 2012) at http://www.bbc.com/news/world-17116882

69 James Gorman, "Considering the Humanity of Nonhumans," *The New York Times* (December 9, 2013) at http://www.nytimes.com/2013/12/10/science/considering-the-humanity-of-nonhumans.html

and the lines being redrawn for different sexual orientations are occurring at the same time. It is only a matter of time before they converge.

And if the discussion of bestiality and zoophilia has been distressing for some, there is still another issue that has to be discussed, again, *not because it should be conflated with homosexuality or any part of the LGBTQI+ community*, but because the logic of the law and the logic of the argument to include sexual orientation in the structures of diversity require us to go there. Brace yourself: things are about to go from distressing to downright ugly.

The pedophilia argument
One mention of the word "pedophilia" in any discussion of LGBTQI+ rights or same-sex marriage will invariably cause the entire room to erupt in paroxysms of rage and anger and disparagement. It is the word that must not be mentioned, the concept that must not be thought, the irrelevant distraction that cannot be allowed to derail the rhetorical train to diversity's utopia. Like any mention of zoophilia, even a passing reference to pedophilia in any discussion of sexual orientation is usually hounded out of the debate so quickly that it is never even considered. This is done partly to show that there is absolutely no link between homosexuality and pedophilia and partly to demonstrate the moral outrage that LGBTQI+ rights activists have toward pedophilia. But here, right now, we are going to have that discussion, because it is a discussion that needs to be had.

Let's start with the claim that there is no link between homosexuality and pedophilia. We are back to the apples and oranges argument—no response is needed because the two have nothing to do with each other. That argument only holds up if we assume that "sexual orientation" is synonymous with homosexuality, which it is not. Homosexuality is a sexual orientation, but as I have said, so too is heterosexuality, and more controversially, zoophilia.

Pedophilia is also a sexual orientation. To say that does not legitimize it, but merely describes it for what it is. So while it would be completely incorrect to raise the issue of pedophilia as somehow a variant of homosexuality, as some very conservative fear-mongers have often tried to do, it is not incorrect to raise the issue of pedophilia in a discussion of sexual orientation, as long as we consider *all* sexual orientations in the discussion. Most but not all pedophiles are heterosexual in terms of sexual orientation, but what creates the substantive divide between heterosexuality and pedophilia as sexual orientations is the issue of *age*. A pedophile is by definition a person who is consistently and sexually attracted to other persons who fall below the legally-defined age of consent for sexual relations. Any person who falls below the legally-defined age of consent cannot offer consent, usually on the grounds that such a person has not yet developed the sufficient capacity to make properly-informed choices about things like sexual relations, and thus is legally an unwilling, non-consenting victim of any sexual act. That is what makes pedophilia a crime, and that is what separates it legally from other sexual orientations such as heterosexuality and homosexuality, which are both legal as long as the persons involved can and have given consent to sexual relations.

Incidentally, if at this point you are having a hard time accepting pedophilia as a sexual orientation, let's revisit that argument one more time. First, what is a sexual orientation? In *McAleer v. Canada* (1996), the courts of Canada responded to a challenge that the idea of sexual orientation was vague and unclear by claiming that sexual orientation was "a precise legal concept" that "deals specifically with an individual's preference in terms of gender." Confusingly, in using the word "preference" the Canadian courts actually reinstated the idea of choice, but we'll sidestep that discussion for now. Or how about the US courts? In *Equality Foundation of Cincinnati v. the City of Cincinnati* (1995), the US District Court stated that "homo-, hetero-, and bisexual orientation is a characteristic beyond the control of the individual," something that "sets in at an early stage, around 3-5 years, and is simply a matter of development beyond that stage." The court also separated all of these from pedophilia, which it places in the category of "deviant sexual practices." Incidentally, according to this opinion, no one is actually *born* gay, but rather, something "sets in" when we are between 3-5 years of age, which immediately raises the question of when exactly something has to "set in" before it is considered an orientation, and what circumstances cause something to "set in" in some individuals but not in others.

Think also of the way we refer to pedophiles. We always say "so-and-so is a pedophile," and never a "heterosexual who engages in acts of pedophilia" or a "person who has sex with children," or some other roundabout form of description. We say of pedophiles that that is what they *are*—innately. In other words, we use the language of sexual orientation. (On a side-note, if you think only of men when you see the word pedophile, think again—women can be pedophiles, too.[70]) We could even refer to the argument made earlier, in relation to homosexuality, that no one would ever *choose* to be gay because there is so much social opprobrium and oppression associated with being gay that one would only be gay if they were born that way. Well, if no one would choose to be gay for those reasons, then certainly no one would choose pedophilia (or zoophilia) either, for similar reasons.[71] I think the US District Court

---

70 And no, female pedophiles are not "exceptions." See, for one example, "23 women found guilty of child pornography," *Radio Sweden* (October 18, 2011) at http://sverigesradio.se/sida/artikel.aspx?programid=2054&artikel=4752927

71 See, for example, Ellie Hooper, "Paedophile nursery worker, 28, demands to be chemically castrated to prevent him reoffending," *Closer* (February 21, 2014) at http://lifestyle.one/closer/news-real-life/real-life/paedophile-nurdery-worker-28-demands-chemically-castrated-prevent-reoffending/

is on very shaky grounds when it assumes that homo-, hetero-, and bisexual orientations are innate but pedophilia is a "deviant sex act." I think what we really have in front of us is an array of sexual orientations, and what makes one illegal and the other legal is not the orientation itself but the object of desire. In other words, it isn't the orientation itself but the target of orientation that is key here. Once upon a time, the only acceptable target of desire was a person of the opposite gender. Currently, we have a shift toward acceptance of homosexuality on the grounds that the orientation is innate and both partners are consenting adults. What separates pedophilia and zoophilia is not that they are "deviant" but rather that the targets of desire, namely children and animals, are unconsenting or unwilling participants in the behavior. There are many sexual activities that deviate from acceptable norms, thereby making them deviant (which is the etymological origin of the word), but they remain legal as long as consent is involved (though it is a little-known fact that most US states still legally categorize anal and oral sex as "deviate [sic] sex acts"). A person with pedophilia as their sexual orientation but who never actually engages in or pursues any act of pedophilia has in fact committed no crime and no act of deviance, just as a person who has racist thoughts but never commits a racist act nor utters a racist statement in public has committed no hate crime.

These legal distinctions are important because law is what generates rights, and since rights are central to securing diversity, the topic simply has to be broached rather than avoided or dismissed as more "apples and oranges." What we have is the same question we saw with zoophilia: can the logic used for legally redrawing the line to move homosexuality to the other side of the line of normativity also be used to move pedophilia closer to or even across that line as well? Again, no matter how loudly one voices moral repugnance for the very thought of pedophilia, moral repugnance cannot be confused with the compelling logic of the law. In the marriage equality debate, for instance, we hear over and over again: if you don't like the idea of gay marriage then that is your choice, but your dislike of it cannot stand in the way of another person's legal right to institutionalize their intimacy through marriage. In short, just because people find pedophilia abhorrent and deviant doesn't mean we should avoid the issue of clarifying the law in an age of shifting lines of normativity.

So let's focus on this issue of consent and see where it gets us. We can start with the point that homosexuality and heterosexuality both involve two (or more) *consenting* adults while pedophilia involves a child that cannot legally consent or is an unwilling victim. Pedophilia therefore necessarily involves criminal victimization. We saw one version of this argument earlier with zoophilia: animals cannot legally consent or are unwilling partners and hence zoophilia is a crime. But the legal consent part is where things unexpectedly start to get complicated and uncomfortable, partly because of the implications of drawing that line firmly and neatly at the age of consent (which in the US is the age of 18) and partly because the age of consent is itself a hotly contested concept in US law and also in international human rights law.

The age of consent
The whole idea of the age of consent is that only at a certain moment in our lives do humans have sufficient knowledge and experience to understand the consequences of our actions and so only from that moment onward can we legitimately express autonomous consent regarding our actions. Before that, other people (parents and guardians) have the legal authority and indeed responsibility to make decisions on our behalf and in our best interest. Currently in the United States, and in international human rights law, that moment happens rather magically and arbitrarily at midnight on the day of a person's eighteenth birthday. At seventeen years and 364 days, a person is too naïve and clueless to understand a sexual

relationship. But when you wake up the next day, all the answers are clear, and the mysteries of life are no longer mysteries at all. At seventeen years, a child does not sufficiently know right from wrong and is unable to make informed decisions about pretty much anything, including sexual orientation. But on the magical day of our eighteenth birthday, suddenly everything changes. We can consent to sex. Inexplicably, in the United States at least, we have to wait three more years before we can consent to alcohol, which is apparently more dangerous than sex.

The chronological line that is drawn at eighteen years, like the line between humans and nonhumans or the lines between sexual orientations, does weird things to thoughts we normally accept as, well, normal. How much control does a child, which is legally anyone under the age of eighteen, actually have over their life? Currently, the parents of a child who exhibits homosexual behavior or who carries the gay gene (if it were ever found) would be perfectly within their rights to alter that behavior or seek out any and all forms of medical treatment or therapy, including gene therapy, to try to turn their son or daughter straight, if they thought it was in their child's best interest. Many states, including California, are passing or considering legislation to ban what is known as "gay conversion therapy," a controversial form of therapy with the intent to turn gay children straight. The premise behind the ban is that gay conversion therapy, which has so far shown a success rate of approximately 0%, is harmful to children. But if sexual orientation is something that "sets in" between 3-5 years of age, then what if parents do everything possible before those years to try to ensure their children are straight? Confusing? Sure—but wait, we're just getting started.

This is partly the impetus behind the search for a gay gene—it would seal the deal on the argument that a child is born gay and so nothing can be done about it and society has no right to intervene in any way to prevent the natural development of the child into a full-fledged, well-adjusted homosexual adult. But when we re-introduce the matter of pedophilia, the argument quickly gets muddled: what happens, for instance, if a child is born a pedophile? What if we discover that there is a pedophile gene? Would society have to let the child grow into a full-fledged adult pedophile?

At this point, someone will usually try to point out that these two possibilities have no relation to each other—apples and oranges. But the awkward fact is—they do. Again, not that homosexuality and pedophilia are one and the same, but the legal argument that is built for one can and indeed already is being used by the other. The search for the gay gene, for instance, has given rise to the search for a pedophile gene. *Gawker*, an online magazine that admittedly pushed lots of buttons until it was shut down by a lawsuit in August 2016, published an article in September 2012 entitled "Born This Way: Sympathy and Science for Those Who Want to Have Sex With Children," which argued that pedophilia is a case of cross-wiring in the architecture of the brain. A "true" pedophile is therefore born that way, at least according to the article, and can do little if nothing to change the way they think and feel. In essence, pedophilia is a sexual orientation. In response to the *Gawker* article, Razib Khan of *Discover* magazine wrote: "Many biological dispositions aren't deterministic, they're probabilistic. That means controlling or channeling them in non-destructive ways entails changing the situations and contexts one is placed in."[72] But if we combine that with the idea that sexual orientation "sets in" between 3-5 years of age, then we've got all sorts of room here for

---

72 Razib Khan, "Pedophiles: born that way?" *Discover* (September 9, 2012) at http://blogs.discovermagazine.com/gnxp/2012/09/pedophiles-born-that-way/#.UVi5Jb_qKnV

parents to be able to control or channel the sexual orientation of their children, and that would be completely within the boundaries of the law, due to the age of consent idea. I can easily see a parent taking a cue from this advice and thinking that as long as their son or daughter is not placed in any type of "gay" context or environment, the homosexual impulse can be eliminated or minimized and their son or daughter will grow up straight.

Many will scoff at citing anything from *Gawker*, so let's look at a few other things to round out the picture. In 2011, for example, a group of scientists in Italy claimed to have isolated a pedophile gene. Neuroscientists at Turin University stated that they had obtained evidence to show that a defective protein was responsible for pedophilia, and expressed hope that in isolating the "pedophile gene," the condition could be cured through proper gene therapy.[73] If the results of this research turn out to be true, then will scientists also offer gene therapy to "fix" homosexuality as well? Will parents be within their rights to request this type of gene therapy for their children? And note too how the language regarding pedophilia and a pedophile gene mirrors the language from just a few decades ago, now discredited, that referred to homosexuality as a "defect" that had to be "cured." The idea now is that homosexuality is innate, and cannot be altered in any way and certainly cannot be "cured" or "fixed," but if we do in fact end up with a pedophile gene, the same rules would also apply—to the pedophile. Again, the only thing we have of substance separating hetero- and homosexuality from pedophilia and zoophilia as sexual orientations is the lack of consent from the target of sexual desire. And that, as I will show, is not as solid a foundation as many think it is.

---

73 Marco Accossato, "Un gene alterato scatena la pedofilia," *La Stampa* (October 21, 2011), at http://www.lastampa.it/2011/10/21/scienza/un-gene-alterato-scatena-la-pedofilia-XF1AMxzArWAl8b5Py8eDSO/pagina.html

Remember the brain scan studies? Well, those have also been done to pedophiles, and as it turns out, pedophiles have brains that are consistently different as well. So if pedophilia is not genetic, then it could credibly claimed to be at least "hard-wired" into an individual's brain, exactly the same argument made in the brain scan studies regarding homosexuality that I discussed earlier. A study carried out by the Centre for Addiction and Mental Research in Toronto, Canada, found that pedophile brains were wired differently from other brains, and so pedophilia might be hard-wired into an individual, rather than something triggered by sexual trauma abuse in childhood, as many existing theories believe. The study carried out by the Centre for Addiction and Mental Research was not the first of its kind either, and in fact backed up and confirmed earlier studies at Yale University that also showed that pedophile brains were wired differently from other brains. But here's a quote that should make everyone pause to think. The lead researcher in the Toronto study, Dr. James Cantor, conceded that pedophiles therefore could not alter the way they thought about sexuality, thereby making pedophilia their sexual orientation, but also added: "Not being able to choose your sexual interests doesn't mean that you can't choose what you do."[74]

We should take a moment here to put things back into perspective—we have many things on the table at this point. Locating a gay gene, seen by many as the definitive "argument over" deal-sealer, may not settle anything at all, especially if there is also a comparable pedophile gene. And trust me on this: every victory that is secured for gay rights on the ground that homosexuality is either genetically determined or something a person is born with will be seized upon by pedophiles and their lawyers to argue that the same rules must be applied to the condition of

---

74 "Brain wiring link to paedophilia," *BBC News* (November 28, 2007) at http://news.bbc.co.uk/2/hi/health/7116506.stm

pedophilia. Because pedophiles are born that way, the argument would go, society cannot discriminate against them, nor can they be despised as perverts. To do so would be to cultivate hate against yet another part of the population who feel they are shunned and marginalized by mainstream society. And to those who voice the objection that pedophiles create victims in a way that homosexuality does not, which is legally true, the response will not be comforting. What we will end up with is a legal situation in which the victims of pedophilia are treated as victims and given assistance by the state to recover from trauma and other emotional damage, but the pedophiles who inflicted the trauma will also be victims since, as their lawyers will no doubt claim, they were born that way.

The age of gayness
As if all that weren't bad enough, there is a whole other issue that relates to the definition of a proper age of consent and the notion of victimization. The definition of eighteen years of age being the legal age of consent is, incidentally, itself the result of a long historical process of redrawing the lines of normativity, in this case regarding childhood. When it comes to sexuality, however, especially when it gets mixed in with the law, things get a bit more complicated. What, for instance, separates the crime of statutory rape from the crime of pedophilia? As it turns out, very few jurisdictions actually use the term "statutory rape," and refer to the act instead as unlawful sex with a minor—a minor being defined as someone under the age of consent, that is, under eighteen. Strictly speaking, that means that any person eighteen years of age or older having sexual relations with anyone under the age of eighteen is engaging in pedophilia. That would mean that if two seventeen year-olds were dating and having sexual relations, and one of them turned eighteen before the other, that person would be a pedophile, at least in a strict reading of the law. Now, any rational person might see that as a bit extreme, but that is exactly the problem: the interpretation of the age of consent has long been open to all sorts of debate and wiggle room.

Consider this scenario: Sir Paul McCartney takes to the stage and begins to sing "I Saw Her Standing There," one of the many iconic hits of the Beatles. The lyrics begin: "Well she was just seventeen, you know what I mean..." Moments later, police take to the stage and arrest Sir Paul for encouraging pedophilia. Afterward, the US Congress debates whether to censor or ban the song—maybe Sir Paul would consent to altering the lyrics to "She was clearly eighteen, you know what I mean?" Sound absurd? Surely, one would think, there is no harm in singing about a hot seventeen-year old girl that one would want to fall in love with after dancing with her—that's just rock and roll, right? And besides, seventeen is "pretty close" to eighteen, and so the girl is close enough, right? Or maybe it was her seventeenth birthday party where she was dancing, and so the day before she was sixteen, and sixteen is pretty close to seventeen, so sixteen is close enough, too, right? After all, the rock band KISS has a song called "Christine Sixteen" about a young girl who is only sixteen years old, and includes lyrics like this: "I don't usually say things like this to girls your age, but when I saw you coming out of school that day, that day I knew, I knew, I've got to have you, I've got to have you." So sixteen seems okay too. But the law says eighteen, while society, or at least rock n' roll, says things are negotiable. Apparently it depends on the circumstances.

Many states put youths who would otherwise legally be children on trial "as an adult," because the courts determined that they were sufficiently aware of what was right and what was wrong to be considered adults in the eyes of the law. In 2011, a judge in Pennsylvania declared Jordan Brown, who was eleven years old when he shot and killed his father's pregnant fiancée, competent as a thirteen-year old to stand trial as an adult, making him the youngest person ever to be considered an adult in the eyes of US law. Others have been tried similarly as adults at the age of twelve, thirteen, and fourteen, and it was only in 2005, in the case of *Roper v. Simmons*, that the US Supreme Court finally did away with the death penalty for persons who had committed their crimes while still children (that is, under the age of eighteen). So, if an eleven year old can understand right from wrong for something as serious as murder, would we be willing to accept that they can understand right from wrong in intimate relations? In other countries, the age of consent for intimate relations is set much lower than the age of eighteen. In Spain, for instance, the age of consent for intimate relations is twelve (which would mean that a relationship condemned as pedophilia in the United States might be considered acceptable and normal in Spain). The law can make a mess of things, even unwittingly, but that only means that the mess has to be cleaned up for proper justice to prevail. Note how we have entered the topic of child murderers being tried as adults, through a discussion of pedophilia launched by a legal parallel with laws that once criminalized homosexuality. The law is fun indeed.

One of the reasons that the law is so unclear on what exactly makes a person a child or an adolescent or a minor is that the normative lines on what childhood is and when it begins have only recently been redrawn. The first juvenile court was created in the United States only in 1899, and before that, the law considered *seven years of age* to be the dividing line on what legally separated the categories of child and adult. Marriages and courtships that would have been considered perfectly normal in the nineteenth century would now be regarded as illegal and perverted. Most of them would be categorized as pedophilia by today's standards. Even then, exceptions are still made all the time: between 2000 and 2010, for instance, 167,000 persons were legally married in the United States below the age of 18, with some as young as 12.[75]

---

[75] Fraidy Reiss, "Why can 12-year-olds still get married in the United States?" *The Washington Post* (February 10, 2017) at https://www.washingtonpost.com/posteverything/wp/2017/02/10/why-does-the-united-states-still-let-12-year-old-girls-get-married/?tid=pm_opinions_pop&utm_term=.201a7b9e8ce1

In other cases, the age of consent is actually raised to "below the age of 19" if the person is still in school, in order to prosecute teachers who pursue sexual relationships with students who are 18 but still in school.[76] And this is precisely the problem that the legal history of pedophilia, past and present, creates for the issues of redefining sexual orientation: when lines of normativity are redrawn, the result can be a whole, uncontrollable mess. No matter how uncomfortable and distasteful it might be, the discussion that no one wants to have—of sexual orientation, pedophilia, and zoophilia—has to take place. Not just the realization of gay rights, but diversity itself, depends on getting it right.

In which the left and the right shake hands
I will end this part of our program as I did with my discussion on zoophilia, by offering an example or two that shows clearly how the things I am discussing here are already in play. These aren't the hypothetical ravings of a lunatic. These are very real and tangible elements that we need to insert into our discussion of diversity if we want diversity to have any chance of success.

If I were called upon to name one intellectual figure who has done more to open the discussion on gay rights and homosexuality than any other, that person would arguably be French philosopher and social critic Michel Foucault. I know there are those who would disagree with me, but I can all but guarantee that even those people would at least rank him in the top five. I will have more to say about Foucault in a later chapter, but for now, let's bring him in to talk about how he opened up the discussion

---

76 Eric Owens, "Charge: Smoking Hot Teacher Victimized 18-Year-Old Male Student with Mind-Blowing Sex Trauma," *The Daily Caller* (January 12, 2015) at http://dailycaller.com/2015/01/12/charge-smoking-hot-teacher-victimized-18-year-old-male-student-with-mind-blowing-sex-trauma/

on gay rights and homosexuality, and why in the eyes of many people, the current achievement of things like marriage equality simply would not have been possible without the philosophical and conceptual contributions of Michel Foucault. His influence in academia is immense, and many if not most scholars in fields that deal with social issues draw heavily on his work, directly or indirectly, for their own.

Foucault's project for much of his life was to unmask the various sources of oppression and control that constrain our lives in ways that are mostly invisible to us. While people living in the modern age were busy convincing themselves that they lived in the best of times, Foucault set about destroying that idea by showing that modernity had only succeeded in creating increasingly sophisticated instruments of surveillance and control. These instruments of surveillance and control exerted an immense normative power, and anything that did not fit within the parameters of normativity had to be isolated and then either exiled, excised, or punished. One of the subjects he focused on in his work was the construction of modern sexuality. As a gay man living in what was supposedly an open, democratic society in France, Foucault felt the normative pressure that pushed homosexuality to the margins, where to his mind the threat it posed was isolated, criminalized, and punished. Foucault wanted to unmask the process through which gay sexuality had been suppressed and criminalized and then dismantle it.

The idea of heteronormativity is central to Foucault's work. It is a word that conveys how society defines what is sexually normal, in this case the heterosexual, monogamous adult, and then pushes anything that does not fit that definition of normal into the realm of the deviant and perverted. Whatever is not normal, as defined by society and enforced through modern instruments of surveillance and control, is thus seen as a threat to society that must be contained and destroyed. The construction of the homosexual as a social deviant, as a pervert, and the criminalization of gay sex, were manifestations of this highly oppressive process. If there was to be any hope of redrawing the normative lines that had rendered homosexuality deviant and criminal, a threat to be exposed and expunged, then the complex apparatus through which that had been accomplished and enforced had to be first outed and then disempowered.

So far, so good, and it should be obvious how Foucault's work has a direct bearing on our discussion of normativity and sexual orientation. Where things get interesting and perhaps a little uncomfortable for those who draw heavily on Foucault's ideas, however, is that Foucault didn't stop there. Foucault also took aim at the age of consent laws in France, arguing that child sexuality, like homosexuality, had also been rendered a threat to society, and like homosexuality, was therefore something to be contained and controlled as well. The two-fold process by which this occurred started first with the construction of the pedophile as a sexual deviant, and then with the desexualization of the child and the construction of childhood as a protected period of asexual innocence. Social fear of child sexuality and the criminalization of pedophilia were linked directly to the social fear and criminalization of homosexuality.

It was this that led Foucault to add his name, along with several other prominent French intellectuals, to a petition to the French parliament in 1977 asking that the age of consent laws in France be scrapped and that consensual sexual relations between adults and children be decriminalized.[77] The petition was linked to two open letters, one published in *Le Monde* (1977) and the other in *Libération* (1979), calling for the release of four adults who were awaiting trial, each accused of having sexual relations with children

---

77 "Quand Libé, Le Monde et la gôche morale défendaient la pédophilie," *24 Heures Actu* (January 2, 2013) at http://24heuresactu.com/2013/01/02/quand-libe-le-monde-et-la-goche-morale-defendaient-la-pedophilie/

(male and female) ranging in age from 6 to 14.[78] The adults should be released, said the open letters, because no crime had been committed. The problem, said the letters and drawing heavily from Foucault, was the social construction of childhood as something separate from adulthood, which resulted in what they saw as the incorrect criminalization of pedophilia. One of the letters argued that if a 13-year old girl could have access to birth control (which was possible in France at the time), then she could consent to sex as well.

For Foucault, in other words, and for those who signed the petition and the open letters, the two issues of homosexuality and pedophilia were not "apples and oranges" as contemporary activists allege, and they weren't even, as I have suggested, different varieties of apples. For Foucault, homosexuality and pedophilia *were* the same apple. Both had been rendered deviant and then criminalized by the same process and for the same reason. Decriminalizing homosexuality didn't just suggest but indeed required the simultaneous decriminalization of pedophilia. Child sexuality, like gay sexuality, had to be liberated, and society just needed to "get over it."

Foucault wasn't just an intellectual. He was also a public activist on the political left. If you might be thinking, well, that was France in the 1970s—crazy times—you should note that in spite of the efforts to dismiss these issues as apples and oranges, the link between them is still showing up as I write, on both the political left and the political right. One of the groups that is directly active in the movement that has become known as Antifa (anti-fascism, as in, opposing Donald Trump), for example, is the Coalition to Defend Affirmative Action, Integration, and immigrant Rights,

---

78 Jon Henley, "Calls for legal child sex rebound on luminaries of May 68," *The Guardian* (February 23, 2001) at https://www.theguardian.com/world/2001/feb/24/jonhenley

and Fight for Equality By Any Means Necessary, known more concisely as BAMN (By Any Means Necessary—a phrase, by the way, coined by another French intellectual, Jean-Paul Sartre). BAMN is clearly a group that emanates from the political left, and operates under the aegis of another left-wing organization known as the Revolutionary Workers League (RWL). A recent release of documents and an investigation by *The Daily Caller* (which admittedly had an interest in making BAMN look hypocritical) showed that the RWL has worked with and directly supported the North American Man-Boy Love Association, also known as NAMBLA, a group that advocates for the decriminalization of pedophilia.[79] My point here is not to discuss NAMBLA, BAMN, or the RWL or even the Antifa movement. My point is to shows that RWL's support of NAMBLA was an extension of their support for gay rights, which is direct descendant of Foucault's work linking the two issues.

Lest anyone think I am singling out the political left on this, let me also remind everyone of what happened to Milo Yiannopoulos, alt-right provocateur and openly-gay Trump supporter. In February 2017 a video surfaced of Yiannopoulos apparently defending pedophilia. In the video, Yiannopoulos is heard saying that sexual relationships between men and young boys are something of a "coming of age" relationship, where older men "help young boys discover who they are." His comments also alluded to the "heavy policing" of consensual adults as a result of social fears about child abuse. Yiannopoulos lost a lucrative book deal and was widely condemned for his remarks. Again, my goal here is not to go after Yiannopoulos or the alt-right or even conservatives in general but rather to point out again how the ghost of Foucault still haunts the

---

79 Peter Hasson, "Documents Tie Berkeley Riot Organizers to Pro-Pedophilia Group, NAMBLA," *The Daily Caller* (April 28, 2017) at http://dailycaller.com/2017/04/28/documents-tie-berkeley-riot-organizers-to-pro-pedophilia-group-nambla/

whole dialogue on normativity and the linking of homosexuality and pedophilia.

I'll end this rather long intermission with an unexpected link of a different kind. The RWL defended NAMBLA and said it was the victim of a social "witch-hunt" for daring to question the oppressive norms of mainstream society. Yiannopoulos also stated he was the victim of a witch-hunt after the video surfaced, again, for daring to question out loud the oppressive norms of mainstream society. Pause for that awkward moment when the alt-right and the radical left shake hands and nod in agreement.

End of intermission

Wading further into the swamp
In the past few decades, a number of professional historians have spent considerable amounts of time and energy documenting the prevalence of homosexuality in different historical epochs and in different cultural environments. Some of them have documented moments of acceptance and tolerance, while others have documented discrimination and oppression. The larger project in all of these histories has been to show how sociologically and historically, homosexuality has been around for almost all of human history, and attempts to ban or suppress it have only driven it underground. Much like the argument surrounding the science of the gay gene, the idea is to show that something so prevalent must clearly be a constant in human society, and therefore we moderns, with the luxury of being able to look back on so many centuries of travesty and tragedy, can finally reflect on this sad history and set things right: accept homosexuality as a part of society and stop trying to find ways to suppress, ban, criminalize, or deny it. There is an undertone of finger-wagging throughout this

collected historical oeuvre, directed at the social hypocrisy of so many different cultures, including our own. So many "fathers" of American democracy extolled the virtues of ancient Greece, for instance, but wait a minute, what's that?—it looks like ancient Greece also tolerated and extolled homosexuality. Oh, what hypocrisy is American democracy! What a travesty it is that the institutions of American democracy claim to have such deep roots in the virtues of ancient Greece, even to the point of designing many key government buildings with ancient Greek architectural models. Yet at the same time they have tried to hide the prevalence of homosexuality in those same deep philosophical roots. Oh, for shame.

That line of argument is certainly compelling, but it runs into another problem very quickly, one that also allows Foucault's ghost back into the room: ancient Greek culture also extolled and encouraged intimate relations between men and boys, especially in the field of education, that were acceptable in those times but would be undeniably pedophilic in ours. We can't just bring in the historical parts we like and leave the others out, for otherwise we are indulging in the same sort of hypocrisy that the historians of homosexuality are trying to condemn. Indeed, in reference to what I stated above in relation to American social history, relations between intimate partners that are now considered illegal and perhaps pedophilic were considered quite normal in the nineteenth century, yet during that time homosexuality was considered illegal. History is full of lines that get redrawn all of the time, and what we have right now on our plates are three lines that have to be sorted out with absolute clarity and with legal precision: the line between homosexual and heterosexual, the line between human and animal, and the line between child and adult.

Let us look a bit closer at the line between child and adult. We have just seen through the work of activist-intellectuals like Michel Foucault that the laws that criminalized homosexuality were produced in tandem with the laws that criminalized pedophilia.

Pedophilia became a crime only with the rise of new normative ideas about childhood, ideas that trace back only a few centuries and have their origins mostly in Western culture. In the 1850s in America, for instance, a ten year-old boy was old enough to work in a factory; in the 1950s, the same thing would have been seen as the exploitation of child labor. There are similar examples from other cultures all over the world, cultures that are now struggling to "reform" their practices in line with new human rights standards that are based on these new normative ideas about the innocence of children and their inability to make autonomous moral decisions until they reach their eighteenth birthday.

Advocates of pedophilia—and yes, there are such people—are watching the shifting normative sands surrounding the redrawing of these lines because they see in them hope and leverage for their legal battles. One could argue, believe it or not, that pedophilia has been tolerated far more throughout human history than homosexuality, and so if the history of homosexuality shows that homosexuality has been consistently prevalent throughout human history, even in the face of efforts to suppress it, and if that prevalence can be used to show that it must somehow be a natural and normal part of the social landscape, then couldn't a similar claim be true of pedophilia? Aren't our current expressions of disgust and outrage at pedophilia based on the redrawing of normative lines made only in the recent past? And aren't these current expressions of disgust and outrage based on our current normative sentiments very similar to the expressions of disgust and outrage that many persons have in America toward opening up the institution of marriage to same-sex couples? The "obviousness" of childhood innocence is no less a normative historical product than the "obviousness" of heterosexual normality. Believing in the first is much like believing in the second.

This debate plays out in some very unexpected areas of research and other forms of creative design. If you haven't been following recent developments in robotics, for instance, then you probably don't know that there are several individuals working arduously to create life-like robots for the sole purpose of serving as intimate partners. As robots become increasingly human-like in their actions, appearance, and speech, robot sex will become more and more of a possibility. The robots would be programmed always to say yes (and never to say no), and so all the anxiety of rejection would be taken out of the process of intimacy. What you also may not know is that there is a debate on whether to build *child* robots, again for the sole purpose of sexual intimacy. Advocates of child sex robots argue that it would eliminate or "treat" pedophilia, since the criminalization of pedophilia hinges not on the sexual orientation itself but on the human age of consent, which would not apply to child sex robots.[80] Opponents of child sex robots argue that it would do the opposite: by "normalizing" sexual relations with child sex robots, it would desensitize society to the horrors of pedophilia and pave the way for normalizing sex with human children.[81]

Again, let me be clear about one point: I differ from Foucault and see homosexuality and pedophilia as different things, different sorts of apples, and I think it undermines the pursuit of justice to link them so closely together. What I *am* saying is that many of the legal and historical arguments that have been invoked to bring about a change in social acceptance and legal permissiveness have a shared logic. My point in this discussion has not been to highlight and champion that link, but rather to show that the part of diversity that deals with gay rights and same-sex marriage

---

80 "Could a child sex robot treat paedophilia?" *BBC News: Echo Chambers* (July 18, 2014) at http://www.bbc.com/news/blogs-echochambers-28353238

81 Jane Wakefield, "Call for a ban on child sex robots," *BBC News* (July 5, 2017) at http://www.bbc.com/news/technology-40428976

has been unfortunately muddled. The result of that might well be a completely accidental open door that gives leverage to other movements whose acceptance is so distasteful to society that it creates a backlash to the very idea of incorporating any part of sexual orientation into the wider project of diversity.

If there is one thing I have said over and over and over again, it is that diversity requires hard work. It also requires good work. I wish I could just look the other way or gesticulate with outrage when someone brings up zoophilia or pedophilia in these debates, or maybe just bark out "apples and oranges" as I smile with the smug satisfaction of exuberant progressivism. But I know enough about how the law works to know that simply assuming one thing is right and the others are "obviously" wrong is not a good way to build a compelling case for anything, especially if it relates to diversity. With diversity, we have to think as much of justice in the present as we do of justice in the future.

Gay culture and other culture
There is one final point to be made in all of this that takes us back to the larger project of diversity. The argument that "being gay" in the United States is like "being Black" or "being Latino" (and so forth) is designed to position the gay community as a minority community in relation to the dominant culture. And of course, what minority communities seek in a democratic context is equality in relation to the dominant community. This just so happens to be the central purpose not just of diversity but also of related programs that are designed to enhance diversity by facilitating the entrance of minority communities into mainstream public life. This does open the question of whether homosexuality, being akin to being a racial or ethnic minority, will become a protected category for diversity programs, including affirmative action (coincidentally, some activists prefer the term "sexual minorities" as opposed to "sexual orientation," since the latter would include heterosexuals).

But that is not my main purpose here. In our earlier discussions of diversity, I made the point that diversity as a general endeavor expects us to understand and also respect cultural differences between different communities and especially between minority communities. But what do we do when those minority communities, the ones who are supposedly analogous to the gay community (if there is such a thing as a unified gay community) and the ones who often seek rights-based protection against the dominant and normative community—what do we do if those minority communities themselves reject homosexuality and anything LGBTQI+?

More to the point, if diversity asks us to respect the beliefs of other cultures, to what extent should a white heterosexual "respect" Latino homophobia? In any other context, if we ask the question of whether a white person should respect the values of Latino culture, we would answer—why yes, of course. That's diversity. If the white person showed disdain for Latino culture, we would call the white person a racist. But if we add a few more specifics into the equation, we get something a bit more complicated. What do we do if a white male homosexual criticizes the pervasive homophobia in Latino culture? In this scenario, it is Latino culture that discriminates, and the white gay man is the champion of progressive justice. One might argue that it would be a good thing to put pressure on the Latino community to rid its culture of the values that give rise to homophobia (such as *machismo*), but if that pressure comes from the white community, is it not also a form of pressure to assimilate to the dominant white community? Or is a white gay male not a part of the white dominant community? Who is dominating whom in these situations? The answers are not clear.

We could also turn our attention away from the Latino community. Perhaps we could look at African-American or other black hip-hop artists and reggae artists. After all, both hip-hop and reggae have deep roots in articulating demands for social justice, so surely here we would expect to find all sorts of tolerance of and advocacy for gay rights and same-sex marriage. But that turns out not to be the case. Homophobic speech is rampant in hip-hop, and though many people associate reggae with the inspirational music of Bob Marley, the reality is often quite different. In recent years, the world has become very aware of just how much anti-gay hate speech shows up in reggae music from Jamaica, to the point where some reggae acts, Vybz Kartel and Elephant Man, for example, have been banned from performing in other countries (such as the United Kingdom) due to their violent, hate-filled, and anti-gay lyrics. Similar examples can be found in the world of hip-hop music, too. None of this is meant to say that Jamaican culture or reggae music or all hip-hop is inherently homophobic—there have been efforts to change attitudes towards homosexuality in both of these musical genres—but it does highlight the awkwardness with which different categories of diversity struggle to coexist. Sometimes non-dominant groups look an awful lot like dominant groups, and sometimes the LGBTQI+ community works well as a minority community and sometimes it doesn't. Sometimes it even creates its own dominant majority center—sending non-conformists to the margins of the LGBTQI+ community they once called home. Diversity is a mess, to be sure. The question is, what does justice in diversity look like?

One step forward two steps back?
The gay rights and same-sex marriage movements are both key examples of why our current approach to diversity continues to fail. Most importantly, it fails because it teaches and encourages identity-based groups to advocate for self-directed rights, which gives us more narcissism and more enclaves that lead away from an integrated society rather than toward it. As I have said repeatedly, I support the granting of equal rights to LGBTQI+ communities, including marriage equality, but I do have some concern for the way the movement has barked down any questions or concerns as so much "homophobia" and "hate" or "apples and oranges." Not

everyone who expresses concern or has questions is a hater—some of them are genuinely concerned about the legal looting that will follow and the endless law suits that will clog the court systems if the redrawing of the normative line is done too quickly or without sufficient scrutiny. Nor is the concern motivated only by a social conservatism that wants slow and gradual change instead of the radical change championed by self-appointed "progressive leaders." Self-directed activism, community by community, without sufficient foresight and cross-community dialog will create more problems and fewer solutions, and the everything now approach—more gay rights, more affirmative action, more everything for me and my community—though it seems rebellious and defiant, will in the long run give us only more bad diversity and more social problems. A fool's rebellion liberates only those who are easily fooled.

CHAPTER 5

COMING IN FIRST: INDIGENOUS IDENTITIES AND DIVERSITY

For my next trick, I will make a claim that will offend pretty much everyone, and then I will spend the rest of the chapter explaining why it's the best and perhaps only way to achieve meaningful justice. The claim, you ask? Well, here it is: *being indigenous means nothing*. I will pause briefly to allow time for those who wish to do so to express outrage, exasperation, indignation, or disbelief—why, I can almost hear the subtly discordant sound of yoga mats being torn in two. Mind you, this isn't a claim I make lightly. I should also point out before I wade into this very difficult and sensitive terrain that I have spent a great deal of my career teaching, researching, and promoting indigenous rights around the world. So at this point you might say, what kind of a person would promote something he finds meaningless? The conundrum is resolved in understanding the qualitative difference between meaning nothing and being meaningless. Being indigenous means nothing, *but that does not mean that the values and life-experiences of indigenous cultures are meaningless*. Indeed, as I will paradoxically argue, the only way to give full and equal respect to indigenous cultures is to reconsider their indigenous status.

The value-systems and world-views of indigenous cultures are an important aspect of the larger vision of an inclusive platform of diversity. They offer yet another perspective through which to view, experience, and interpret the complexity of life, just as all cultures do. In the world of diversity, this is something of extraordinary value that benefits indigenous peoples as much as it benefits everyone else. It is another way to view ourselves among others, another way to see the world through someone else's eyes. Yet at the same time I can claim that being indigenous means nothing, indeed I must claim it to be so, because there is nothing about being indigenous that justifies or explains the special distinctions that are made between indigenous and non-indigenous cultures. Simply because a culture has been around longer than another culture, or because it came first, does not make that culture or its value-systems inherently good or intrinsically more valuable. Nor does it make it more important than other cultures, simply because it occupied quite by chance an earlier chronological niche. And as I will show, the status of being indigenous ends up creating a permanent state of infantilization for indigenous peoples that seems permanently to treat them as children in the adult world of diversity.

I know there are many people out there, some of them indigenous and some of them not, who want to believe that since time immemorial, the diurnal schedule of indigenous life, wherever it was found, went something like this:

Morning: wake up, worship Mother Earth, make organic breakfast to eat communally and then promote harmony and world peace

Afternoon: achieve unity with the Universe while farming with organic and sustainable methods

Late afternoon: engage in harmonious actions, meditate, and periodically hug trees, hug children, and hug each other

Evening: listen to the Elders tell beautiful stories that everyone believes because all are good and true; organic dinner is served and it is environmentally and nutritionally perfect; a simple life without war is cultivated; Mother Earth is honored

Night: sleep smugly and peacefully while dreaming indigenous dreams; the dreams are also environmentally sustainable

We all know how this beautiful story ends: the White Man came and ruined everything. But is that the way it really happened? In a word, Yes, but we need more than one word here, in which case the answer becomes more complex and more difficult to discern clearly. To recall a few things discussed in earlier chapters, I always find it interesting how calls for diversity disappear when it comes to taking responsibility for the tragedies and atrocities of the world. For one thing, we ought to say the White *People* came. Though feminists might never champion this version of equality, it is worth pointing out that white women played an equally active role in this truly sad and despicable story of a cultural encounter gone horribly wrong. More than this, it was not just white people who came to undermine indigenous cultures: people of color around the world have had encounters with indigenous peoples, and guess what? The story is pretty much the same and quite often it is even worse. Moreover, and here is the central focus of this chapter, indigenous cultures themselves don't have the most innocent of histories. Indigenous history, as I will explain shortly, is just as much a distasteful mess as is the rest of human history, which again, is why I feel compelled to point out that being indigenous means nothing.

Historical fictions are the perennial nemesis of a diversity that is meaningful, constructive, and accessible for all. In the case of indigenous peoples, we can clearly see how a perverse misreading of history creates an untenable and unsustainable situation in the present with regard to identity, and therefore with regard to diversity. The challenge is to demonstrate how letting go of old ideals about the past will free us to create new ideals for the present. Here, we bump up against the same conceptual paradox that we have hit time and time again in this narrative journey about diversity, only this time through the elements of indigenous history. The only way to create a system of equal rights and mutual respect for indigenous cultures, and the only way to create an equal and equally dignified seat at the great feast of diversity, is to first liberate ourselves from all of the deeply-held beliefs we have about what it means to be indigenous. And liberation, in case you didn't know, never comes easy.

Indigenizing history
The city of Berkeley is a very strange place. It is, for instance, one of the very few places in the world where a driver can experience the perplexing confusion of road rage from someone at the wheel of a Prius. Nothing induces fear and gets the heart racing and adrenaline flowing like the fury of angry acceleration— from a silent engine, mind you—followed by a drive-by glance of disdainful superiority and a middle-finger salute out the driver-side window, all brought to a close by the disconcerting vision of a "Cultivate World Peace" bumper sticker receding at an environmentally safe pace in the direction of Whole Foods (that's a true story, by the way). Berkeley is also one of the many places in the

United States where the holiday-formerly-known-as-Columbus Day was changed to Indigenous Peoples Day. The reason for this transformation was that the city of Berkeley decided that it was wrong to celebrate the tragedy of 1492, when the White Man, in the form of one Christopher Columbus, showed up in the neighborhood to inaugurate five hundred (plus) years of imperialism against the innocent and beautiful and peace-loving indigenous peoples of North America. The city of Berkeley therefore turned the holiday upside-down and now uses it to recognize the inherent goodness of the only "real" Americans—the Native Americans—and to excoriate the white colonizers who ruined their perfect way of life.

Living in Berkeley, one becomes gradually accustomed to interacting with a special sort of people, many of whom I would describe as hard on the eyes and soft on the brain, and some of whom also engage in differential levels of olfactory assault that test the limits of what might be considered nonviolent. These are the people who want to believe, among other things, that all that is good and all that is indigenous in the world are essentially the same thing. But on this particular point, of viewing the moment of arrival of the White Man as *the moment when everything changed*—we need to step back and seriously reconsider the basis of the claim. We need to do that because like everything else I have discussed, it impinges on and greatly influences the way we look at diversity. My point here is not to question the idea of whether the White Man actually engaged in the disturbingly violent actions of which he is accused in the encounter with indigenous peoples in America. The historical record speaks for itself on that account, and when it speaks, it offends and assaults even our most rudimentary sense of ethical and moral values. Instead, what I want to question is whether it makes sense, whether it if justifiable, to keep our focus on this one moment in history—the arrival of the White Man—as *the moment when everything changed*, to see if it really merits its exceptional and extraordinary consideration. We need to do this because every aspect of the importance attached to being indigenous emanates from this one moment in time.

In the case of indigenous peoples, the way we look at this historical moment determines and influences everything we do to find a way to include indigenous peoples in our vision of diversity. But indigenous peoples are also treated differently and viewed separately in discussions of diversity, as there is a sense that indigenous identities are something very different from all the other types of identities we have discussed so far. The one similarity we do have, however, is that the past, in the form of history, plays some sort of foundational role in how diversity in the present is constructed. We still have this idea that at some point, on Columbus Day in 1492, for instance, history somehow went off course, and diversity in the present is the answer to putting history back on track, of setting right all the things that went wrong. These notions are not just insipid and misinformed, they are actually counterproductive and corrosive to the very idea of what diversity is and what it can accomplish. For that reason, the question of indigenous identities warrants a closer look, no matter how painful the alterations of identity may be.

The first part of diversity
Let's start with the most fundamental claim of what it means to be indigenous: namely, that one was here *first*. This is a central component of what it means to be indigenous—Canada for example refers to its indigenous peoples as First Nations—and yet, what does it really mean to be first? Why is it considered special? There are two ways of looking at this idea of being first. One is to look at it as an absolute value, that being indigenous meant you were here

before anyone else was ever here, that you were the first humans to arrive and settle (note interestingly that if we extended indigenous status to nonhuman species, no humans would be indigenous anywhere). If that is the case—and there are very few actual examples of this—then the question is, why is this special? The problem with ascribing special meaning to the idea of being first and therefore of being indigenous is that it means nothing because we cannot attribute any significance either to timing or to intent. Did the indigenous people know that all of those lands were uninhabited when they first arrived? If the lands were not uninhabited, did these settlers intend to wipe out those who lived there to take the lands for themselves? That is, did they go with the expectation of colonizing those lands and taking them from others who might have been there "more first"? If this is true then it would make them no different from the Europeans who showed up centuries later. The main point is, if they did not know the lands were open, then we cannot ascribe any innocent intention to them. They simply lucked out that they ventured into territories where other human settlements were not yet present. Had Christopher Columbus showed up and had the lands he came upon been truly uninhabited, would we consider him "indigenous" and would we admire how peaceful he was? It's easy to look peaceful when there is nothing and no one in the way.

What is lacking from our justification to give exceptional value to indigenous cultures is any ability to evaluate original intent. When first peoples colonized the lands they found, they were uninhabited simply by chance. It is easy and perhaps understandable to mistake what is in fact a fortuitous historical accident—lands were discovered that were not inhabited—for a cultural disposition towards peace and fairness. We often think of other latecomers to the Americas, for example the Europeans, as the vicious and violent thieves of indigenous lands, an assessment that is sadly not altogether inaccurate, but we cannot compare the two moments of historical arrival in any meaningful way because the circumstances were so vastly different. We cannot say, when the indigenous peoples came they were peaceful and good, but the Europeans were violent and bad, because we don't know what the indigenous peoples would have done had they encountered other people on the lands they wanted, and we don't know what the Europeans would have done if they encountered no one on the lands they wanted. We cannot confuse historical luck with cultural disposition. Indeed, if we look more closely at indigenous histories, which we will do in a moment, we find that most indigenous cultures, when placed in situations more akin to what the Europeans encountered upon arrival, tend to act in pretty much the same way the Europeans did. Nothing special, and nothing especially different, happened. But for now, let's continue along this line of argument to understand what, if anything, "firstness" should mean in looking at cultural difference.

Why coming in first is sometimes irrelevant
The second thing about this idea of absolute firstness, of ascribing special value to being the first to arrive in a place, is that human settlement has never really been a race or a competition, so arriving first as a settler is not like arriving first at the finish line of a marathon. Arrival, in other words, is not an achievement or an accomplishment. On top of that, very little in the chronology of human settlement speaks to the idea of fairness. Just because one group of people show up in a new place due to unforeseen historical circumstances—the formation of a land bridge into a new continent due to climatic change, for instance (as happened according to one of the prevailing theories of how Native Americans first came to the Americas)—and just because they do so before anyone else has a chance to get there and before the Europeans found out, how is that a special thing? It's certainly a *lucky* thing, but it's not a special accomplishment.

Imagine walking through the forest and by chance a number of trees have fallen in such a way as to create a perfect room in which to live. Imagine you decide that since no one else is there, it's yours for the taking and you decide to live in it. Now imagine that twenty years later, someone else is walking through the forest, and decides that like you, she really likes the forest and wants to live there, if only there were a place to live. When she comes across the room where you live, a room you have to yourself only because you happened to stumble upon it twenty years previously when no one else had found it, suppose she wants to live there, too. Does she have an equal claim to be there, if she came across it later than you through no fault of her own? You came across it first, by luck, and now she has come across it, too, also by luck, but twenty years later. Would you be the innocent and peaceful one, the one indigenous to the room, and would she be greedy for thinking she might be able to live there, too? If you wrote your personal history to describe how wonderful your life was as the indigenous inhabitant, about how idyllic your life was until "she" came and ruined everything, would we be justified in extolling your wonderful virtues, and vilifying that woman who came and arrogantly thought she could live there, too?

I realize in this example, as hypothetical as it is, I am leaving out the subsequent violence that took place in the process of the European colonization of the Americas. Right now I am focusing on the idea of firstness—later I will open up the question of violence. So let me offer a less hypothetical example of how firstness, in and of itself, means nothing. Some readers may have heard of a thing called the internet, and for those that have, you may have suffered the frustration of trying to create a domain name or an email address that perfectly reflects who you are (or who you *think* you are), only to find out that someone got there first and took the name you wanted. Suppose your name is Maria Ramirez, and you were born in the year 2000. You hit your tenth birthday and decide it's time for you to celebrate your arrival into the second decade of life by opening your very own gmail account. You start with Maria Ramirez@gmail.com, but you quickly get the message that someone else already has that address, someone named Maria Ramirez who was born in 1990 and who grabbed that address before you were even born. So of course, you try other addresses: Maria@gmail.com (already taken), MariaR@gmail.com (already taken), MRamirez@gmail.com (already taken), TheRealMariaRamirez@gmail.com (already taken)—yes, pretty much every variation you can think of is already taken. You could resign yourself to your utter lack of uniqueness and accept something like MariaRamirez189948653904698722@gmail.com (the first one you find that is not already taken), or you can try something you think is really different like Cutepuppy@gmail.com, or Thugpuppy@gmail.com, or Puppythug@gmail.com, or Puppykitty@gmail.com, only to discover they, too, are all already taken. So in anger you start thinking of things like ihatepeople@gmail.com, sadanddepressed@gmail.com, theinternetsucks@gmail.com, only to discover that, alas, all of those have been taken, too.

Meanwhile, you quickly learn that somewhere out there is a person with the email address john@gmail.com. John, it seems, got to the internet very early simply because he was born earlier than you. The point is, would it make sense to consider people like john@gmail.com indigenous to the internet? Just because they were born at an earlier time, and just because they were able to create email addresses and domain names that were unique and simply because they were able to get to the internet before others, does that make them special to the internet? Should we revere them because of their of their firstness in cyberspace? Should we assume that because John entered the internet at a time before there were (computer) viruses, that John and people like him are inherently good people who would never consider engaging in malicious behavior on the internet? I think there are very few people, if any at all, who would see the claim to firstness as anything other than chronological luck. And settling the earth and settling the internet are very much alike, except that settling the earth required getting outside into the environment and doing arduous physical exertion, whereas settling the internet required sitting inside and obtaining sustenance from frozen foods, instant ramen, and home-delivery pizza.

There is one other related element to all of this that is often cited as a reason to attribute special value to indigenous peoples due to their firstness. This element is that indigenous peoples, as the oldest inhabitants of the lands upon which they live, also have the oldest traditions and belief-systems in relation to all other peoples in America. For that reason, we are told, indigenous cultures should be respected and revered, to a special extent above and beyond what is shown to others. Indigenous peoples are truly a link to our past, a link that we must protect, respect, and revere. The problem with this argument is that we really have no reason to revere something just because it is old. The same political platform that tells us that we should honor and revere the indigenous peoples of the world (or that we should rename Columbus Day as Indigenous Peoples Day) because they are old and wise and traditional and close to nature also tells us that things like patriarchy and traditional marriage need to be bulldozed into oblivion because they are antiquated ideas of the past that have no relevance in the present. In other words, patriarchy is old (and, I might add, one deeply entrenched in many indigenous cultures): so why aren't we revering that? And of all the old ideas and practices we have, none is as old as war—people have been killing each other for as long as there have been people to kill, and yet, at no point do I hear anyone claiming we should revere, protect, and cherish war, or that the world would be a better place if we just returned to our roots and had more war. So again, firstness doesn't help us here. Just because something has been around for a long time, doesn't make it special. We will need something more, and if my suspicions serve me well, then something tells me that the next section will discuss this further.

Historicizing indigeneity

I mentioned there were two ways of determining what it means to be indigenous. The first one, as we have just seen, is to claim that being indigenous is an absolute value: you were here first. No one else lived where you live before you did, and you have lived there ever since. As it turns out, however, the historical record shows us very few, if any, instances where that definition holds true or is even verifiable. Yes, there are many among us who would like to believe that indigenous peoples settled their indigenous lands shortly after the big bang, even before clouds of interstellar gas began to cool into the solidified spheres we call planets. They were just somehow always here. Not only do we have no credible historical evidence that this is the way things went, but also, and more importantly, we *do* have an ever-increasing body of historical evidence that tends to show that the people we consider indigenous in various parts of North America were not in fact the first people to settle the land on which they settled. And by the way, if they settled here, then that makes them settlers—colonizers, in a word—which means they came from somewhere else originally. That should make them at least *less* indigenous, but as it turns out we don't like to qualify the word indigenous with different strengths of meaning. It's a bit like being pregnant—you either are or you aren't. Something is clearly amiss, and we need to take a closer look at this to try to make sense of what it means to be indigenous.

First, I should give at least an example of the type of historical evidence I am referring to when I speak to the idea that the peoples we now consider indigenous might not have been the first to arrive and settle their lands. In 1990, a landmark piece of legislation was passed into US federal law known as the Native American Graves Protection and Repatriation Act (NAGPRA). This piece of legislation was designed to give Native American tribes an enhanced degree of cultural autonomy by giving them control over their ancestral remains and territorial domains. What this means in practice is that if Native American burial grounds were unearthed, for instance, then scientists and art opportunists could not take any cultural artifacts or remains away and use them (or sell them) without the express consent of the tribe on whose lands those remains and artifacts had been found. If the tribes did not want to give consent, then the scientists or other relevant persons had to return the skeletal remains and any related cultural artifacts to the tribe, if any had been taken. It is easy to see the intent behind the act, and the general and basic intent is, I think, a good one. But what has happened since the passing into law of NAGPRA in 1990 is something that has less to do with cultural autonomy and more to do with an attempt to preclude meaningful investigation into the past, largely because that investigation calls into question the very definition of what it means to be indigenous.

From time to time, scientists and other researchers will unearth a skeleton on Native American grounds, which from a scholarly perspective is a rich and rare moment to help answer questions that have hitherto been unanswerable. Although some of these skeletal remains were unearthed before the passage of NAGPRA, Native American tribes can make retroactive claims to get these remains back from museums and universities. What has been of considerable interest and even more considerable controversy, however, is that quite often, a close study of these artifacts turns up evidence that the skeletal remains that have been discovered are not in fact related to the Native American group on whose lands the remains were found. In other words, it calls into question whether the indigenous people are truly indigenous on their land, whether they were latecomers who might have forced earlier groups out. Because the entire basis of indigenous rights through NAGPRA is based on the acceptance that a particular group is in fact indigenous, what has evolved since the passage of NAGPRA are various legal battles between Native American tribes who want to get the discovered remains back as quickly as possible, literally to bury the evidence, and researchers who want to scrutinize the evidence. Some of that evidence, it seems, calls into question nearly everything we thought we knew about how indigenous peoples came to settle and inhabit their lands.

The University of California, for instance, has been locked in a lawsuit with the Kumeyaay tribe since 2000 over a pair of skeletal remains. The remains were discovered in 1976 during an excavation of University House in La Jolla (San Diego), which is the official residence of the Chancellor of the University of California, San Diego. The Kumeyaay want the remains of the their ancestors returned for proper burial, whereas a handful of researchers have dug in their heels after producing evidence that the skeletal remains are most likely from an entirely different group, and therefore are not ancestors of the Kumeyaay at all.[82] (The Kumeyaay, for instance, tended to cremate their dead, not bury them.) A legal clarification to NAGPRA by the Department of the Interior then produced a ruling that Native American tribes do not have to prove that such remains are culturally related to the present-day tribe that inhabits the land, though they do have to prove that the remains are at least related to *some* indigenous group. If that

---

82 Samantha Masunaga, "UC professors in legal battle with Native American tribe over rights to ancient skeletons," *Daily Bruin* (July 8, 2012) at http://dailybruin.com/2012/07/08/uc-professors-in-legal-battle-with-native-american-tribe-over-rights-to-ancient-skeletons/

cannot be done, only then does NAGPRA not apply and the researchers can continue their analysis.

Another example of this kind of feud involves the discovery of what has become known (famously and infamously) as Kennewick Man in 1996, so named because of the discovery of the skeleton in Kennewick in the state of Washington. Though local Native American tribes demanded the skeletal remains be returned for reburial, scientists were quick to claim that the skeletal remains were not related to any of the local indigenous groups.[83] In 2004, after a bitterly rancorous legal dispute, the United States Court of Appeal for the Ninth Circuit initially ruled that indigenous groups could not prove any meaningful genetic or cultural link between the skeletal remains and their current cultural practice or genetic composition, and so allowed scientists to retain access to the remains for further research. A 2015 study by a research team in Denmark, however, was finally able to establish a genetic link to modern Native Americans, a result that was subsequently confirmed by the US Army Corps of Engineers through a different research team at the University of Chicago.[84] This means that NAGPRA does in fact apply and Kennewick Man is to be returned to the Native American cultural environment, where the Ancient One, as he has been named, will receive a proper burial. No doubt there will be more cases like this, and more legal battles, in the years to come. Nevertheless, it does leave open an interesting line

---

[83] John Carlin, "Who are the true native Americans?" *The Independent* (October 5, 1996) at http://www.independent.co.uk/news/world/who-are-the-true-native-americans-are-red-men-true-native-americans-who-really-were-the-first-1356972.html

[84] Sarah Pruitt, "Army Corps of Engineers Confirms Kennewick Man is Native American," *History* (May 2, 2016) at http://www.history.com/news/army-corps-of-engineers-confirms-kennewick-man-is-native-american

of inquiry into what exactly we mean when we refer to something as indigenous.

This brings us back to the two ways of interpreting what indigenous might mean. In relation to Kennewick Man, for instance, one leader from the Umatilla tribe claimed that "[f]rom our oral histories, we know that our people have been a part of this land since the beginning of time."[85] That's a comment drawn from a specific belief system, but the historical reality is that there is no evidence of any tribe, let alone any humans, being there or anywhere on earth since the beginning of time. Even without the evidence from Kennewick Man, new archaeological digs are continuously and consistently pointing to information that suggest the possibility that the groups we now consider indigenous in America were not in fact the first colonizers to arrive.[86] If that turns out to be the case, then what happened to those first peoples? Were they assimilated, forcibly or not, to the second wave of colonizers who came after them? Were they wiped out? Displaced? If so, should we still consider Native Americans as indigenous peoples? (I'll talk more broadly about indigenousness in history in volume 3 of this series.)

So, if indigenous does not mean something that is *absolutely* first, then what else do we have? The second way of looking at this question is to look at it in *relative* rather than absolute terms. Something or someone is indigenous, we might say, if they were there first in relation to something else. In other words, if you are indigenous, you were perhaps not the absolute first person to

---

85 Tasneem Raja, "A Long, Complicated Battle over 9,000-year-old Bones is Finally Over," *NPR: Code Switch* (May 5, 2016) at http://www.npr.org/sections/codeswitch/2016/05/05/476631934/a-long-complicated-battle-over-9-000-year-old-bones-is-finally-over

86 Paul Rincon and Jonathan Amos, "Stone tools 'demand new American story'," *BBC News* (March 24, 2011) at http://www.bbc.com/news/science-environment-12851772

arrive and settle, but you were at least there before some other group of people arrived. In a strange way, it means you were the last to be there before the first arrival of some other group. But here is where things get even more interesting. This definition of indigenous requires some sort of benchmark, some moment in history where the arrival of one group becomes a chronological marker before which things are indigenous and after which they are not. Not surprisingly, in the light of what I discussed in the previous chapters, that defining moment in historical time was the arrival of Europeans, aka the White Man.

Before I get into some of the mistaken interpretations that flow from this way of defining indigenousness, I would first like to point out some of the illogical peculiarities that this definition suggests. If what makes Native Americans special is that they arrived here before the White Man, then what we are really valuing here is *prior* arrival (as opposed to first arrival). Native Americans are special and deserve special valuation because they arrived earlier than the White Man. But if prior arrival is something to value, then it should be valued in all situations. Yet this would imply that descendants of white settlers who immigrated to the United States in the eighteenth and nineteenth centuries are more "special" and more "native" than later immigrants, since prior arrival contains an inherent value. This leads to still more unsettling questions. The differential treatment given to Asians and other immigrant groups whose arrival came much later in American history must be to a certain extent understandable and even justifiable, right? It's not racism—it's just an expression of valuing prior arrival as a special quality, right? Obviously these claims are *not* right, but they do show the problems we have if prior arrival is given some inherent superior value.

If you are struggling to suppress your outrage at the suggestion that white settlers who arrived before others are "more American" than later arrivals, it must mean that prior arrival contains no special or inherent value, which calls into question, once again, the value we attribute to the quality of being indigenous, if indigenous means only that you arrived at any point before the White Man came. For now, however, let us accept this interesting if somewhat arbitrary chronological distinction that says that those who were here before the White Man are indigenous, and those who came at the time of the White Man or after, whatever they are called, cannot be considered indigenous. *Ever.*

The biggest flaw in this line of thinking is to confuse what is in essence a chronological distinction—the question of when—with a qualitative one. We assume that because the (white) imperialists were bad and guilty, the non-imperialists (the indigenous) must be good and innocent. But the leap from chronological distinction to qualitative distinction is neither logical nor justifiable. Just because someone came earlier does not mean that they had a way of life that was inherently better or superior, nor does it mean that the actions that had occurred among indigenous groups prior to the arrival of the White Man were necessarily benevolent, innocent, or nonviolent. Of the two distinctions, chronological or qualitative, it is the qualitative one that is most important to questions of diversity. Trying to use diversity to "correct" history only gives us bad diversity and bad history. The discomfiting news is that we need to let go of all those notions about the past, of how we think that when the White Man arrived in 1492 history went "off course," of how diversity can magically put history back "on course" and right the wrongs of the past. The good news is that once we do that, once we let go of the delusion that we can somehow set the past right by using diversity in the present, we can finally create a framework for diversity in the present that offers equal dignity to all.

Indigenous vignettes: a short and disjointed drama

With that in mind, let's revisit this question of the past, of the role that history plays in crafting, or in most cases warping, our approaches to diversity in the present.

Scene One: In which slavery makes an unexpected appearance
We can start with one of the more disturbing aspects of American history, all summed up in a word whose very mention creates bitter memories of the past and divisive polarization in the present: *slavery*. Now, if you have been through the educational system in the United States, you will know that slavery is something that whites did to blacks, that it was horrible (and it was), that countless lives were ended or irreparably altered through the institution of slavery, and that a civil war—*the* Civil War—nearly split the country in two over the issue of whether freedom was for everyone of just for some. If you also read the part of American history that talks about the unfortunate and equally reprehensible tale of the "encounter" between the White Man and Native Americans, another story filled with exploitation, mistreatment, violence, and plunder, you might find yourself asking the question: what kind of a person would do this? How could the White Man do this? I don't have an answer for why the White Man would engage in slavery. When I look through human history I have no answer for why so many people did the tragic and brutal things they did. But in the focus of this discussion, let me offer an answer that probably didn't show up in your standard American history textbooks. I may not know why the White Man did what he did when he decided that slavery was acceptable, but I at least know how he did it. I know how the White Man did what he did because I also know how the Native Man did the same thing before the White Man ever arrived. In both cases, slavery was a form of exploitation that was justified through the value system of the dominant group. Yes, you heard that right: indigenous America also had

indigenous slavery, and indigenous America also had dominant indigenous cultures.

Slaves in indigenous societies came from a number of different sources. Most but not all were captives (from violent warfare, which was endemic among and between Native American groups). And while there were different regional variations in indigenous slavery systems, the commonalities between them will sound a lot like the slavery we associate with the United States: slaves were property, the owner of the slave had absolute power over the slave (to sell as property in indigenous slave markets, to exploit for work, or to kill without penalty), and the slave had a humiliating and dishonorably low status that was permanent. As with African slavery in the United States, captives could try to find a way to work the system and improve their lot, sometimes by accepting or at least pretending to accept their lowly status in exchange for special treatment, but at the end of the day, everything about a slave's life and condition of living was dependent upon the whim of the indigenous master. Indigenous slave owners also had full rights of access to female slaves, in every sense of the word, and the female slave had no right of refusal. There were even examples where a White Man was captured and enslaved by Native Americans. Charles Bishop, for instance, was held as a captive slave by the Cumshewa Haida for two years in 1794-1795. During that time he was "kept naked, forced to work hard...and treated badly by everyone, including other slaves."[87] Like the infamous Buffalo Soldiers, the African slaves who were forced to fight the White Man's war, indigenous slaves (including white ones) were also forced to fight in the wars of their indigenous owners. We know that slaves of the Native Americans were at great risk of being killed by their captors and owners, especially at the early stages of their enslavement, but as long as they

---

87 Leland Donald, *Aboriginal Slavery on the Northwest Coast of North America* (University of California Press, 1997), p. 75

submitted to their status and became good and compliant slaves, that risk subsided over time, though it never fully disappeared.[88]

Students of American history are often shocked to learn, if they are in a class that cares to discuss it, that Native Americans continued to engage in slave trading and slave owning well into the period of White Man expansion and settlement. In other words, Native Americans purchased and owned African slaves. During the reprehensible series of events that led to what is known as the Trail of Tears, in which several Native American tribes were forced to travel on a long and arduous and deadly journey as part of a coercive relocation program started in 1830 to open new lands for white settlement, the Native American tribes were at least allowed—as a small concession—to take their property with them. For many of the Native Americans, that property included African slaves, who were also forced to make the long and perilous journey with their owners. When the Native Americans resettled in their new reservations—hardly hospitable places by any account—their slaves settled with them.

And yet, as disturbing as the whole incident was in the past, it ends up being a tragedy that continues into the present. Over time, those African slaves and their freed descendants considered themselves to be a part of the tribal groups that originally owned them. But with the strengthening of Native American rights in the past several decades, and with the rise of increased tribal revenue and enhanced government benefits, many Native American tribes decided it was time to tighten up their borders by redefining tribal membership. In 2007, the Cherokee Nation voted overwhelmingly to eject black slave descendants as members, and so black descendants were stripped of tribal membership and tribal citizenship. Interestingly, the US federal government—the government of the White Man, as many see it—through the Bureau of Indian Affairs,

---

88 *Ibid.*, p. 266 (Note 8)

sent a strongly-worded letter to the Cherokee Nation urging them to reinstate full membership and citizenship (voting) rights to the black slave descendants. But the tribal leadership pushed back and stood its ground in the name of indigenous self-governance, with the Cherokee Supreme Court confirming in 2011 that only persons with sufficient Cherokee genetic purity could be considered true Cherokee citizens.[89] If there was one thing this indigenous group didn't want among its ranks, it was diversity, so the minority within the tribe was given the indigenous boot.

Scene Two: In which violence plays a leading role
Native American activists are often fond of pointing out that the much-vaunted American Democracy of the founding fathers was deeply influenced by the democratic ideals of the indigenous peoples of America, in particular of the Iroquois tribes. Benjamin Franklin was said to be quite taken with the democratic ideals of the Native American peoples, and allegedly used the model of the Iroquois Confederacy, in which the Five Iroquois nations made a democratic bond of peace and amity, as a potential model for early American democracy. In other words, although Greek and Roman and "classical" ideas of virtue are usually given the credit for the philosophical foundations of American democracy, the Native American contribution has been carefully occluded, since it would mean that the "civilized" White Man borrowed from the so-called "savage" Indigenous Man. While part of the story may in fact be true, it is the other part of the story—the one the activists don't tell—that shows how Native Americans and Non-native Americans have a lot more in common than either side cares to admit.

---

[89] James MacKay, "The Cherokee nation must be free to expel black freedmen," *The Guardian* (September 17, 2011) at https://www.theguardian.com/commentisfree/2011/sep/17/cherokee-nation-black-freedmen

Let's take a closer look at the foundation of the democratic entity known as the Iroquois Confederacy or the League of the Iroquois. If we were to drop ourselves into Iroquois territory in, say, the sixteenth century—before the White Man came—we might walk into an Iroquois village and be struck by how closely the community was put together, both physically and socially. Of course we would struck by this, you might say, since we all know that the Native Americans lived harmonious and organic lives where close-knit families were happy and the peacefulness of nature was matched only by the peacefulness of the people. Unfortunately, we'd also be wrong—very wrong. Iroquois villages were closely put together in the sixteenth century not as a result of organic and harmonious social solidarity but as a defensive gesture, since violent and predatory warfare was endemic between the various Iroquois tribes. The tight-knit village societies were not a virtue but a necessity—conformity to social values was demanded and enforced because any division in village society could weaken the social fabric and spell disaster in terms of vulnerability to outside raiding parties. Warfare was as constant as it was brutal, with endless cycles of reprisal and vengeance generating layer upon escalating layer of organized violence that would clearly violate any currently existing set of guidelines for humane conduct in war (such as the Geneva Conventions). Among other things, victorious war parties often tortured and then slaughtered their enemies en masse, or else marched them back to their home villages where they literally had to run the gauntlet—in front of other villagers who lined up to watch the macabre spectacle. Some captives were tortured and then enslaved while others were scalped or met other gruesome ends. We often see images of proud Native American warriors in contemporary depictions of Native Americans, but we forget that the reason those warriors existed was that fierce warfare raged throughout much of Native America, long before the arrival of the White Man.

So then, what of the League of the Iroquois, the indigenous democracy that may have been an inspirational model for American democracy? The League certainly existed, though its main purpose was not to celebrate the virtues of democracy. Rather, it was to find a collective way to stop the ongoing problem of spending so much time killing each other in what amounted to an endless civil war among the Iroquois tribes. The League was indeed put together, and myths were invented to justify its existence (all societies do this, even white ones), but its democratic credentials were a bit different from what ultimately became American democracy. For one thing, democracy in the League consisted of decision by unanimity rather than by plurality. Everyone had to agree on the same thing, or the matter at hand was rejected. Moreover, the peace that was created by the League of the Iroquois was an *internal* peace only. Outsiders, as in other non-Iroquois Native American tribes, were now treated as collective enemies of all the Iroquois, and this in an area where warfare between different Native American groups was violent and endemic. Peace within the Iroquois community meant a collective peace for insiders and a collective hostility toward outsiders. The Susquehannock tribe, for instance, were closely related to the Iroquois, but never became a formal part of the League. The Iroquois nations, now united through their democratic League, took advantage of the disarray created by a complex conflict involving European settlers, the Iroquois Nations, and the Susquehannock, and perhaps with an eye to taking over their lucrative trade networks, the Iroquois confederacy displaced the Susquehannock out of their territory and ultimately the Susquehannock disappeared entirely.

I don't want to downplay the complexity of the situation. Like so many other Native American tribes, the Susquehannock were greatly weakened and decimated by smallpox and other diseases, so my point here is not to cover that up, nor is it to blame the Iroquois confederacy alone for the what happened to the Susquehannock.

It would be easy to argue that none of this would ever have happened were it not for the arrival of the Europeans, but it would also be a facile argument. Warfare over territory, over economic resources and trade, and over any one of a long list of reasons why humans have historically decided it's time to start killing each other—all were endemic in Native America long before the first Europeans arrived. European settlers did not introduce violence where there had hitherto been peace. They introduced new forms of violence into an already violent landscape. Yes, there is a surprising amount in common between Native and non-native America, both historically and culturally, and not all of it is nice. The point in time when the White Man arrived, the point we like to think of as *the moment when everything changed,* looks less and less like the one defining moment and more and more like one moment among many, a variation on a theme already well in motion before the moment of white arrival. At least in terms of the long perspective on American history, the White Man may have changed the color of events, but not necessarily the tone.

Scene Three: In which imperialists find themselves in good company
One of the great blind spots we have in world history occurs in discussions of imperialism: somehow we refuse to notice that the "divide-and-rule" tactics we often ascribe to the dirty tricks of the Western imperialists are in fact common tactics found in *all* empires. Not surprisingly, they show up in a good deal of Native American warfare as well. Before the Iroquois tribes came together to form their confederacy, that is, during the time when they were at war with themselves, nearly destroying their own social organization in the struggle for power, many individual chiefs engaged in similar tactics to gain an advantage over rival chiefs and tribes. Chiefs would manipulate various tribal loyalties and affinities, or exploit divisions and antagonisms, to build alliances that might allow them to defeat and destroy their enemies, thereby attaining

more power. The Iroquois ultimately put an end to their fighting, as we have seen, through the formation of the League, but other Native American groups went in a different direction and actually engaged in various forays into empire building. Although our simplified narratives tell us that Native American society existed in its peaceful simplicity until Western imperialism came along and either ruined or stole everything (or both), the reality is that when Western settlers arrived in the lands of the Native Americans, they often found various forms of indigenous imperialism already at work.

One example of this can be found in the Comanche peoples of the American Southwest. Using what one historian has referred to as "transnational (or trans-imperial) networks of violence," networks that included pillaging and slave-raiding (the Comanches built the largest slave-based economy in the Southwest), the Comanches built a formidable empire in the American Southwest that clearly predated the arrival of the White Man. At least in this part of what later became the United States, "it was Comanches, not Euro-Americans, who mastered the policies of divide and rule."[90] As with the League of the Iroquois, outsiders who incurred the wrath of the Comanche or stood in their way of seeking to control lucrative trade networks faced a full-on onslaught of imperialist violence, up to and including dispossession from native lands (which were then colonized by the Comanche). When the White Man arrived in the American Southwest in the late eighteenth and nineteenth centuries, he found a formidable and formidably violent empire already in full swing, and much of the struggle to wrest control of this region came *not* in the form of Western imperialists stealing land from peace-loving indigenous communities, but in the form of foreign imperialists battling indigenous ones.

---

90 Pekka Hämäläinen, *The Comanche Empire* (New Haven: Yale UP, 2008), p. 8-9

Many of our diversity-related histories in the present "revise" these awkward and distasteful realities and prefer instead to list the positive accomplishments of the indigenous peoples. And indeed, those accomplishments are noteworthy and *should* be added to the record of the evolution of what ultimately becomes the multiplexity of America. But it is important to remember that not all of those accomplishments were the beautiful actions of small grassroots communities of people living in indigenous harmony with nature. The irony is that, in relation to things like imperialism, the Native Americans showed an equal capacity for violence and predation, which again, makes that carved-in-stone dividing line between Native American life and the arrival of Christopher Columbus as *the moment that changed everything* seem much more like a blurred, slow-motion transition. It starts looking more like the gradual transition when one set of violent forces were supplanted by another. Such an understanding will forever change our collective understanding of how America became what it was then and what it is now. But this changed understanding is absolutely essential to correcting our warped and simplified visions of the indigenous past, and more importantly, to building a viable and constructive framework for diversity in the present that restores the necessary dignity and agency to indigenous peoples and to all other peoples in equal measure.

Scene Four: In which things don't seem so great
In the heart of Honolulu, across the street from the 'Iolani palace and right in front of Ali'iolani Hale (the headquarters of *Hawai'i Five-0* in TV land), stands the most well-known statue of King Kamehameha the Great. What makes Kamehameha so Great, among other things, is that he is credited with the incredible feat of uniting the peoples of Hawai'i—the native peoples, that is—from all of the islands into a single, unified kingdom, something he accomplished in 1810. Before that, and much like what

was occurring among the Native Americans back on the continent, the different groups of native Hawai'ians spent much of their time battling each other, going to war, and vying for supremacy. Every June 11th is Kamehameha Day, in which the extraordinary accomplishments of Kamehameha—and some of them indeed are quite extraordinary—are commemorated and honored. Many native Hawai'ian people revere Kamehameha so much because the unification of Hawai'i allowed the native peoples to offer more united resistance to the encroachment of Western interests—the arrival of the White Man—and even though that resistance ultimately failed to keep the Western interests at bay, there is at least the idea that the native peoples put up a good, indigenous fight. Still to this day, there are groups of native Hawai'ians who feel that Hawai'i was and still is illegally colonized and annexed by the West and that full sovereignty (independence) should be reinstated. Hawai'i, they say, is occupied land.

I'm not going to take up the question of sovereignty here, but I am very interested in taking a closer look at the story surrounding the unification of Hawai'i into a kingdom under one ruler, the first of which was Kamehameha himself. Note how the use of the word "unification" implies that the native peoples of Hawai'i were a people destined to be together, a sort of logically teleological tale whose ending could only be a unified, indigenous kingdom. Destiny called, and Kamehameha answered. But one wonders why this idea was not present from the beginning, why the native peoples of Hawai'i spent so much time fighting each other in bitter and divisive battles rather than just coming together as they naturally were supposed to do. The reason for that becomes clearer if we use a different word for what happened in 1810. How about instead of stating that Kamehameha *unified* the peoples of Hawai'i, we say instead that he *conquered* them. The latter term is historically more accurate (as I will explain in a moment), but note how the whole impression of what happened changes dramatically if we see Kamehameha's project as one of conquest or even imperialism. In essence, a unified Hawai'i is really an imperial Hawai'i—a unity forged out of native imperialism. Much like the Comanche empire of the American Southwest, the arrival of Western interests looks very different in this perspective, more like the arrival of one empire into the realm of another.

The word unification implies that all participants were willing participants, that the peoples of Hawai'i voluntarily and gladly came together to achieve the unity they were destined to achieve. To refer to Kamehameha's enterprise as an empire and a conquest, however, implies reluctance and coercion, which means we would expect to find evidence of resistance (just as those native Hawai'ians who believe in the restoration of full sovereignty like to point out native resistance to Western imperialism). Does such evidence exist? Indeed it does. A bit further inland on the island of O'ahu (where Honolulu is located), on the route from Honolulu to Kailua, one will come across a beautiful mountainous ridge that is today called the Nu'uanu Pali Lookout. It is called a Lookout because of the panoramic views that can be enjoyed from the summit. But the name Lookout masks the rather tragic history of the Nu'uanu Pali, in particular what happened there in 1795, during Kamehameha's efforts to conquer the island of O'ahu. In 1795, in what is now known as the Battle of Nu'uanu, the forces of Kamehameha, which interestingly included a number of non-native foreigners, were battling the indigenous warriors who were resisting Kamehameha's attempt to conquer the island of Oahu. As Kamehameha's fighters began to prevail, the resistance slowly retreated up the slope side of Nu'uanu Pali. At the top of Nu'uanu Pali, there is a sheer cliff (*pali* means cliff in Hawai'ian), so once you retreat up to the cliff's edge, you essentially face a surrender-or-die situation. The resistance fighters, fighting under the leadership of Kalanikupule, chose to go over the cliff and fall to their deaths rather than submit to Kamehameha's conquest and rule, making this ultimately one of the bloodiest battles in Hawai'ian history.

What I find most interesting about the events that led up to the violent tragedy of Nu'uanu Pali is not that they are somehow excised from the historical record—the events are well-known in Hawai'ian history—but rather how what is clearly a violent bid for conquest and control has been reinterpreted as a heroic sacrifice for the inevitable and necessary unification of the Hawai'ian peoples under Kamehameha. In essence, the unification of Hawai'i was so glorious and such an important achievement that Kamehameha is extolled for doing whatever was necessary to make it happen. Ends justify means. That's what makes him Kamehameha the Great. The reason I find it so interesting is that this story almost exactly parallels what used to be the standard history of America. The Westward expansion, the incorporation of peoples who lived there and the struggles against those who resisted, and so forth, all led up to the creation of the great and glorious United States, which in the original narrative seemed as inevitable as it was necessary. Yet the same people who want us to believe that America is an imperialist country that used violence to subjugate the peoples who opposed its expansion (that is, its unification) also want us to believe that a king who forced warriors to jump off of a cliff to their violent death if they did not want to submit to his conquest and rule was a "heroic sacrifice" for the establishment of a great kingdom. If you are going to ask us to accept the slaughter of people as a necessary part of Hawai'ian unification, then you would also have to accept the violence of American expansion as a necessary part of the creation of America. The peoples of Hawai'I stand in relation to American imperialism as the warriors of Nu'uanu Pali did to Kamehameha's. That's not something to celebrate in either situation, but it is grounds for a fruitful discussion, an accounting of the past, a "robust exchange of ideas," which as we know, is exactly what diversity is supposed to offer. Instead, we have a situation where we can question and critique one of those historical moments (the White Man) but not the other, which is considered off limits. Diversity once again gives us not the robust exchange of ideas, but another long silence brought about by censorship.

Epilog
Diversity is about equality, and equality comes in different flavors. One of those formats comes in giving both *equal respect* and *equal scrutiny* to the stories we all tell about how America came to be. When I hear the story of what happened at Nu'uanu Pali, it troubles me, almost as much as it troubles me to hear it incorporated into a heroic narrative of glorious unification. When I hear someone refer to Kamehameha the Great, I think of those resistance fighters who jumped to their death rather than capitulate to Kamehameha's empire, and I find myself responding to the word Great in Kamehameha's title in the same way I respond to the name of China's so-called Great Wall: it doesn't seem all that Great to me, once you know the entire story. Diversity has created a mad rush to tear apart every part of the White Man's history, but to question the non-White histories of others is denounced as "hate speech." Clearly, diversity has failed us on this.

We live in a moment where the idea of a wall at the US-Mexico border is seen by many as little more than a monument to racism and fear, and yet we simultaneously are asked to praise the Great Wall of China as a monument to civilizational accomplishment and cultural sophistication. For what it is worth, I agree that building a wall at the US-Mexico border is a grotesquely misguided idea born of racist hate, but I also see the misnamed Great Wall of China in exactly the same way. Giant walls are never built with great intentions. I am also arguing the same thing from a different angle when I talk of the history of Hawai'i: we cannot view the slaughter of warriors at Nu'uanu Pali as a justifiable and necessary act to unify the peoples of Hawai'i (some of whom clearly did not want to be "unified"), and then view the story of how the White

Man showed up to unify America against the will of the native peoples as an exceptional tragedy. I agree that much of the story of America is filled with tragedy, and it bothers me greatly every time I think about it. But I can remain equally troubled by other tragedies in other histories as well. We can't build diversity on airbrushed histories, and if diversity is going to give us equality, part of that equality must necessarily involve equal scrutiny of our collective pasts.

I also find it somewhat hypocritical that the pro-sovereignty activists in Hawai'I think of restoring what was lost: what they want restored is the glorious moment of unification created by Kamehameha and his successors. That is, they want to return to a time *before* the White Man came but *after* Hawai'i was unified. Why not go back to the time before Kamehameha? Why not restore the original, separate sovereignty for all the islands and replicate the disunity and antagonism that was present before Kamehameha built his empire? Much like many of the conservative voices in America who want naively to go back to a time when American was allegedly "simpler" (what I sometimes call *Mad Men* nostalgia), sovereignty activists in Hawai'i are advocating a convenient utopia that ignores the complexities of the story.

End of historical vignettes

A reflection on the presents of the past
As a surfer, I have cultivated a sense of respect for a number of things: respect for other surfers, respect for the unwritten rules of surfing culture, respect for the power of the wave and the power of the ocean, respect for the myriad creatures that call the ocean home, and respect for the Pacific Island cultures that gave surfing

to the world, including Hawai'ian culture. Indeed, I have spent many years of my life in the study of Pacific Island cultures, many of which have influenced the way I view my place in the world. I also understand the complex historical processes that came together to allow me the moment when I can grab a board and surf the waves whenever I want and wherever I want. You see, in its origins, surfing was stratified by status, and only Hawai'ian elites and nobles were permitted to surf the best waves at the best beaches on the best boards. Commoners were not allowed to do so. And yes, there were cultural reasons for all of that. But somewhere along the way, spirited individuals, such as Duke Kahanamoku (1890-1968)—someone who in my book *would* deserve the title of "The Great"—found a way to translate those cultural values into a more democratic spirit, and made it possible for persons like me to learn this wonderful thing called surfing and the values associated with it. I am quite sure that there are many people out there who are very confused. How can I have such a critical stance toward historical events like the tragedy of Nu'uanu Pali or toward the actions of revered individuals like King Kamehameha, and then at the same time talk of my deep respect for the Pacific Islander values associated with surfing? Aren't I the one engaging in hypocrisy?

I can assure those of you who might think so that there is no hypocrisy involved. I can accept and respect Pacific Islander culture without having to accept every part of it uncritically. I wish Kamehameha would have done things differently at Nu'uanu Pali. I wish he would have found a way to avoid the tragedy that occurred, to talk those resistance fighters down from the cliff and find a different way to make peace.

I wish the American government would have done things differently in the expansion into the Western frontier, too. I wish they would have found a way to respect and negotiate with the Native American groups they encountered along the way. I wish the dealings would have been honest and not duplicitous, honorable and not shameful. I wish the American government would have found a way to create peace and dignity in the way that the country grew into the country that it became. I wish that a lot of things would have happened differently in American history. But just because they didn't, it doesn't mean I need to be a cultural nihilist. Nor does it mean that everything is necessarily all good or all bad. I might disagree with many of the things that Kamehameha did and many other things that are a part of Hawai'ian culture and history, but that does not diminish the respect I have for the native peoples of Hawai'i, their history, their cultural values, and their way of life, without which I would never have become the person I have become. I might disagree with many of the things that have happened in American history, but that does not diminish the deep respect I have for the values of American democracy and the individual freedom it provides, without which I would never have become the person I have become.

Diversity is a part of that democratic spirit and a part of that individual freedom, and we cannot permit this thing called diversity to take away our ability to think things through, to evaluate them with a critical lens. It is what separates the consumption of cultural propaganda from the cultivation of cultural respect. Yes, I wish a lot of things would have been different in the past, but they weren't. This is why the attempt to use diversity to fix the past is an impossible and delusional effort, especially if it involves censoring history to make it more convenient. What we *can* do is use diversity to make a better America, a better Hawai'i, and indeed, a better world, in the present—not by fixing the past, but by making sure we do not repeat it.

Something from nothing: A redemption song
I started this chapter with the claim that being indigenous means nothing. I also claimed that I would be able to show that in making that claim, I was actually opening the door to justice and not

closing it. And so, here is the moment where I redeem myself, or at least try to. When I said that being indigenous means nothing, I was not denying the existence of indigenous peoples, nor was I saying that indigenous culture amounted to nothing or was worth nothing. When I said it means nothing, I meant that it means nothing inherently special beyond any other category of existence. For some reason, we want to believe that indigenous peoples around the world, including Native Americans, are inherently better people, both in the present and in the past, and in the process we have transformed them into some sort of foil in relation to the presumed badness of the modern West, globalization, and every other thing out there that makes the world seem like a violent and scary place. People believe in indigenous peoples the way that children believe in things like Santa Claus, and it helps no one—most of all indigenous peoples—in the process. Indigenous peoples are not the goodness of the past that we lost in the badness of the present. They are people just like everyone else, whose cultures are just as rich and just as flawed as any other. By linking indigenous peoples with some imagined utopian moment in the past, we end up with a situation where we focus far more on the preservation of the imagined culture in the past than on the renovation of dignity in the present.

In unearthing some of the more problematic moments of indigenous history in the American past, my intention was not to humiliate, nor was it to try to make a claim that indigenous rights or any other policy designed to create dignity among and between indigenous peoples was unjustified or undeserved. My intention was in fact to create a sobering moment of equality between the indigenous peoples of America and the non-indigenous Americans with whom they live and with whom they interact. That is the space where diversity is supposed to do its work, in creating a shared, intercultural space to situate ourselves among others and to do so in a way where we can enter as strangers and depart as friends, regardless of how we got there and regardless of where we are going. What is *not* being said or suggested here is that Native Americans somehow deserved the treatment they got. Yes, the evidence we have shows that there was often little difference between the actions of indigenous America and the actions of the other settlers who came later. There was all too much violence and thievery and imperialism, and all of it was justified by cultural and religious value systems that were invoked more often out of convenience than conviction. There is much to be shocked by in all of these histories, including the shock that imperialism is not just a moment in time when the White Man arrived, but rather a continuous experience in the long perspective of American history, and indeed, of world history. Ditching Columbus Day for Indigenous Peoples Day is a feel-good gesture at best, like offering a band-aid to someone who really needs a heart transplant.

I understand that much of American history consists of negative depictions of Native Americans and indigenous peoples, and I understand and support all efforts to replace those images with something that more accurately reflects the richness that indigenous culture holds and offers to those who want to know it better. But it is just as destructive to *undervalue* indigenous culture as it is to *overvalue* it. When I said that being indigenous means nothing, I was not undervaluing indigenous culture or indigenous peoples. Nor was I overvaluing them. What I am doing is to state that indigenous cultures carry an equal weight in the complex array of identities that constitute this place we call America, and that weight is not based on some child-like innocence or inherent goodness or timeless traditions or any other of the infantilizing simplifications we make about indigenous cultures. Nor is it based on some sort of calculus of guilt or innocence from the past, about who did bad things to whom and when. Diversity in the present is based on equal dignity and mutual understanding. If America is worth its weight in anything, and if diversity is going to have any credibility as an agent of change for the better, then dignity and understanding should be our guide, rather than blame and guilt.

I have made the argument in every chapter of this book so far that diversity is about understanding difference rather than simply being different. With that in mind, I have often pondered and just as often lamented the fact that the richness and complexity of indigenous cultures in America do not play a more central role in the curriculum of American education. Why, for instance, do we offer in any standard high school curriculum the option to study French, German, Spanish, and perhaps Mandarin or Japanese, but not Hawai'ian or Choctaw or Navajo or Cherokee? I know there are parents out there who would object to this and say it is absurdly impractical—shouldn't little Suzie learn French or some other language that will help her get a job in the real world, or at least help her become more cultured and cosmopolitan? Well, in my experience, if Suzie is like pretty much every other high school student in America, if she takes even two years of French in high school, by the time she hits the five-year class reunion she won't remember enough of it to know a *croissant* from a *douche*. My point here is not a cynical one. It is only to point out that an unjustified assumption about educational impracticality should not be an obstacle to putting indigenous cultures more deeply into the American curriculum for *all* Americans to study (and not just Native Americans). Why not make it possible for Suzie to learn Hawai'ian? What she remembers of it will be an invaluable asset for diversity. Besides, when Suzie finally makes it to Paris and ends up suffering the snooty laughter of a Parisian waiter who finds her American accent uncouth and unrefined, she can just smile and cut them down to size with a barrage of eloquent insults in fluent Hawai'ian.

To act, perchance to resist
To bring this chapter to a close, I'd like to revisit a more recent event in United States history, and that would be the protests over

the construction of the Dakota Access Pipeline (DAPL) that started in April 2016. You might think that given everything I've discussed in this chapter, that I would have no sympathy or concern for the Native American groups involved, especially the Standing Rock Sioux who were at the heart of the controversy. You might think I would simply say let people build whatever they want wherever they want because being indigenous means nothing. In fact, and this may come as a surprise, the opposite is true. I think the whole affair was handled poorly and disgracefully, and I think a better solution could and should have been tried that offered full and equal respect not just to the Standing Rock Sioux, but to all of the Native American groups that got involved with the protests in support of the Standing Rock Sioux.

So in the end, am I contradicting myself? How can I support the claims of the Standing Rock Sioux if I think that being indigenous means nothing? As a reminder, I did say that being indigenous means nothing, but I also said quite clearly that that does *not* mean that indigenous culture is meaningless. One of the things that is common to indigenous cultures, not just in the United States but all around the world, is a special connection to the land. That's not necessarily unique to indigenous cultures, but let's keep the focus on indigenous groups for now. When I refer to a special connection to the land, I refer to a spiritual, cosmological connection to the land—not in some New Age fetishization of indigenous spirituality, and not in a way that caricatures Native American cultures into people who have some innate, pure spirituality that the rest of us non-indigenous moderns have lost. This is not a trivial point. Think, for instance, of how a Christian would feel on the grounds of a church, or how a Muslim would feel on the grounds of a Muslim cemetery. If someone wanted to build a pipeline that traversed the grounds of the church or the cemetery, most of us would have no problem thinking that something was clearly wrong and clearly insensitive about that. No amount of studies showing that the pipeline would have no adverse effect on the church or the cemetery would solve the problem, because safety isn't really the issue. And offering to reroute the pipeline along the edge of the property of the church or cemetery wouldn't solve the problem either. Yes, it would now be technically off the property, but it's still in a very general sense simply disrespectful. It's as if a rancher had bought a parcel of land right next to the Muslim cemetery with the intent to create a massive pig farm. Legally she has every right to do so, and every right to make her livelihood however she wants—it's her property, after all. But law and economics should not be the only two things that determine the best outcome.

Speaking of law, and getting back to the DAPL issue, there is also the issue of the treaties that exist between the US Federal Government and Native American tribes, treaties that have a long history of being ignored, disrespected, or conveniently (one-sidedly) reinterpreted. Whether or not you like the treaties is irrelevant—they are there, and if the rule of law means anything, it means giving full and equal respect to matters of the law, regardless of whether one party is more powerful than the other.

What was lost in the DAPL project was the chance for all involved parties to find a way to make everything work in the best way possible. As long as we depend on oil, pipelines will be a necessary part of the landscape, and companies that want to build pipelines are entitled to the returns of their economic investment. Part of the fiasco with the DAPL was that Energy Transfer Partners had already been given a green light with the project, so when the federal government tried to reassess the situation, it was already too late to do anything about it (and US Federal courts agreed). If diversity is, as I have argued throughout this whole project, about understanding difference, then it is clear that in the whole process through which the DAPL was conceived and implemented, no one really took the time to understand how this would look to and what it would mean for the Standing Rock Sioux. Yes, there were consultations, many of them in fact, but the consultation process on projects like these was and remains terribly flawed and imperfect. It's embarrassing how poorly the whole issue was handled, and I can only hope that if there are any future pipelines to be built like this, that someone takes the time to do what diversity asks us to do: listen to and learn from the words of others, and ask ourselves how we would feel if we were in their shoes.

Lastly, I want to revisit a concept that comes up over and over again in discussions of indigenous peoples in America and indeed, in any sort of discussion involving diversity. It is something I have mentioned in passing from time to time and one I should finally address directly. I refer here to the idea of *resistance*. There is something romantically appealing about considering oneself part of the resistance, because in most contexts, those who belong to the resistance are the good guys, the ones battling the bad guys. During the protests that occurred in 1992, protests against the idea of celebrating Columbus Day since that meant honoring the oppressor, the imperialist, the bad guy, the White Man, and so on, there were signs held high by protesters that read "500 years of indigenous resistance," or any one of several variations on that theme. The idea was that indigenous peoples had been collectively unified as one gigantic act of resistance against Western imperialism, which gives us the simplified tale of the good guy (native resistance) against the bad guy (the White Man). That is also, incidentally, how many people viewed the resistance to the DAPL project.

If nothing else, I hope some of the information conveyed in this chapter shows that these narratives not only betray the substantive reality of history, they also undermine the possibility of a diversity that works equally for all. I mean, why stop at 500 years of resistance? Why not call it a 1000 years of resistance, or 1500 years, since indigenous peoples were resisting each other's acts of violence and conquest before, during, and after the arrival of Columbus? It's less heroic and less romantic, to be sure, but it is also more accurate and more constructive in situating ourselves among others, historically and presently. Diversity cannot be built on myths and fantasies, and it is as important to reflect on the good parts of our collective histories as it is to reflect on the bad. Resistance can be a good thing, but it does no one any good to use resistance as a distraction to gloss over the unpleasant events of the past and present. If I have questions about the history of indigenous peoples, it is not "resistance" to shout me down or evade the questions with accusations of hate and racism. Diversity requires, indeed demands that we confront everything that has transpired and continues to transpire around us and between us. It requires not just action, but also pensive reflection. Sure, everyone would like to imagine themselves as the hero that resisted tyranny and oppression, but if there is one thing my observations on social justice and diversity have taught me, it is this: *Resistance without reflection is simply the mobilization of idiocy.*

CHAPTER 6

FEAR, IGNORANCE, STUPIDITY, DIVERSITY

One of the many unfortunate stereotypes that exist in the world is the one about the "stupid American." Americans, it seems, are so spoiled in wealth and self-indulgent privilege that they just stopped learning long ago, and now exist in a self-absorbed microcosm of complete ignorance about the rest of the world. I will certainly admit that there are a lot of stupid Americans. I know this because I have spent more of my life than I care to ponder dealing with them. The bumper-sticker adage that tells us, "if you think education is expensive, try ignorance," is absolutely correct. But there is a bit of fallacious reasoning here in the image of the ignorant American that suggests that the non-American part of the world is therefore non-ignorant, as in, insightful and well-informed about themselves and about others. If there is one thing I have learned in my many years of research and travel, it is that no country or culture, not even America, has a monopoly on ignorance. The rest of the world is equally as stupid and sometimes even more stupid than America. If you are an American and you find comfort and even cause for celebration in that point, think very clearly about what you are applauding: the diversity of ignorance, in America and around the world, is not something we should celebrate. It is something we should lament.

But let's return to the idea of the ignorant American, and go through a short exercise. When someone mentions or invokes the idea of the ignorant American, what image comes to mind? My guess is that we think of someone who is "white." If someone asks me to think of an ignorant American and I conjure up a Latino male or a black woman, no doubt I would be called a racist. No one would applaud my efforts to expand diversity by including a wider array of identity-based groups in the category of "stupid Americans."

I am quite certain that in the world of diversity and in the endeavor to create a more inclusive society in America, at least as they current exist in practice, the absolute preference is to incorporate non-dominant and minority groups only into positive categories of existence. If I am writing a book on innovative corporate leaders in America, I will be strongly encouraged to include profiles of women and minorities in each chapter of the book. If I am writing a book on flatulent psychopaths who harm children by pelting them with puppies, no one will complain if I have not included the Latino contribution to this rather specialized and peculiar demographic. But ignorance and stupidity are special categories when it comes to diversity, because diversity as policy and practice is in part packaged with the premise that diversity will help *eliminate* ignorance in America. The more diversity we have in America, we are told, the less we will suffer the ignominy of ignorance. And why does this happen? It happens because we believe that things like discrimination and racism and prejudice all occur due to the ignorance of their practitioners, and that ignorance is based on a lack of familiarity with the sorts of people against whom they project their invective and disdain. If diversity puts us in the company of other kinds of people, if diversity helps us to situate ourselves among others, the argument goes, then they will become familiar to us. The more familiarity we have with them, the less ignorance we will retain about them, and without ignorance, the basis for racism and prejudice and discrimination will disappear. World peace breaks out, cross-cultural hugs become endemic, and cute kitten videos are enjoyed by all. The only problem is that clearly, none of this has happened, so it is time for us to delve into the complex relationship that ignorance and stupidity have with diversity and identity.

Earlier I mentioned one of the dreaded moments that happens in nearly every discussion of diversity, when someone shuts down the conversation with the dismissive claim that a person "just doesn't get it." In these moments, the person who "doesn't get it" is without fail a person from the dominant or majority group. I find it interesting that this question is not evoked in relation to members of minority groups. If a Latino makes an ignorant statement about an Asian, he clearly "doesn't get it," but there is a reluctance to point this out. There is a bizarre offensiveness to this, insofar as implies that we should expect a Latino to be ignorant, but a person from the dominant group, a white person—well, we should expect more from them. But what if we *all* "don't get it"? What if diversity fails because we are all equally ignorant? In fact, this is one of the main areas where diversity fails. It isn't that white people don't understand minority cultures. It is that people in one culture rarely take the time to understand people in another. When we package diversity to reward ourselves for promoting our own identity, which presumably we "get," we then get a diversity that separates rather one that integrates. Enclave mindsets are created by and in turn create ignorance. Diversity is not about understanding and appreciating one's own identity. Nor is it about celebrating difference. It is about understanding different, understanding other people's identities, and that is a responsibility we all hold equally, regardless of what group or groups we like to call home.

Ignorance and Phobia part 1: Ignorance
There are a lot of buzz words that get thrown around in any discussion of diversity, and two of the most important are the dynamic duo of *ignorance* and *phobia*. The two are clearly interrelated, and like most buzz words in the dislocated dialogue of diversity, they are more often than not invoked less for any intrinsic meaning or relevance they contain and more for the emotive response they generate. Though they are often associated with calls for better understanding and calls to end prejudice by being better informed about other cultures, they usually motivate in the opposite direction. That is, they tend to shut down the process of understanding and they tend to exacerbate prejudice through the amplification of frustration. What I want to do now is pull these two interrelated terms apart—not completely, but just enough to show how these two words that should be advancing the project of diversity actually end up jeopardizing and undermining that project. This is not to say that ignorance and phobia are not ever present in the convoluted rhetorical jumble that composes the contentious dialogue on diversity and all things related. Rather it is to say that ignorance and phobia are often attributed where none is actually present, and are often employed as a strategic tactic to *avoid* some of the most sensitive and difficult parts of the dialogue on diversity, when what we really need is to engage with them. In other words, those who incorrectly and unjustifiably attribute these two qualities of ignorance and phobia to others do just as much to dismantle the promise of diversity as those who actually display and deploy those two negative qualities in their everyday actions.

Sadly, there is an almost endless supply of examples I could draw on to show how ignorance and phobia saturate the world of diversity, but I suppose I need to start somewhere, and so I will start with a scene from a movie that is ironically about minority identities. In Wayne Wang's film *Eat a Bowl of Tea* (1989), based on Louis Chu's novel of the same name published in 1961, we get yet another work of expressive art that depicts the disorientation of identity among immigrant communities in America and the difficulties and struggles of adopting to ways of life in America, in this case focusing on Chinese-American communities in New York City. The film, like the book, focuses on the complexities of Chinese identity in America, but the scene I want to explore is one that would otherwise be just an amusing and brief detraction that turns the lens ever-so-briefly away from Chinese identity. In one scene in the movie, a non-Chinese American man (aka, a "white guy") comes into a Chinese restaurant to eat, and the Chinese staff at the Chinese restaurant have a bit of fun with the "foreigner." First, the wait-staff have already written down the order in advance because apparently all white people always order the same dishes in a Chinese restaurant (sweet and sour pork, etc.). White people, the inside joke goes, are too stupid to understand "real" Chinese cuisine. This is just the standard "let's stereotype outsiders because it is funny to laugh at them" type of scene. But later in the same scene, when the "white guy" orders a cup of Chinese tea, he also requests milk and sugar, which he then puts into the tea while the Chinese wait-staff stare at the ignorant foreigner who is apparently too stupid to know that Chinese tea is not drunk with milk and sugar—that simply isn't the "Chinese way" to drink tea.

What I find remarkable about this scene is that in a film (and a novel) that is in large part about the difficulties and challenges of articulating a Chinese identity in a non-Chinese environment ("America"), the scene shows that such difficulties and challenges are situational and not unique to specific minority groups. In the situation where a non-Chinese person is in a Chinese restaurant that is run by a Chinese staff, the non-Chinese person is ridiculed because he has not properly assimilated to the dominant ways of the cultural micro-environment of which he is now a part. The lesson of the scene seems to be that you should assimilate to your environment and do things as locals do: don't bring your own ways with you, and if you do, it is acceptable to laugh at you. Yet in so much of the literature that relates to the identity challenges of minority communities, Chinese-American literature included, much of the struggle centers on the difficulty of negotiating the pressure to assimilate and of finding the right balance between one's "native" culture and the new cultural environment of which one is a part. In this scene, however, the tables are turned as the non-Chinese character finds himself in a new and unfamiliar environment, while the Chinese staff are in a position of cultural familiarity and "dominance." In ridiculing the non-Chinese character for drinking Chinese tea in a way that reveals his native and non-Chinese background, rather than assimilating to the dominant values of the environment in which he finds himself, the Chinese characters are in fact laughing at the person who is doing exactly what they are trying to do. Clearly, they don't "get it."

How power corrupts diversity
One excuse that is often offered to explain how the two situations—that of the Chinese person in a non-Chinese environment and that of a non-Chinese person in a Chinese environment—are entirely different is that such a comparison overlooks the difference in the "power dynamic" that exists in each circumstance. Because the Chinese community has less power than the dominant community, when members of the dominant community laugh at the Chinese person who struggles to assimilate, it is considered racism. But when Chinese people laugh at the non-Chinese person in a Chinese environment, it is seen as a form of "resistance." As I argued earlier, however, these excuses rely upon facile and convenient interpretations of power. The attraction of defining racism as prejudice + power and then claiming that only white people have power, as I discussed earlier, is that the definition makes it impossible for people of color to be racist. It's a definition that

people of color cling to because it allows for ignorance without responsibility.

The power dynamic is never simple in any situation where diversity exists, and there are multiple power dynamics within different groups and not just between them (consider for instance how many people in minority communities in the US ridicule the "FOBs"—people Fresh Off the Boat, aka new arrivals—in their own communities). Moreover, as I made clear in an earlier chapter, power is not the central issue in these situations. Prejudice is the central issue, and prejudice is independent of power. Prejudice is itself generated by ignorance and so ignorance should be confronted and addressed wherever it exists, whether in majority or minority communities. Once we take power out of the equation, then the two situations mentioned above become similar: the Chinese people are as ignorant of other cultures as non-Chinese are of Chinese culture. The lesson we learn is that we *all* have work to do when it comes to diversity.

Ignorance and prejudice abound in a diverse world. Browsing in the foreign language section of the campus bookstore at UC Berkeley one day, for instance, two students walked over to search for a book related to one of their classes. One of them happened to see a Hindi-language dictionary on the shelf with Hindi writing (Devanagari) on the spine, and took the book from the shelf while saying "what kind of language is this?" As they flipped through the pages of the dictionary, they began laughing hysterically. One said to the other "this is fu__d up," and the two shook their heads in disbelief at such a "ridiculous" language and continued laughing as they put the book back on the shelf. Ignorance? Absolutely. But here's an additional detail that at this point might not have been clear when I started narrating this incident. The two students were both Chicano, and both had MEChA (*Movimiento Estudiantil Chican@ de Aztlan*) buttons on their backpacks.

This detail is an important one. In so many conversations and arguments on diversity in America, someone will make the claim that the problem is that "white people" do not understand minority cultures, as in, white people don't "get" the cultures of Chicanos, Latinos, Koreans, Chinese, etc. Not only do white people not get these cultures, but also they actively distort public perception about these cultures. As a result, what passes for diversity education in the United States, a form of education that is supposed to combat the ignorance that frustrates the potential of diversity, is a form of education in which students from minority groups clamor to study their own culture, taught by professors from their own groups—in order to correct the "distorted" view that would be offered by non-native professors—and students from dominant groups are encouraged to take these classes as a way to overcome what is assumed to be their inherent ignorance. But does this type of diversity education do anything to help diversity flourish? Ignorance is really a reflection on the quality of knowledge, or lack thereof, that a person possesses. Majority or minority, dominant or non-dominant are entirely irrelevant here, as they do not affect the quality of knowledge nor do they affect the responsibility to seek and obtain the knowledge necessary to make diversity work, a responsibility that falls equally on everyone in a diverse society (making it therefore, as I have said, a civic responsibility). If we are going to ask questions such as "Why don't white people know more about Latino culture?" then we must also ask questions such as "Why don't Latinos know more about Korean culture?" and so forth. Knowing one's own culture really well does almost nothing for diversity.

The obsession with the idea that only majority cultures need to learn diversity, while minorities just somehow have it, is what brings us to our currently untenable and unproductive position in America, where the burdens of diversity are not apportioned equally. To put it bluntly, white people are expected to know about all other cultures, while non-whites need only know their own. What diversity requires in order to succeed is to have similar expectations—and yes, sacrifices—from all identity groups. I agree with the position that whites in America should be more informed about other cultures, but I agree with it as part of a more general position that holds that all cultures should be more informed about other cultures (that is, cultures other than their own). Minorities are just as ignorant of other cultures as are whites, and so the civic duty of battling ignorance falls equally on all identity-based groups. If we expect or advocate anything different, then what we have is not diversity but hypocrisy.

Ignorance and Phobia part 2: Phobia
Ignorance and fear tend to work in the same direction, and more often than not, one is the catalyst for the other. So it should come as no surprise to find that fear rears its ugly and ignorant head in nearly every discussion that engages the elements of diversity. Nevertheless, the two phenomena are clearly distinct: to be ignorant of another culture is not the same thing as having a fear of it. Yet ironically the idea of fear is frequently invoked where ignorance is at play, and the invocation of fear, almost always in the form of some sort of *phobia*, does more to shut down the process of interpersonal and intercultural understanding than nearly any other concept. Even stranger is that this usually happens because the person invoking some sort of phobia is ignorant of what a phobia actually is. A phobia is an extreme and irrational fear of something, and so it is a particular kind of fear and not just fear itself. At a debate at UC Berkeley on the wearing of headscarves by Muslim women, when one audience member asked how the wearing of a headscarf could be seen as a Muslim obligation since many Muslim women choose not to wear a headscarf, one of the women on the panel—a Muslim woman wearing a headscarf—refused to answer the question because she said the question itself was *Islamophobic*. I

can see how the question might be attributed to a certain kind of ignorance about Islamic practices, but I cannot see how the question is linked to an extreme or irrational fear of Islam. This moment from the debate highlights how the invocation of fear in the form of phobias counters the work of diversity: rather than provide an answer that informs the questioner and thereby diminishes his or her ignorance of Islam, the respondent instead refuses to provide the knowledge sought by the questioner by shifting the problem away from inconsistencies created by the diversity within Islam and toward the attributed flaws of the questioner. The result is that the ignorance is never dispelled and the conversation is truncated: neither questioner nor respondent learns or resolves anything. In that moment, diversity fails.

This is not to suggest that identity-based phobias do not exist. But I do mean to suggest that the invoking of "phobias" when none are present—calling someone a "phobe" is usually a convenient way of avoiding a difficult question that has no easy or pleasant answer—is counterproductive if not outright destructive to the project of diversity. Central to the diversity project is the idea of understanding what is different, and this is where the problem of phobia-saturated rhetoric corrodes the whole framework: invoking the shibboleth of "phobia" forces us to bypass deep understanding and go straight to acceptance. But diversity is not about acceptance as much as it is about understanding. Understanding is inextricably linked to asking questions, so if we censor the right to ask questions and demand unquestioning acceptance, we get only stifled misunderstandings. To demand acceptance without question is to throw kerosene on the fire of resentment.

Who's afraid of diversity?
The two most common phobias that show up in debates and discussions on diversity are Islamophobia and homophobia. For

now I will focus on Islamophobia. In a strict definitional sense, Islamophobia would be an extreme or irrational fear of Islam or Muslims. As I demonstrated through my anecdote earlier, sometimes the charge of Islamophobia is invoked in order to shut down a dialogue or censor out difficult questions. At various events at college campuses in the United States, for instance, I have seen questions such as "why are there so many Muslim suicide bombers?" or "doesn't Islam forbid terrorism?" or "do Muslims really believe that terrorists will get seventy-two virgins in heaven?" or "why are women in the Islamic world denied equal rights?" all go unanswered because the person asking the question is simply accused of being Islamophobic. The questions are not worth answering, the argument goes, because they are based on irrational fear and ignorance. But it seems to me, the best way to battle ignorance is to offer knowledge. These are crucial moments when information could be offered to dispel all varieties of ignorance and prejudice, and yet the idea is that these kinds of questions reveal a "phobia" among non-Muslims that is not worth engaging. The result is that there is now an additional fear: the fear of asking questions. And ironically, when the questions stop, that is precisely when Islamophobia festers.

To demonstrate how unhelpful and frustrating this can be, I can introduce an educational tactic that is rarely used in discussions on diversity, and this is the tactic of *shifting the contextual perspective*. Let us imagine a discussion, led by a group of citizens from Israel, on operations by the Israeli military in the West Bank and Gaza. Now let us imagine that a person in the audience raises the question of why Israeli actions are not denounced by the United Nations or by the United States, or why there is not some sort of war crimes investigation for actions undertaken by the Israeli military. At that point, imagine where the discussion would go if the response was this: "I'm sorry, but those questions are very Judeophobic." Where would the discussion go? It would go nowhere, that's where it would go, and it would go there immediately.

The reason it would go nowhere is that the response is in fact a non-response, one that shuts down any possibility of understanding. It is a response that says: if you question anything the Israeli military does, it is because you have an extreme and irrational fear of Jewish people, and it is because you are ignorant. At this point, one might even recommend some sort of diversity education program for those who question the actions of Israel, to dispel these irrational fears and to provide a remedy for the ignorance that generates them. And how do you know when a sufficient amount of diversity education has been consumed? Why, that's easy: when you stop asking questions about Israeli actions in the West Bank and Gaza and simply accept them without questioning them. If you weren't so ignorant and you "truly" understood Judaism and the history of Israel, the argument would go, then you would stop asking questions and just accept things as they are.

At this point, one might quibble with the parallel: after all, the Israeli military is an official part of the Israeli state, whereas terrorists who claim to act in the name of Islam are not an official part of any Muslim state (and the Islamic State is not in fact a state). The problem is easily addressed: we could talk about the various settlements set up by Israeli settlers in the occupied territories, for instance. The end result, however, would be the same: if anyone who questions the settlements is accused of being Judeophobic, the discussion simply goes nowhere. There will be no cross-cultural or interfaith understanding, no resolution of issues or disputes, no sense of empathy, no peace, no nothing. There will just be a group of people who say you must accept everything we do without question, or else you are Judeophobic.

We could also do the same thing with the idea of Americaphobia. Imagine if anyone anywhere in the world, or even in the United States, questioned the way America acted in the world or questioned the behavior of Americans, and the response was simply to call anyone who raised those questions "Americaphobic." Does America have racism, you ask? Stop being Americaphobic. There would be no end to the frustration and resentment of people if every time someone raised a question about American foreign policy, the response was something like this: "Your ignorance-based Americaphobia is the problem, not America's foreign policy." And again, there is the circular reasoning that says the cure for the irrational phobia is to dispel the ignorance, and the point where we know the ignorance is gone is the point where the person ceases to question American foreign policy. Accept what America does without questioning it—otherwise, you are Americaphobic.

Of course, one could also counter that there actually *are* people who are truly Islamophobic, but the fact is, there are also people who are truly Judeophobic and Americaphobic. There are Americans who are killed in many places around the world because the actions of a small number of people (policy makers, for example) are somehow attributed to all Americans, in exactly the same way that Muslims face discrimination because the actions of a small number of Muslims (radical militants) are somehow attributed to all Muslims. Indeed, the same people who often refer to all of America as Islamophobic do so because *some* Americans think that all Muslims support Islamic terrorism.

If that sounds like an extreme simplification, then consider the following. When one of my students at UC Berkeley came to me with the idea of setting up a chapter of the Olive Tree Initiative—an organization that tries to foster peace in the Middle East by establishing cross-cultural and interfaith dialogues among Muslims and Jews and Israelis and Palestinians—we drew up a list of faculty at UC Berkeley who might be interested in or relevant to the goals of the Olive Tree Initiative. One of the faculty members on that list turned out to be entirely dismissive of the project. There is no point for Muslims to speak with Jews or Israelis about peace, he said, because that would be like asking a slave to speak to his master about freedom. It's an interesting perversion of the Golden Rule: instead of do unto others as you would have them do unto you, it is demand that others know, accept, and never question all that you do while you dismiss, criticize and remain ignorant of what they do. Or even more simply, it is wrong for you to do to me what I think is right to do to you. If only we could all set our goals lower: instead of wanting diversity and peace, perhaps we should aspire to stupidity and violence, in which case we can most certainly say we have already arrived at our desired destination.

Learning to be ignorant
With so much ignorance to be found in America, and sadly in the rest of the world as well, it naturally raises the question of where it all comes from. The surprising answer is that much of the ignorance people exhibit is actually a byproduct of the learning process. Education makes us ignorant, and diversity education, at least as it is currently packaged, makes us even more ignorant. That might seem like a rather cynical claim from someone who has spent his entire professional career in the field of education, but I can assure you, this is no claim sourced from cynicism. The short explanation to this is the way that diversity education is currently offered. Especially at the university level, students are encouraged to affirm themselves by learning about themselves. That is, students aren't just drawn to classes and majors that tell them all about themselves, they are actually encouraged to take them in the name of diversity. These courses are more often than not taught by people from within those identity groups and whose scholarly "activism" consists of reaffirming all the positive values of their culture of community. Asian-Americans are drawn to Asian Studies and Asian-American Studies, African-Americans are drawn to African Studies and African-American Studies, Latinos are drawn to Latino Studies, Native Americans are drawn

to Native American Studies, and so on. In courses where the topic is not identity specific, students usually end up, as I have pointed out, choosing topics for their research that are centered on their own identities. Diversity education rewards students for indulging in a self-affirming and self-indulgent education about their own identity, and does nothing to encourage or require or reward them to learn about others. This is one of the biggest flaws of diversity: we are continuously encouraged and rewarded to learn about ourselves, and are offered no incentives to learn about others. As long as that is the case, diversity education will simply continue to churn out ignorant champions of triumphant narcissism.

Too harsh? I don't think so. Consider, for instance, the case of the student who once came to my office (when I was still a graduate student) to say that she and her fellow students of Indian heritage were organizing a protest against American racism. When I asked what the protest was about, the student responded that students of Indian descent were offended by the Alanis Morissette song "Thank U," which at the time was receiving a tremendous amount of airplay. According to the student, the song mentioned India, but it also mentioned the words "death" and "starving" in one of the lines, and therefore, it was just one more example of an ignorant white American entrenching stereotypes of India as a country of poor and starving people. This type of colonial racism could not go unanswered, and so the resistance had answered the call of duty. When I asked the student if she had actually read the lyrics of the song or knew what it was about, the response was that she did not need to do that, as the facts were clear: a white person was singing (a white woman at that), the song mentioned India, and the song mentioned negative things like "starving." Voila! American racism. The fact that Alanis Morissette is Canadian seemed irrelevant—all Westerners are just the same, apparently. When I pointed out that the song was not meant as an act of racism or sarcasm or satire or irony (keeping in mind that many are skeptical about whether

Alanis Morissette actually understands the concept of irony), but rather as an homage to India for the positive effect that it had on Alanis Morissette when she visited the country, the student was dumbfounded. The desire to hold a protest to claim that anything regarding India should only be spoken of by Indians—who were ethnically predisposed to always "get it"—and to denounce white people for presuming they could speak about India in anything other than paeans of praise, quickly dissipated into disappointment. The protest never occurred. Thank U, intelligence.

More recently I had a moment in a seminar with college seniors where, in the midst of a discussion about the relationship of warlord militias in war zones and violent inner-city gangs in the United States, a white female student took the opportunity to interrupt the discussion in order to—as she saw it—set all the other students straight. As the other, apparently misinformed and ignorant students discussed the war zones at home, of neighborhoods torn apart by gang-related violence, this particular student, armed with knowledge apparently gleaned from a "radical" class on identity, decided to stop the discussion and critique her fellow students for "buying into the dominant image of gangs in poor communities of color." Inner-city gangs, she continued, were actually "community-oriented service groups" (that's a direct quote) that provided essential services to neighborhoods that were neglected or oppressed by governments that served only the needs of the dominant group. I remember this comment so well because it was one of the few times in my professional career where I actually had to choke back my own vomit. I reflected on all of the instances of lives destroyed and lives ended far too early that I had encountered in my research on sex trafficking—young women who had been punished for trying to escape the gangs that exploited them by being pinned down and gang-raped repeatedly until their bodies were destroyed—and wondered how anyone could seduce themselves into such a torpor of ignorance that they could somehow see that as an act of community service. Radical? Radically stupid perhaps, and that's being charitable. And yet, it's all a part of how the university system currently packages diversity education as a corrective to all the ignorance we didn't know we had. In reality, it merely exchanges one type of ignorance for another. Radical indeed.

The trade in ignorance is generated by the illogical nature of our current thinking on diversity: academics who fancy themselves advocates of social justice use the classroom as a recruitment platform rather than a space for the robust exchange of diverse ideas, and students are thus fed a heavy and dyspeptic diet of rhetorical propaganda that encourages them to sort themselves out by identity—to find their own kind—and then display their new-found group identity as part of diversity. Students don't learn to *think*, they learn to *identify*. Instead of learning the active process of thinking, they learn the passive process of just being something. Ironically, and lamentably, the passive act of being something is then packaged as a form of activism. What students learn is that *being different* is all it takes to create diversity, when in fact the mere passive act of being different means and signifies nothing. Diversity is not about preening and displaying one's own identity, but rather about trying to understand the identity of others. Only when we work to understand others—something that requires active thinking and critical reflection—can we understand ourselves. In other words, until our classrooms teach students to study and learn and understand things *other* than themselves, we will have a diversity based on willful ignorance. And a diversity based on willful ignorance is an absolute waste of time.

The point is, when we say that American culture is ignorant, we need to remember that we are all in this together, for the good and the bad. Ignorance is bad, and if America is ignorant, then we all share in the blame. If we are going to open up the subject of Islamophobia, for instance, then we should at least open it up completely, whether in the classroom or in other public discussions or even among friends. If America is Islamophobic because it is ignorant of the real tenets and practices of Islam, then we need and must acknowledge that that ignorance is spread diversely throughout the population. There are Hindus who are ignorant of Islam, and there are Latinos who are ignorant of Islam, and there are Asians who are ignorant of Islam, all of whom harbor distorted if not abhorrent views towards Islam. If we only focus on what the dominant groups says and thinks, we are missing a large part of the problem.

But wait, you might say—since Muslims and these other minority groups are all "communities of color" (keep in mind that giving a color to a religion is pure idiocy), surely they all just "get it" and understand each other, right? Not quite. Consider the case of Julissa Fikri, a resident of East Harlem with Puerto Rican-Dominican heritage, who found comfort in and ultimately converted to Islam during a period of personal difficulty in her life. Did she face Islamophobic prejudice in America? Yes she did—but she faced it from her Latino and Hispanic community, the very community she grew up in.[91] Said one Latino man: "Oh, so she changed her race. Now she's Arab." Another called her a terrorist. Her own mother told her to take off her "Arab" clothing, because the family was Hispanic, and "we don't wear that." So there's plenty of Latino and Hispanic Islamophobia to discuss in our classrooms, but you'll search in vain for a class on Latino Islamophobia on any university campus.

Remember, too, that ignorance is ubiquitous, thanks to our acceptance of diversity as a strange display of separate but equal

---

91 Michael J. Feeney, "Hispanic woman who converted to Islam experiences prejudice from fellow East Harlem residents," *New York Daily News* (August 31, 2011) at http://www.nydailynews.com/new-york/uptown/hispanic-woman-converted-islam-experiences-prejudice-fellow-east-harlem-residents-article-1.946543

identities. A question about how much Muslims know about Latino culture or Hinduism or Christianity is just as important as a question about how much whites or Latinos know about Islam. Muslims can be victims of Latino Islamophobia, while Latinos can be victims of Muslim Latinophobia. If Muslims expect the rest of America to learn more about them, then Muslims should also be doing the same thing—learning about others. In fact, everyone should be doing this. It is the most important work of diversity.

Ignorance in action
It is easy to forget that diversity is more than just an act of public policy and more than just another item on the pedagogical agenda for a school curriculum. Diversity is lived experience and it is something we encounter every day. We participate in diversity every time we interact with others. The tensions and problems we encounter through those interactions are ours to reflect upon and ours to resolve. To the extent that our social circulation is confined to those like ourselves, to those of our kind, to "our people," we engage in a sort of self-segregation that undermines everything that diversity should offer. In those moments, it isn't someone else's fault and it isn't the dominant group oppressing everyone. It is ourselves failing to do what diversity asks us to do. There is always a litany of excuses to justify why someone else is to blame—I hang out with my own kind because we have to stick together in the face of oppression, I live in a neighborhood full of my own people because it resists the efforts by the dominant group to divide and conquer—but in the end it is just a collective epic fail. Diversity remains forever stuck in a rut because we continuously generate excuses to blame others for the everyday errors and mistakes we commit all by ourselves.

In San Francisco I once accompanied a group of people from India and of Indian descent on a tour of various sites, and one of those sites was the exquisitely beautiful Grace Cathedral. I noticed as we looked around that they were quite bored, especially the younger ones (mostly in their 20s), and so when we exited the brief tour I asked what they thought of the cathedral. I received an earful from several in the group, about how churches were "cold places" and that Christianity as a religion made no sense. Some guy in a robe waving his arms around and "screaming hallelujah" (their words, not mine) and giving out wafers of bread just made no sense to them. By contrast, I was told, Hindu temples were "warm places" that were full of energy and spirituality. The incense, the chanting, the oil lamps, the crowds—everything was exactly what a religion should be. It was a classic example of how people mistake what is familiar with what is superior. Hindu temples were better and more religious than Christian churches because as Hindus, everything in Hinduism was familiar to them and therefore made sense. I tried to explain the meaning of the architecture of the cathedral and some of the ceremonies of Christianity, but there was just no interest from them. In fact, the discussion led to a question of some frustration: how could Indians convert to Christianity when their own religion (assuming Hinduism was the natural religion of Indian people) was so much better?

When I asked how they felt among non-Indian Americans getting involved with Hinduism (such as white Americans converting to Hinduism), they welcomed this and thought it something that contributed to diversity. When I asked why they did not have similar views of people converting to Christianity in India, they replied that Christianity was too "foreign" for India. India has a strong culture, they pointed out, whereas America does not. Christianity in India was therefore bad and foreign, but in America, anyone who thought Hinduism was bad and foreign was apparently ignorant and racist. In other words, my difference is good for you, but your difference is bad for me. And there it is: another random act of ignorance, brought to us by members of what we are supposed to call a "community of color," that shows why there is still so much work to do to move diversity forward.

Jump-cut to a different scene: standing in line at a Walgreens drug store, I witness a brief interaction between an African-American woman and two Muslim women, both of whom were wearing a veil, though one was fully covered (hair and face) and the other was partially covered (hair only). The African-American woman was staring at both of them, to the point where the two Muslim women noticed and seemed somewhat uncomfortable, and then the African-American woman suddenly initiated a conversation. "Can I ask you a question?" she said. "Both of you are Muslims, right?" The two Muslim women, who appeared somewhat startled by the question, replied in the affirmative. "Why do you cover your head like that? Does it mean you are married?" The two Muslim women exchanged glances with each other, and then one of them said that no, it was not a sign of being married. It was part of being a Muslim. "Then why are you two dressed differently? I mean, you're all covered up but I can see her face." Again, there was a palpable sense of discomfort, until again one of the Muslim women, the one whose face was not covered, said that it was simply a matter of personal preference. "So you don't have to cover yourselves up?" asked the African-American woman, which was followed by, "Aren't those things really hot to wear?" At this point, the two Muslim women were clearly trying to find a way to extricate themselves from the increasingly awkward conversation, an opportunity that was provided when a cashier station opened up and they could proceed along their way.

I remember thinking about how each of the participants in that exchange would tell a very different story of what happened. The two Muslim women would no doubt think that the whole line of questioning from the African-American woman was Islamophobic. The African-American woman would no doubt still wonder why

Muslim women wore head coverings, and left the conversation, it seemed to me, just as ignorant as she was when it started (that is, she had no real answer to her questions and so learned nothing in the exchange). In a moment when two perspectives and two different cultural points of view came together, neither side seems to have learned anything. A moment of diversity produced nothing but an affirmation of stereotypes.

I sometimes use that story in my classes. Sometimes when I tell the story, I initially leave out the detail that the woman asking the questions was an African-American woman. When I do that, students without fail assume the woman was white and do not hesitate to label the situation as a glaring example of Islamophobia. When I later add the detail that the woman was African-American, the classroom suddenly becomes uncomfortable and awkward. Interestingly, the interpretation undergoes a curious transformative revision: now, the accusations of Islamophobia are withdrawn and the whole incident is simply labeled a cultural misunderstanding. It becomes difficult to ascribe ignorance and Islamophobia to a person from a minority group, even though no other detail of the story is altered, and even though just a few moments before students did not hesitate to call the conversation Islamophobic if not downright racist. If I ask students why they changed their interpretations, the discomfort in the room grows even more palpable—such is the level of awkward and unproductive dialogue created by our current policies to promote diversity. Some students will come to office hours and tell me one-on-one that they felt uncomfortable attributing ignorance to a person of color because they feared it would look like racism. Others would repeat the nonsensical belief that people of color cannot be racist or Islamophobic, and therefore it is a different situation altogether (it isn't). Others would admit that the African-American woman was racist but would attribute that to the poor quality of education offered to communities of color in the United States, so the African-American woman was ignorant but was not responsible for that ignorance. None of these interpretations can be verified because I did not know the personal background of the three women involved in the discussion at Walgreens. But I do find it disconcerting that even at face value, most students who hear the story unwittingly assume that if the questioner were white, we can and should expect a higher state of awareness and intelligence than if the questioner were a person of color. A white person should know better, it seems, but for a person of color we should apparently lower our expectations and excuse any display of ignorance. If this is the best we can do right now, then it is no wonder diversity is such a mess in America.

Discovering our inner idiot
One of the biggest fallacies we currently have in the context of experiencing diversity is the assumption that people within a specific identity group know their culture perfectly and know their culture better than any outsider ever could. Many people believe that we are all cultural experts of the group with which we identify, an expertise that is transmitted genetically since it seems to occur naturally without any need for learning or understanding. In so many discussions that revolve around diversity or identity-related issues, I hear sentences like this: "Well, I'm Latino and this is how it is…" or "As a woman, this is how it is…" or "As a person of color, I can say…" The idea behind these sentences is that what follows must be taken as unquestioned fact and no one outside of that category may question the wisdom or point of view that is then articulated. What is presented as an enhancement to the conversation is actually something that shuts down the conversation, since it precludes the possibility of any sort of questioning. The absurdity of these statements can be revealed through the use of a hypothetical situation: what if in the midst of a discussion on racism in the United States, a white person were to offer the following statement: "As a white person, I can say that there is no racism in the

white community." Is there anyone stupid enough to believe that all the non-white persons in the same room would not be competent to question that statement?

The fact is, most people do not understand their own culture, and it is a dangerous and foolish assumption to think that they do. Anyone familiar with American television knows various late-night hosts often have a bit of fun with American ignorance and stupidity. In different skits, the hosts will quiz random people on the street about basic facts of American culture—the words to the national anthem, the name of the current vice-president, and so on—and the humor comes from the fact that most Americans have no idea about basic elements of American culture and politics. More often than not, Americans do not understand America. Is it sad? Yes. But it is not uncommon. We could do the same sort of skit and query persons about their own culture and they would just as frequently get things wrong.

In India, for instance, I have asked many, many people about the significance of a *bhindi* (which also goes by different names, such as *pottu* in Tamil). Outside of India, this is often known as that "little red dot" that Indian women often have on their forehead. For clarification, not every Indian woman wears one, though it is most common among those who are Hindu. Also, not just women wear them, but back to the main point. The most common answer I get? "That's just what we do." In other words, someone was brought up in a culture where they do that, so it must be part of the culture. I've received lots of other answers, too—that it is the third eye of wisdom, that the color shows whether a woman is married or not, and even that it absorbs harmful UV radiation, showing that Indian culture was thousands of years ahead of the West (not kidding on that one). In fact, I've received a different answer from nearly everyone I've asked, to the point where I could say that in spite of the fact that nearly every Hindu woman in India wears one, there seems to be absolutely no agreement or collectively shared understanding as to why that is. It just is.

A harmless observation? Perhaps. But then things like this happen. In April 2013, pop star Selena Gomez performed the song "Come and Get It" at the MTV Movie Awards, dressed in an outfit reminiscent of a Bollywood dance routine and sporting a bhindi on her forehead. The singer, along with her backup dancers, even gesticulated with hands pressed together and bowing, in the way that many people in India often greet one another (while saying *namaste,* or *vanakkam* in Tamil). Almost immediately, Hindu activists demanded an apology for Gomez's insensitivity to Hindu culture—how dare a non-Hindu wear a Hindu symbol without understanding the meaning of it! How dare a non-Hindu wear a Hindu symbol while singing and dancing! Keep in mind, by the way, that Selena Gomez is Latina and so we also get to revisit the debate once again about whether communities of color automatically "get" things like culture and diversity in a way that whites don't (which as I have argued is pure nonsense). Given the information I just shared about how very few Hindu women in India understand the origins and meaning of the very same symbol, and given the fact that many a Bollywood actress wears the very same symbol while gyrating suggestively for the camera, I find the absence of any similar protest quite noticeable. Hindu "activists" claim to be demanding respect for their culture, but the reality is that they only have a problem if a non-Hindu and non-Indian person is involved. In essence, if you are "brown," you are automatically authentic and may do as you please, regardless of how ignorant you are about your culture or religion.

Sometimes people from within a culture are attacked for not being "authentic" enough, which is another way of calling out a member of the group for not assimilating to the dominant values of that group. In May 2017, for instance, actress Priyanka Chopra met with Indian prime minister Narendra Modi. She shared a picture of the meeting, which showed Priyanka Chopra in a dress cut at the knee and thus revealing her bare legs. Chopra was immediately attacked and trolled on social media for betraying her Indian heritage. Showing one's legs as a woman in front of a man was "offensive" to Indian cultural values, said her detractors. Chopra was unapologetic about her actions, offending others in the process but at the same time also inspiring others for her defiance of cultural norms. She was attacked for not being Indian enough, and yet the reaction showed that there is little agreement on what it means to be Indian. In the ongoing discussion of diversity in America, there is a growing emphasis on "preserving" culture (usually in the face of white hegemony). But as the example of Priyanka Chopra shows, culture is too diverse to be preserved. Culture changes all the time, and sometimes, it really needs to change.

The sin that Selena Gomez allegedly committed was the sin of cultural appropriation. As I discussed earlier, I understand how the misuse of someone else's culture can be very offensive, especially if the misuse is intentional. But what concerns me in the case of Selena Gomez and other cases like it is how the idea of cultural appropriation becomes a form of segregation and censorship. If a singer of Indian descent wears a bhindi, no one will question whether he or she has any idea of what it means. Indeed, many will praise the act as a sign of courage or a sign of embracing her or his identity with pride—resistance against Western hegemony, and so forth. But implicit in the idea of telling Selena Gomez that she has no right to wear a bhindi because she is not Indian is the idea that the only cultural symbols we can wear or display are those of our own culture, which means we have to figure out which culture we have and then *only be that*. If that is the rule, then meaningful diversity becomes absolutely impossible. Sure, it passes for diversity now, but that is because we are infatuated with the idea that participating in diversity means to passively display ourselves and our cultures to others. Preen and be seen, as it were. But as I have argued over and over again, that is not diversity. Diversity is not about posturing what you are; it is about learning and understanding the posturing of everything you are not. *Cultural appropriation is a central part of how diversity works.* If everything outside our own frame of cultural reference is off limits, or if we are precluded from venturing into the cultural worlds of others, then diversity will simply fail over and over again.

Riding the bull in the china shop
What currently passes for diversity amounts to a fragile collection of porcelain dolls, each decorated like some haplessly simplistic cultural icon. When we enter the shop we are immediately directed to the part of the store where the dolls are "just like us." Imagine such a shop, a cute little boutique called "Diversity." As you enter, the entire shop is sectioned off: here are Latino dolls, there are China dolls, and over there are Filipino dolls, and so forth. Now imagine the boutique full of shoppers, separated into the different sections, each group ignoring the dolls of other cultures and going straight to their predetermined section: "Welcome, Miss, I see that you are Filipino, so I am sure you will be interested in the Filipino collection. It must feel so comforting for a Filipino to be among Filipino things. Right this way." The shop is filled with people happily segregated among their own kind, ignoring the dolls of others, but admiring the dolls that look like them, beaming with narcissistic pride on how beautiful they are. Every now and then a customer will hold a doll up, so that those in other sections can see it, to display its magnificent beauty: "Look upon this doll, those of you who are different. But remember, you may only admire and praise, never criticize or question. Look, but don't touch." If this is your idea of diversity then you are most certainly part of the problem. What we really need in this situation is not to learn which part of the boutique to shop in. No, what we really need here is for

someone to ride a bull through the shop and smash everything to pieces.

I'm no nihilist and so of course I would not want to just leave the ruins of Diversity (the shop) as so many shards of smashed porcelain on the ground. Being from Berkeley, I would make sure it was all cleaned up using environmentally sound and organic materials, powered by solar energy and transported in a convoy of low-emission vehicles, and I would be sure to have the SPCA on site to confirm that no bulls were harmed in the destruction of the shop. Of course I would do that. And I would also want to rebuild the shop, because I think that Diversity is important. So the question is really quite simple: what sort of shop would we build to replace the original?

The sad reality is that the momentum of our current narrow-minded approach toward diversity will generate a desire to rebuild the same thing, only this time with each group clamoring for a larger section of dolls in their own image. In essence, we will have a bigger version of a shop that was already irrelevant and counterproductive the first time it was built. Latino activists will demand more Latino dolls, African-American activists will demand more African-American dolls, feminists will demand more feminist dolls, and at some point whites will ask for more white dolls, but the others will call them racist for doing so. But the accusation is disingenuous—the reality is that all the groups in this shop are participating in racism. As long as diversity creates self-directed and narcissistic advocacy, we will get more racism and inter-group enmity, not less. We become hypersensitive to the racism of others, but blind to our own.

Here is an example of what that looks like. Not everyone likes a doll shop, so I will switch to something that has more universal appeal: music. In a discussion that emerged in one of my classes at UC Berkeley, I was talking about the many ways that biases creep into our lives and how we often use music to entrench our own, preexisting biases. One student, who just so happened to be white, begged to differ. He made the claim that he preferred a specific kind of music because it was good music, and not for instance because the artists were white or somehow "like him." An African-American student chimed in to say quite bluntly that the artists the white student had mentioned "sucked" and were mostly "white people singing about white problems." The African-American student then challenged the white student about the music he had in his music collection, and went through a list of influential African-American artists—mostly from the genres of r&b and hip-hop—to ask if he had any of that in his collection. When the white student said no, that he had none of that in his collection, the African-American student denounced his obvious and strong white bias and declared that the white student needed to add some diversity to his music collection.

A few other students applauded the presumed victory of the African-American in this impromptu slam session, but at that point I decided to push the issue a little further. I agreed with the suggestion that the white student should diversify his music tastes, but I also began to query the African-American student, going through a list of Hispanic and Latino and Pacific Islander musicians to see how many of those were in *his* collection. With each negative response, it became clear that the African-American student had a collection full of African-American music and little else. But there was a sudden shift in the atmosphere of the classroom—it had become decidedly uncomfortable. When I asked if this did not reveal a similar bias in the African-American student's music collection, there was a clear hesitation for anyone to speak up. Finally a student who identified herself as Latino said that it was not a bias because the music of minority groups was marginalized and censored by the mainstream media and so listening to music by musicians from one's own identity-group was a political act of solidarity, or as she put it, the "voice of my community." In other words, a white person listening to white music showed a lack of diversity and a bias that bordered on racism, but an African-American or a Latino listening only to African-American or Latino music respectively showed no bias whatsoever. Indeed, it was seen as a positive display of *diversity*.

Whether it is the doll shop or the music shop, our current failed state of diversity leads us down the same problematic pathways time and time again. Diversity is always someone else's problem and someone else's responsibility to fix, and while we assign the task to others to fix things, we lull ourselves to sleep with a soporific soundtrack of our own narcissistic lullabies. But that doll shop needs to be smashed and that soundtrack needs to rendered into noisome noise: what once seduced us must now repel us. Diversity requires a new sound, a new shop, a new dance, and a new everything.

What would that look like? Well, let's return for a moment to the site of devastation at the doll shop. While self-styled community activists begin to gather around the site, with so many bullhorns blaring so much bombast and bull—"more of my kind, more of me"—inside a real revolution is taking place. With the real bull (the one who so selflessly destroyed the shop in the first place) standing guard at the door, the store becomes partitioned into different sections, but instead of sections labeled "Asian" or "Latino" or "African-American" or whatever other identity groups people clamor for, now we have a whole different and infinitely variable set of sections. Now we have things like "People who like the sound of a cello" and "People who think sunsets are exquisite" and "People who are religious" and "People who are atheists" and "People who are atheists but respect people who are religious" and "People who wish Justin Bieber was a woman" and "People who think Justin Bieber *is* a woman" and "People who think math is poetry" and "People who lack money and want more" and "People who have money but want less" and "People who lack money but don't care" and "Bulls who smash doll shops" and "Dogs that get along with cats" and "Cats that get along with pigs" and "Pigs who get along with bulls who smash doll shops" and so forth. Gone is the old straitjacket of identity—you are Asian and so should like Asian things—and here now we have a shop of infinite size and infinite possibilities. Everywhere throughout the store you hear people saying things like "You, too? I never knew…" And it's not that Asianness and Latinoness and Whiteness and everything else just disappears. It's that it now appears as remarkably irrelevant. There are simply too many other things to discover, too many other ways to bring people together and think new thoughts and speak new languages and try new things and make new connections. The same opportunities are open to all, and the same expectations are asked of everyone. And that, it seems to me, is what diversity ought to offer.

Of roots, trees, leaves, and forests
One of the things we hear over and over again in relation to the identity we profess is to "never forget our roots." More often than not, the meaning of our "roots" means some essential or primordial aspect of our identity—race, ethnicity, and so forth. Apparently, this part of our identity is "where we came from." Just as a tree cannot survive without its roots, we are told, a person cannot survive without her or his roots to hold them up and support them. So many times, in confessional discussions about diversity, we hear stories of people who rediscover their roots after "drifting" for so long, and return to their community and do things to embrace those who are "just like them" and feel the warm and comforting blanket of some primordial identity. I'm not sure the roots analogy is a good one for diversity or for our identity in general. Sure, a tree cannot survive without its roots, but the roots are only one part of the tree, and without the tree growing as it will, the roots are useless anyway. If you keep a tree close to its roots, it will never

grow to be a tree. Anyone who walks through a forest looks up to admire how the tree has grown in its own individual way. No one has ever walked through a redwood forest only to stare at the roots. The only way for a tree to return to its roots is to chop it down and kill it. The tree prospers by growing *out* of its roots. So if we are going to put our roots in the picture, perhaps we should focus more on the trees we become and the forest we are a part of, rather than always trying to climb back to our roots.

Remember, too, that the roots metaphor is not what people think it is. We think of roots as a collective thing, but in reality, every tree has a different set of roots. "Not forgetting our roots" doesn't mean remembering the group we came from or are a part of. It means remembering who we are *as individuals*. Every tree is a different tree. The forest is a very diverse place.

I know many people who spend much of their life trying to forget where they came from. Our origins are not always happy, and to idealize them or romanticize them or to fall prey to the siren call of returning to "where we came from" is just as easily something to stunt our future growth as it is to remember our newly invented past. If it is important not to forget where we came from, it is equally important not to forget where we are now and also where we want to be in the future. And if the answer to the three questions of "where did you come from?" and "where are you now?" and "where do you want to be in the future?" is the same, then you lack any real sense of what diversity is. Sticking so close to "our own kind" is like a horse running at full gallop with blinders on. Sure, the horse will run in a straight line and it will run very fast, but if you remove the blinders, the horse will buck the saddle and run free, dashing off at its own pace for parts unknown.

Our roots and our cultures are like training wheels—they help us get a feel for how to do things and help us gain a sense of balance. But as anyone who has learned to ride a bicycle knows, at some point the training wheels have to come off and we have to learn how to keep our balance on our own and eventually we move on to bigger and different bikes. We break free. A college student or a forty year-old man who begs to have the training wheels put back on and cries to ride on a child's bike is not a moment of dignity. Putting the training wheels back on is akin to returning to "where you came from," but it is a regressive and bewildering choice. The obsession with finding our culture that populates so much of the current landscape of diversity infantilizes our society and undermines our ability to wander free and make new connections. If diversity is going to deliver on its promise and potential, then we need to learn to remove the training wheels for good, start a new journey of our own, and, like a horse without its blinders, ride free in every and any direction we can go.

INDEX

A
age of consent, 151-153
animals
    as the new queer, 144-147

B
bigamy, 118-119

C
Chopra, Priyanka, 237-238
Clinton, Hillary, 77-81
Comanche tribe
    and imperialism, 197
cultural appropriation, 48-53, 238

D
Dakota Access Pipeline (DAPL), 209-212
didgeridoo
    for men only, 65
diversity education
    as undiverse, 226-227
DNA
    and identity, 48, 101
domestic violence
    and men, 74-75
Duke Kahanamoku, 204
Duong Thu Huong, 73

E
education
    and diversity, 2
equality, negative, 78-81

F
feminist histories
    as disempowering, 64
feminist transphobia, 111-113
Florida

anti-zoophilia legislation,
142-144
foreign language
and diversity, 42-44
Foucault, Michel
and child sexuality, 162

G
gay gene, 99
gay racism, 124
Gayborhood (Philadelphia)
racism and discrimination in,
126
genocide
and gender, 56
Cambodia, 6, 56
Germany
court case on zoophilia,
139-141
Silvesternacht attacks, 86
glass ceiling, 88-89
Gomez, Selena, 237
Great Wall of China
as not so great, 202

H
heritage
and pride, 34
heritage learning, 36, 43
herstory, 67
heteronormativity, 117
homonormativity, 122
homophobia
and Islamophobia, 222-223
homophobic speech
in reggae and hip-hop, 170
homosexuality
and brain scans, 101-102
as hard-wired, 98
like race, 114-115, 168-169

I
ignorance
diversity of, 220-221
India
Siddi community, 13
indigenous
meaning of, 177
Indigenous Peoples Day, 176
indigenous societies
and slavery, 190-193
involution
identity-based, 8
Iroquois Confederacy,
194-195
Islamophobia, 9, 222-225, 229,
230, 234

K
Kamehameha the Great,
198-202
Kennewick Man, 186-187

L
Lady Gaga, 98
Larry Craig scandal, 96

LGBTQI+
    and culture, 113-114
    defined, 110

M
Monogamy
    as normative, 119
Morissette, Alanis, 227

N
National Front (France)
    LGBTQI+ support for, 125
Native American Graves Protection and Repatriation Act (NAGPRA), 184-185
New Zealand
    animal and gay rights, 145
Nonhuman Rights Project, 146
Nyiramasuhuko, Pauline, 56

P
patriarchy, 62-77, 182
pedophilia, 178
    as hard-wired, 150
    as sexual orientation, 148
phobia
    and identity, 221-222
polyamorous relations, 119
polygamy, 118, 129
Portland, Oregon
    food cart scandal, 50
prejudice
    and racism, 17
Presley, Domino, 111

R
Race
    as social construct, 19-20
    as Western concept, 20-21
racism
    diversity of, 28
    flawed definition of, 17-18
Rambler, Terry
    and blackface, 30-31
rape culture
    and 2016 elections, 79-80
Rau, Johannes, 33
resistance, 212
robot sex
    and pedophilia, 167
roots
    as individual, 243-244
Roy and Silo
    as gay penguins, 130-131

S
same-sex marriage
    diversity of opposition to, 114-115
San Francisco
    and Beijing Olympics, 40-41
sexual assault
    and gender, 85-86
sexual orientation
    definition of, 148-149

Shinde, Tarabai, 69-72
slave trade
    Islamic, 10
South Korea
    and discrimination, 40
stupid Americans, 214
surfing, 203-204
Sweden
    and Bravalla festival, 84

T
Thailand
    and skin color, 28-29
trafficking, 76, 228
    and women, 83
Trump, Donald, 77-82, 163

V
vegetarianism, 64

    and marriage equality, 138-141
Veterinarians Against Zoophilia, 137

W
Whale Rider, 65-66

X
XYY Syndrome, 105

Y
Yiannopoulos, Milo, 163-164
Yugoslavia, 1
    gender in conflict, 59

Z
zoophilia, 132-147

ABOUT THE AUTHOR

D. C. Zook is a writer, musician, and filmmaker who also happens to be a professor at the University of California, Berkeley, in the departments of Global Studies and Political Science. He writes both fiction and nonfiction, and cultivates both sense and nonsense. He is currently at work on two books, one on new frontiers of human rights and the other on the changing landscape of cybersecurity. He is also plotting his next novel, and plotting many other things as well.

Visit D. C. Zook at dczook.com

www.ingramcontent.com/pod-product-compliance
Lightning Source LLC
Chambersburg PA
CBHW051533020426
42333CB00016B/1913